David Jones: artist and writer

David Blamires

David Jones
artist and writer

Manchester University Press

© 1971 David Blamires

All rights reserved

Published by
Manchester University Press
Oxford Road
Manchester M13 9PL

Second edition in paper covers 1978
ISBN 0 7190 0730 5

British Library cataloguing in publication data

Blamires, David
   David Jones. – [1st ed. reprinted]; with new preface.
   1. Jones, David, b.1895 – Criticism and interpretation
   I. Title
   821'.9'12   PR6019.053Z/

ISBN 0 7190 0730 5

Printed in Great Britain
by The Scolar Press Ltd
Ilkley, West Yorkshire

Contents

	List of plates	*page* vi
	Preface	vii
	Preface to the second edition	ix
1	Introduction	1
2	Observations on art	15
3	The visual arts	35
4	*In Parenthesis*	74
5	*The Anathemata*	113
6	The work in progress	151
7	Essays and occasional writings	168
8	The Arthurian World	176
9	Conclusion	193
	Select bibliography	207
	Index	214

List of plates

1 *The Chester Play of the Deluge* (1927), wood-engraving,
  No. 10, 'The Oblation of Noah' *opposite page* 40

2 *The Rime of the Ancient Mariner* (1929), copper-engraving,
  No. 2, 'I shot the ALBATROSS' 41

3 *Portrait of a Boy* (1928), pencil and watercolour,
  Whitworth Art Gallery, Manchester 56

4 *The Terrace* (1929), watercolour, Tate Gallery, London 57

5 *Thorn Cup* (1932), watercolour drawing,
  Coll. the late Miss Helen Sutherland 68

6 *Vexilla Regis* (1947), watercolour drawing,
  Kettle's Yard Collection, Cambridge 69

Preface

The writing of a book is rarely a solitary affair. The author is everywhere indebted to other people who show their interest and give their help to what he is personally involved in. During the time that I have worked on this book, which has meant some lessening of hours spent on German language and literature, I have valued the friendly interest of Professors R. E. Keller and Idris Parry and my other colleagues in the German Department at Manchester University in what I was doing. Colleagues in the English Department have been similarly indulgent towards me, and I am grateful to John Chapple in particular for making helpful suggestions on both the Introduction and the Conclusion. In the Department of Comparative Literary Studies Lilian Furst and Simon Curtis have enabled me to present some of my chapter on *In Parenthesis* within the framework of a course on Experimentation in the Modern Novel.

In venturing from the field of literary studies into that of art history I have reason to be grateful to several people. Mrs Nicolete Gray and Mr H. S. Ede were kind enough to take me round their collections of David Jones's paintings, drawings, engravings and inscriptions. Miss Margaret Pilkington very generously lent me her copies of several of the books that David Jones has illustrated. The Whitworth Art Gallery, Manchester, the City of Salford Art Gallery and the Tate all made special arrangements for me to see the works they own. My chapter on the visual arts has benefited immensely from the patient and helpful criticism of Charles Sewter of the History of Art Department at Manchester.

PREFACE

I was first encouraged to write this book by Professor Norman Jeffares, who accepted a short article I wrote on *The Anathemata* for publication in *A Review of English Literature*. Subsequently this article was reprinted with minor alterations in the special issue of *Agenda* devoted to the work of David Jones, and it forms the basis of my chapter on *The Anathemata* in this book. Similarly, the chapter on 'The Arthurian World' is a revised version of an article entitled 'Kynge Arthur ys nat dede' that was specially written for *Agenda*. I thank the Editor, William Cookson, for permission to include it here.

The BBC Programme Correspondence Section provided me with useful information about broadcasts of David Jones's work. Mr Ian Cave, of Manchester University Library, helped me to get a microfilm from the United States with extraordinary speed, and for assistance in typing I have to thank Miss Pat Horne and Jane Walper (as she was then).

In the course of writing a book like this many of one's friends get to know about it and in this way share in its gestation. The members of the Book Club that used to meet most times at the Friends Meeting House, Wythenshawe, until William and Anne Ashmore moved elsewhere, deserve a special mention for their enthusiasm and continuing interest.

More than anyone I have to thank David Jones himself for all the help he has given me in writing this book. His letters have given me all kinds of detailed information about points that were unclear to me, and I have enjoyed talking to him on a variety of subjects in his crowded room in Harrow. I hope there are no serious errors in what I have written, but certainly David Jones has seen to it that there are fewer than when I first started out.

D B

Preface to the second edition

David Jones died on 28 October 1974 in the Calvary Nursing Home of the Little Company of Mary at Sudbury Hill, Harrow, aged 78. He had been there since 1970 following a slight stroke and an accident in which he broke his hip. Despite the considerable difficulties imposed on him by this incapacity and by being separated from most of his books and working papers, he continued to write and lived to see various pieces of his 'work in progress', together with an extract from an earlier, abandoned writing called *The Book of Balaam's Ass*, published under the title of *The Sleeping Lord and Other Fragments* (Faber, 1974). Two further poetic fragments also appeared around the same time—*The Narrows* (first published in the *Anglo-Welsh Review*, vol. 22, no. 50, Autumn 1973, and reprinted in the second David Jones Special Issue of *Agenda*, Autumn/Winter 1973–4) and *The Kensington Mass* (also in the *Agenda* Special Issue). The latter poem was subsequently published in book form, along with transcripts and reproductions of such further work-sheets as could be found and with an introduction by René Hague (Agenda Editions, 1975). Because of their fragmentary state and lack of an explicit larger context these two poems are difficult to comment on with any authority. The former is obviously allied, in its subject-matter and treatment, to the 'Middle-Sea and Lear-Sea' section of *The Anathemata* and, more especially, to the various poems that constitute *The Sleeping Lord*. Its rhythms and particular phrases link closely with 'The Wall' and 'The Fatigue' (not to

PREFACE TO THE SECOND EDITION

exclude other sections of that book). *The Kensington Mass* clearly reverts to the underlying meditative pattern of *The Anathemata*, but is more personal in its evocation of the celebrant, the initials of the dedication referring to Fr John O'Connor. René Hague's comment on the book version makes clear that all we have here is the very beginning of what was intended as an ambitious long poem, its themes as yet only lightly sketched in, but with images drawn from as wide a range as those in *The Anathemata*. The diction and approach of these two poems is all of a piece with David Jones's earlier writing.

In the Queen's Birthday Honours of the June before he died David Jones's unique contribution to art and letters was recognized through his being made, however tardily, a Companion of Honour. This recognition moved him deeply. Since his death interest in all aspects of his work has grown. Exhibitions in London, Cambridge, Stirling, Manchester and various locations in Wales have enabled lots of people to see splendid selections of his paintings, drawings, engravings and inscriptions, including many that have rarely or never been publicly shown before. Through the goodwill and generosity of the Trustees of the David Jones Estate several major works have been acquired by public institutions in various parts of the United Kingdom, especially in Wales. A second limited edition of his woodengravings for *The Chester Play of the Deluge* was published by the Clover Hill Editions in 1977. In the literary field there have been two main types of posthumous publication – occasional writings and personal letters.

Harman Grisewood, the editor of *Epoch and Artist*, has sifted the vast quantity of papers that David Jones left behind and chosen from them material comparable in scope and quality with the earlier collection of essays, reviews and occasional writings. They have been published under the title of *The Dying Gaul and Other Writings* (Faber, 1978). The title essay has already been commented on below (see p. 173), and indeed about half the items in this new collection have appeared previously elsewhere, in places or forms that are now largely

PREFACE TO THE SECOND EDITION

inaccessible. The autobiographical sketch *'In illo tempore'* provides fascinating glimpses of David Jones's childhood and formative years, with further remarks that lead into the period of the First World War and the beginnings of *In Parenthesis*, dated here at 1928 and not a year earlier as I indicated on p. 7 below. Almost all of the essays contain autobiographical side-lights, for it is the mark of the unity of his life and work that they can hardly be separated from each other.

Several of the other pieces dwell on his life-long striving to correlate the English and Welsh elements in his own family heritage and to assimilate the minutest details of Welsh tradition and national feeling. In this task he was always painfully conscious of his lack of the Welsh language, except for what he could puzzle out slowly from books. His observations on 'Wales and Visual Form' are peculiarly interesting in view of his own stature as an artist and of his struggle, while living in London, to analyse and interpret the nature and limitations of the Welsh achievement. The brief note on 'The Death of Harold', written in the centenary year of the Battle of Hastings, provides a highly characteristic juxtaposition of Welsh and English. One of the medieval Welsh chronicles, only translated into English in 1952, contains a reference to a tradition that Harold was not killed at Hastings, but escaped to live as an anchorite at Chester, where a body supposed to be his was disinterred in the fourteenth century. Such notes as this are important in disclosing the deep and intricate quality of David Jones's involvement with Wales, but they are also significant in that through one man's patience and enthusiasm they open up traditions and moods of Wales that are so often otherwise literally a closed book to English speakers.

The Dying Gaul contains two major essays – major in terms of length and subject-matter. The first, 'Art in Relation to War', written in 1942–3 and revised in 1946, should be read alongside 'Art and Sacrament', published in *Epoch and Artist*. Considering the time at which this was written, it is an extraordinary performance and ranges much more widely and in parts much more narrowly than the title would suggest, for it is an impassioned statement of David Jones's aesthetics and has little to say on the topic of morality in regard to war. The level of argument is theoretical and abstract; it is not concerned with particular details of the writer's own problems in translating into artforms his own experience of war. But following the initial discussion of the strategies of war as part and parcel of man's very being as an artist, replete with examples, the essay revolves around the abiding theme of the meaning of culture and the destruction of it through the inflexible dominance of the machine. Like so much of David Jones's writing, it resists summary.

The second major essay is 'An Introduction to *The Rime of the Ancient Mariner*', originally published as a separate book by Clover Hill Editions in 1972. The essay is the fruit of almost a lifetime's involvement with Coleridge's poem and provides a commentary on the engravings that he did for Douglas Cleverdon in 1929. There is more of a meander to his writing here, the effect of age on his many-threaded imagination and memory, but the essay is a very serious attempt to disentangle certain details and penetrate the underlying symbolism of the poem, dwelling especially on the theme of penance and David Jones's judgement that Coleridge's notion of sacramental penance was misconceived. In its range of allusion and the eclecticism of its treatment this essay must surely be one of the most amazing that *The Ancient Mariner* has ever elicited.

The posthumous poetry and prose mentioned above simply amplify what David Jones saw fit to publish in his own lifetime. Since his death, however, several people have published transcripts of letters from him, for he was an accomplished exponent of this informal art, writing extensively about his work and life to a large number of correspondents, both personal friends and academic enquirers. Two collections of letters have been or are shortly about to be published in book form – *Letters to Vernon Watkins*, edited by Ruth Pryor (University of Wales Press, 1976) and *Letters to William Hayward*, edited by Colin Wilcockson (Agenda Editions, 1978). Single or small numbers of letters to Saunders Lewis, Wyn Griffith and Colin Wilcockson have also appeared in magazines. Tony Stoneburner, in *A List of Letters by David Jones* (Limekiln Press, 1977), has provided brief biblio-

PREFACE TO THE SECOND EDITION

graphical details of some 700 letters to about 75 persons, ranging from as early as 1921 up to just before David Jones's death. Such a mass of material will doubtless contain much duplication of information, but a volume of selected letters would add greatly to our knowledge and growing appreciation of this innocent, lovable man.

The printing of a second edition of this book enables me to correct some errors in the first. On p. 103 the bracketed reference to 'Mametz Wood' should be corrected to 'Biez Wood'. Two allusions on p. 186 can now be identified through the help of correspondents as noted: the eating of grass as a token of the sacrament comes from *The High History of the Holy Graal*, branch XX, title XIII, translated by Sebastian Evans (Norman Yendell), and the words 'and but we avoid wisely there is but death' comes from Malory, book I, ch. 16 (Colin Hughes). Paul Hills points out that Plate 5 is normally called 'Briar Cup'. I ought also to make clear that the details of owners of pictures given in this book are not necessarily correct for 1971 or now, as I unwarily followed the information given in Ironside without further checking. A preliminary 'List of Works in Public Collections by David Jones' was published by Paul Hills in the second David Jones Special Issue of *Agenda* (Autumn/Winter 1973–4), but many additions now need to be made to this. With regard to the private collections some minor corrections should be made. The *Annunciation to Shepherds* (p. 70) is more usually referred to as *Eclogue IV*. *The Lamb* (p. 70) and *Pigotts* (p. 57) never belonged to Miss Helen Sutherland, but rather to Mrs Nicolete Gray. On p. 7 the list of places where David Jones did watercolours and drawings should include Northumberland, where he frequently stayed at Rock Hall before Helen Sutherland moved to Cockley Moor in the Lake District.

The frontispiece portrait of David Jones, by Sally Soames, was provided by the David Jones estate.

For further bibliographical information the reader is referred to my own supplementary bibliography in *David Jones: Eight Essays on His Work as Writer and Artist*, edited by Roland Mathias

(Llandysul: Gomer Press, 1976) and to the much fuller book by Samuel Rees, *David Jones: An Annotated Bibliography and Guide to Research* (New York: Garland Publishing, 1977). Continuing bibliographical material and other information is provided in the *David Jones Society Newsletter*, edited by myself from the Department of German, The University, Manchester, M13 9PL, since 1976.

DB
1978

To Gerow

I

Introduction

> To see a World in a Grain of Sand
> And a Heaven in a Wild Flower,
> Hold Infinity in the palm of your hand
> And Eternity in an hour.

These introductory lines from Blake's *Auguries of Innocence* may aptly serve as a double introduction to a study of David Jones, for Blake is the most distinguished of that small number of men, including such diverse talents as D. G. Rossetti, William Morris and Percy Wyndham Lewis, who have enriched English culture, as David Jones has done, in the fields of both literature and the visual arts. And Blake, together with El Greco, is one of the artists in the great mystical tradition that most move David Jones, and with whom he feels his own work to be allied.[1] This is not, of course, to assume an identity of vision between the two poet-artists: Blake's outlook on life expresses a much stronger awareness of the forces of darkness, of the evil that rends the world, than is ever apparent in David Jones's work. The lines that follow those already quoted from the *Auguries of Innocence* are a clear epitome of Blake's views. Yet the first four give a remarkable summary of the qualities inherent in almost all of David Jones's varied achievements. Look at a painting such as *Thorn Cup* (1932) or *Guenever* (1940), take practically any page from *In Parenthesis* (1937) or *The Anathemata* (1952), and you can hardly fail to realize that the loving attention paid to the

---

[1] John Rothenstein, *Modern English Painters. Lewis to Moore* (Eyre & Spottiswoode, 1956), p. 296.

particular has as its aim a depiction of the universal and that the tangible world points beyond itself to the transcendental.

But we are already perhaps moving too quickly, for even among those who reckon themselves usually well-informed David Jones is not very well known, and this despite the fact that *The Anathemata*, for example, has been hailed by one critic as one of the five 'major poetic efforts of our era'[1] in English (the others being Eliot's *Waste Land*, Pound's *Cantos*, Hugh MacDiarmid's *In Memoriam James Joyce*, and William Carlos Williams's *Paterson*). In the sphere of the visual arts, especially in watercolours and engraving, he is probably better known than in the field of literature, and this may well be due to the fact that it was as a painter that he started his career. He held his first exhibition at the St George's Gallery in Grosvenor St in 1927 and has continued exhibiting ever since,[2] but it was not until ten years later that he published his first book, *In Parenthesis*.

David Jones was born on 1 November 1895 at Brockley in Kent.[3] His father, James Jones, was a printer's overseer and had come to London from Holywell, Flintshire, about 1885, but the small boy became aware of his Welsh blood and his Welsh heritage through such things as hearing his father sing 'Mae hen wlad fy nhadau' and 'Ar hyd y nos' and going on an early visit to his grandfather, John Jones, a plasterer, whom he remembers sitting on the sea-shore near the oratory of St Trillo at Rhos. His mother was called Alice Ann and was the daugher of Ebenezer Bradshaw, a mast-and-block maker from Rotherhithe, who figures prominently in *The Anathemata* in the section entitled 'Redriff'. As his mother had an aptitude for drawing in her younger days and his father's job made a familiarity with books and illustrations a natural state of affairs, David Jones's early preoccupation with drawing was properly encouraged. One of his earliest drawings, still extant, is of a *Dancing Bear*, done at the age of seven and possessed of a naturalistic vision and a sense of pity unusual in children. Not much later he

---

[1] David Wright in the Introduction to *Longer Contemporary Poems* (Penguin, 1966), p. 9.

[2] Rothenstein, *op. cit.*, p. 301.

[3] Biographical information is given in 'Autobiographical Talk' (*Epoch and Artist* = *E & A*); H. S. Ede, 'David Jones' (*Horizon* VIII, 1943); Robin Ironside, *David Jones* (Penguin, 1949); Rothenstein, *op. cit.*

INTRODUCTION

began to exhibit with the Royal Drawing Society, showing mainly drawings of animals, but the special gifts of early childhood were soon overlaid by a growing dependence on the popular art current in magazines and old Royal Academy catalogues. From 1909 to 1914 he studied at the Camberwell Art School under A. S. Hartrick, Reginald Savage and Herbert Cole, and through them he was introduced to modern French painting, to the Pre-Raphaelites and the English illustrators of the nineteenth century—Pinwell, Sandys, Beardsley, etc. During this period, though he says he was 'completely muddle-headed as to the function of the arts in general', he gradually formed the idea of becoming either an illustrator of Welsh historical and legendary themes or an animal painter.

The First World War broke as rudely into David Jones's life as anyone else's and on 2 January 1915 he enlisted in the Royal Welch Fusiliers, with whom he served as a private on the Western Front from December 1915 until March 1918. This experience, especially of the brutality of trench warfare, but also of the comradeship of soldiers, was to provide the basis of one of the most important works of English literature to emerge from the Great War—his first book, *In Parenthesis*. For David Jones this period of life as a soldier has been a continuing experience: it was not entirely or merely the parenthesis in the rest of a man's life that the title suggests. In fact it was not until 1927 that he began to write the first sentences that led ten years later to the publication of *In Parenthesis*. Nor did this concern with the effects of warfare and the experience of a soldier die out after this. In a modified form it has run over into the series of extracts, published from 1955 onwards, from a work in progress on themes connected with the life of Roman soldiers in the Near East at about the time of Christ. Even *The Hunt* (1965), which is largely Arthurian in inspiration, has reminiscences of 'the wounded men in the thick greenery of Mametz Wood'. 'Wounded trees and wounded men,' writes David Jones, 'are very much an abiding image in my mind as a hang-over from the War.'[1] The account of the War in *In Parenthesis* is one of the most vivid and detailed written of a war that made a

[1] In a letter to me of 9 September 1966.

deep impact on English letters, but although it is a distillation of actual events and emotions it could not have been written until considerably later. It was only after the War that David Jones began to focus his experience as an artist and as a person in such a way as to be able to form a coherent vision of what he had seen and lived through.

In 1919 he went on a Government grant to the Westminster School of Art, where he profited from the teaching and encouragement of Walter Bayes and Bernard Meninsky and became acquainted with the painters of the School of Paris. But it was the English watercolourists and Blake who were his particular enthusiasm. However, the training afforded by an art school did not properly satisfy his deeper and perhaps less conscious desires, which went further than simply learning the tools of a trade. He seems to have been searching for something that would make use of his discrete perceptions of the world and of his own place within it. He had not yet discovered his vocation.

The religious background of the Jones family was that of the Church of England. But during the course of the War, probably in 1917 and in the neighbourhood of Ypres, he began considering the Catholic tradition and on 7 September 1921 was received into the Roman Catholic Church. In a life that shows a gradual progression in self-awareness and accomplishment, from the tentative pencil lines of the *Dancing Bear* to the subtle colouring and complex unified vision of the *Aphrodite in Aulis* (1941), from the observations of concrete detail with which *In Parenthesis* begins to the rich reverberations of ritual and image in *The Anathemata* and the later poems, this step of entering the Catholic Church was surely the most decisive. For through the Catholic tradition David Jones found a mode of seeing things which made sense of the variety of human experience, and he could envisage a place for himself in a body with a continuous, growing, objective tradition of some nineteen centuries of history. Not that he could ever be called a religious artist or writer in the conventional sense of the word. For him there is none of the facile distinction between the sacred and the secular, the religious and the worldly, but rather a comprehensive vision of the wholeness of life. But if becoming a Catholic was the decisive step in the right direction, it was nonetheless only the first one. The Catholic tradition represented a potential, a possibility, which required translation into the actuality of creative artistic activity. One man who particularly helped David Jones to realize his potentialities was Eric Gill.

When David Jones and Eric Gill first met, Gill was nearly forty. He had made a striking reputation as a sculptor, engraver and letterer and had, together with Hilary Pepler, founded the Guild of St Joseph and St Dominic in 1921 as a craft guild and 'a religious fraternity for those who make things with their hands'.[1] When David Jones first went to Ditchling, where Gill had already been living for some time, it was on a casual afternoon visit with a friend from the Westminster Art School on 29 January 1921. He was very impressed by what he saw and found in Eric Gill a man who had thought long and deeply on the most fundamental questions of the nature of art and its relationship with the job of living. Though he did not always agree with Gill's views or the way in which he sometimes translated his ideas into practice, David Jones was stimulated by the clarity and sharpness of Gill's questions into working out where he stood himself. During the summer vacation of 1921 he paid a longer visit to Ditchling, went again in the late autumn and in January 1922 returned to join the community on a more permanent basis. He tried to acquire the skill of carpentry under George Maxwell, but was hopeless at it. But under the tuition of Desmond Chute, in whom he recognized 'a man fully perceptive of the implications of our western Christian cultural and spiritual heritage' as well as a practising artist and a scholar,[2] he successfully learnt the art of engraving on wood and copper and later produced such fine illustrations as those for *The Chester Play of the Deluge* (1927) and *The Rime of the Ancient Mariner* (1929).

The friendship with Eric Gill that started with David Jones's apprenticeship at Ditchling lasted until Gill's death in 1940 and was one of mutual respect and affection. Eric Gill wrote the first article

---

[1] Robert Speaight, *The Life of Eric Gill* (Methuen, 1966), p. 110, quoting Eric Gill from *The Game* (Sept. 1921).
[2] See his letter to the *Tablet*, 20 October 1962, p. 994.

published on David Jones's work in *Artwork* in 1930, and David Jones wrote a very discerning appreciation of Gill's life and work for the *Tablet* almost immediately after his death. He followed this up by a short essay on his sculpture, published in *Blackfriars* in 1941. He also did a watercolour portrait in 1930, which captures something of the philosopher in Gill. Moreover, the whole atmosphere and ethos of the Ditchling community enabled David Jones to develop his own individual talents and views from the stability of a community dedicated to aims with which he profoundly sympathized. The organization of the Guild seems to have been sufficiently elastic for David Jones not to know whether he was formally made a member of it.

In August 1924 the Gills, seeking a less troubled life than that at Ditchling, moved to Capel-y-ffin, and David Jones returned somewhat later to London. However, in December of the same year he joined them again in their remote mountain valley, staying there with interludes in such spots as the Benedictine monastery on Caldy Island until 1927, when he went back to live with his parents in Brockley. It is from this period with the Gills in Wales that David Jones's maturity as an artist dates, with watercolours mainly of landscapes from the area. Further stays with the Gills at Salies de Béarn in the Pyrenees in 1928 and at Pigotts, their Buckinghamshire home from October 1928, provided more material and models for pictures, including two of Petra, the Gills' second daughter, to whom David Jones was for some time engaged. Though Eric Gill's influence is important in David Jones's development as a painter and engraver, there are occasional sidelights to be spotted in his poetry. A solitary sentence from *In Parenthesis* (p. 77) picks out sharply an everyday experience from Capel-y-ffin: 'The water in the trench-drain ran as fast as stream in Nant Honddu in the early months, when you go to get milk from Pen-y-maes.' The stay at Salies de Béarn is reflected in another passage in the same book (p. 163). It was at Capel-y-ffin that David Jones met René Hague, whose printing press he painted and who was mainly responsible for the typography of the original edition of *In Parenthesis*. Through his translation *The Song of Roland* became part of David Jones's *materia poetica*, and he was, as appears in a note to

The Anathemata (p. 238), once literally a 'freer of the waters'. It is interesting to note that Eric Gill shared David Jones's delight in Malory and used to read him aloud to the assembled family.[1]

The period from about 1926 to 1933 is the most prolific in David Jones's career. In 1927 he joined the Society of Wood Engravers, and in 1928 he was elected to the Seven and Five Society, which included among its members Ivon Hitchens, Ben Nicholson, Barbara Hepworth, Henry Moore, John Piper and Edward Bawden. From 1925 onwards he had done a large number of engravings for the Golden Cockerel Press, including illustrations for *The Book of Jonah* (1926) and *The Chester Play of the Deluge*, and also for the St Dominic's Press at Ditchling. He also did some illustrations for poems published by Faber, and this association was rounded off by those to T. S. Eliot's poem *The Cultivation of Christmas Trees* (1954), though the reproduction fails to do justice to the subtle and varied colours of the original. David Jones's considerable talents as an engraver and illustrator were nonetheless exceeded by his devotion to watercolour painting and drawing. Many of these are landscapes and seascapes from Wales, Buckinghamshire, the South coast, London, and the Lake District, at the home of the late Miss Helen Sutherland, who possessed the largest private collection of David Jones's works. (Almost the whole of the Helen Sutherland Collection has recently been exhibited at the Hayward Gallery; the catalogue has a fascinating introduction by Mrs Nicolete Gray.)[2] But there are also a few portraits, some splendidly proud animal drawings, and a good number of interiors with bowls of flowers and household objects. The conventional expression 'still life' seems extraordinarily inappropriate for these vibrant compositions. The richness of David Jones's output from this period is still not exhausted, for it saw also his first essays on themes of a literary or mythological character that were not done specifically as illustrations to a book. Among these perhaps the most striking are the mysterious *Merlin Appears in the Form of a Young Child to Arthur Sleeping* (1930) and *The Chapel Perilous* (1932). There is another

---

[1] Speaight, *op. cit.*, p. 157.
[2] Mrs Gray's first name is found spelled both with a double 't' and a single 't'. I have standardized this to a single 't' throughout, even in bibliographical references.

painting of about the same date that is very similar indeed to the last mentioned Arthurian picture, and it is called simply *Chapel in the Park*. This is strongly indicative of the way in which David Jones can and does transmute the ordinary 'into something rich and strange'. What may at first appear firm, earthbound and separate becomes part of an ethereal vision, suffused with a delicately luminous beauty, and almost absorbing the viewer into it. The organization of the paintings of this period is careful and complex (though not as complex as some of the later ones), but there nonetheless emerges a sense of childlike innocence and delight that David Jones has never lost.

In the midst of all this artistic creativity, once when he was staying with his parents in their bungalow at Portslade in Sussex, David Jones thought he would see if he could manage to do in words something of what he had been doing with paint and pencil. These initial sentences, written tentatively in 1927, were ultimately completed by the publication of his first book, *In Parenthesis*, in 1937. In this highly original account of the First World War several strands of his experience were twisted into a strong thread. As a basis, of course, there was his own experience of life in the trenches of Flanders, minutely and accurately recalled, which was for him, as for most of the men who survived, a continuing, unforgettable experience. This was seen through the mingled lives of those Welshmen and Londoners who were his companions in the Royal Welch Fusiliers, and through the history and culture of these two groups, which he himself shared equally by the accidents of birth. It took a long time for David Jones to shape the data of his personal experience, to give it a formal coherence, and to see in it something other than the immediate sense of despair, anger and compassion that marks the great lyric poetry of the War. Time gave a perspective to the picture, but it was the development of his own *Weltanschauung* resulting from his entering the Catholic Church and his association with Eric Gill, together with the realization of his powers as an artist, which made it possible for him to attempt the ambitious project of writing *In Parenthesis*. It is a unique piece of work, quite unlike any other book written about the First World War, and owing little to contemporary literary trends apart from

The Waste Land (1922) and the poems of Gerard Manley Hopkins, first published by Robert Bridges in 1918.

Since 1933 David Jones has been dogged by repeated periods of ill-health, but when his strength has permitted he has continued both painting and writing. His work has, even in such difficult circumstances, developed and deepened in quality, technique and range. He is not one of those artists or writers whose life-work consists in a continual re-working of one obsessive idea. He has progressively refined his work in certain already chosen and established directions, but he has also embarked on theoretical and critical writings on a variety of topics, of which perhaps the most important are his clearly articulated views on the nature of art in such essays as 'Art and Democracy', written in 1942–3, and 'Art and Sacrament' (1955).

The 1940s saw an increasing pre-occupation with themes from myth and legend, especially but not exclusively from Arthurian romance. This fascination with the Matter of Britain goes back to early childhood, when David Jones particularly enjoyed listening to the stories of King Arthur and the Knights of the Round Table. In his early years as an art student he had thought he would like to be an illustrator of subjects from Welsh history, and his Arthur is very much a Welshman. Now the scattered Malorian allusions of *In Parenthesis* and the small number of Arthurian pictures from the early 1930s were to be followed up and find a consummation in *Guenever* (1940) and *The Four Queens* (1941), and in the long and vital account of the historical and cultural importance of the Arthurian tradition in the essay entitled 'The Myth of Arthur', written for a volume in honour of Hilaire Belloc and published in 1942. The two pictures, both owned by the Tate Gallery, together with *Aphrodite in Aulis* (1941), *Vexilla Regis* (1947), *Trystan ac Essyllt* (c. 1962) and *The Annunciation* (c. 1963), represent the culmination of David Jones's achievement in the visual arts. The complexity of their design and the skilful combination of lavish detail into a unified whole are paralleled by the richness of spiritual meaning that these works reveal. They are the fruit of a lifetime's dedication to the pursuit of truth.

The concern for tradition in its many forms provided much of the motive forces for David Jones's second book, *The Anathemata*, published fifteen years after *In Parenthesis*. It has a lot in common with the earlier work, particularly in its mixture of prose and verse and its allusive, polyglot technique, but it is a more ambitious and a finer work. Unlike *In Parenthesis* it has no plot, but attempts to distil the essence of civilization as manifested in the historical, cultural and spiritual deposits of the British Isles. In scope and accomplishment it is the most impressive of all David Jones's work. I do not think there is anyone else who has interpreted the diversity of tradition in Britain so unerringly or who has expressed the significance of the Welsh tradition for England with such illumination.

David Jones has not spent very much of his life in Wales: the longest period was what he spent with the Gill family at Capel-y-ffin in the mid 1920s. Nor does he speak or read Welsh, but manages to puzzle out the meaning of words and phrases with extreme difficulty. Nonetheless he has identified himself with Wales and Welsh culture in an altogether remarkable way. Not many English people, even half-English people, not even the many English people living in Wales, have tried to find out about and assimilate anything of the Welsh tradition or Welsh literature. There seems to be a persistent streak of colonial xenophobia in the general English attitude towards Wales, which is always more readily identified with the grim industrialism of the mining valleys and the narrow zeal of the chapels than with the richness of Welsh poetry and the unspoilt beauty of the mountains and the sea. David Jones has, I think, penetrated the heart of the Welsh tradition and demonstrated its centrality for anyone who wishes to understand our island heritage properly. Nor has Wales been slow to reciprocate: it was the Welsh Committee of the Arts Council of Great Britain that organized the largest exhibition of David Jones's work in 1954–5, and in 1960 the University of Wales awarded him the honorary degree of Doctor of Letters. In 1955 the distinction of his work was more generally recognized with the award of the C.B.E. In 1968 he won the Corporation of London's first midsummer prize, valued at £1,500, which is awarded for 'the artist, writer, musician, man of letters or science, who has made a major

INTRODUCTION

contribution to British cultural heritage, but who has received little recompense for his or her work'.

Since *The Anathemata* appeared David Jones has been working on another book of poetry centred on themes derived from the experience of Roman soldiers in the Near East at the time of Christ. A number of extracts have been published, the first, called *The Wall*, in 1955. One recent extract, *The Fatigue*, was privately printed for his seventieth birthday by a number of friends and admirers. The initial impetus for this work seems to derive from a visit that David Jones made to Palestine in 1934, joining up with Eric Gill, who was carving some panels for the Palestine Archaeological Museum in Jerusalem. These shorter poems, which will ultimately form a coherent whole, are perhaps, by their very compactness and episodic character, more easily accessible than *The Anathemata* or even *In Parenthesis*.

Another sphere in which David Jones has made a very individual contribution in recent years is that of calligraphy. A number of these inscriptions, dating from 1948 to 1952, were incorporated into *The Anathemata*, though most of them are reproduced in a drab grey that totally fails to impart their real character. The words chosen for these, as always, extremely varied inscriptions are most frequently key quotations in David Jones's *materia poetica*. More often than not they are in Latin, less frequently in Welsh or English. Each letter in every word is carefully and individually shaped so that the whole word or group of letters will form a tightly balanced unit on the sheet. The use of colour is integral to the total conception, whether that of the paper or of the letters, and reproduction in monotone can only obscure or spoil the artist's intention. David Jones's style in inscriptions, as in his paintings, is quite unmistakable. Anyone who is at all familiar with it will not fail to notice that not all the words on the book-cover to the American edition of *Epoch and Artist* are from his hand. Very appropriately, David Jones's contribution to the volume published to celebrate Eliot's seventieth birthday was an inscription including the opening lines of *The Waste Land*.

The range of David Jones's contributions to both art and literature is extraordinarily wide. There are few men who have made their mark in so many diverse fields without somewhere or other being dilettantes, but this accusation cannot be levelled against him. He has always first learnt the tools of his trade so that what he has exhibited or published is polished and properly finished. The writing of *In Parenthesis* took some six or seven years, that of *The Anathemata* about twelve or thirteen. They are considered works, their themes and modes of expression deeply pondered and perfected. Most of this study will be concerned with analysing and evaluating these two works, first and foremost from their own internal structure and use of language, according to their own logic, but a few words need to be said here about the raw material that the poet has hewn and moulded, because it is here that David Jones is most obviously an outsider in the literary world.

The prevalent tendency in modern English poetry is a microscopic examination of details of personal experience, possibly an attempt to find the universal in the completely subjective experience of a private world. In cases where its triviality would otherwise be blatant, the subject is lost in its degeneration into a preoccupation with formal structure or even typography. The reader, if he has difficulty in understanding what is offered to him, experiences this on account of the private nature of the poet's imagination. I exaggerate in order to focus the contrast with David Jones's work. His material, indeed his whole concern as a poet, is non-subjective. If this is true of his attempt to show the essence of a tradition in *The Anathemata*, it is equally so when one considers *In Parenthesis*. Most of the enduring literature of the First World War consists of autobiographical prose or lyric poetry of a deeply emotional, strongly subjective nature. But although *In Parenthesis* could only be based on personal experience, it lacks any simple autobiographical character. It is not about 'I'. It distils a common objective experience, and one of the means whereby this is achieved is the constant reference to an objective tradition of the poetry of war, exemplified superlatively in such works as *Henry V*, Malory's *Morte d'Arthur*, *The Song of Roland*, *The Battle of Brunanburh*, and the Old Welsh poem *Y Gododdin*. No one else, in writing about the War, sought to relate his personal woes, his anger and insights, to this common literary heritage. In her review of *The Anathemata*

INTRODUCTION

Kathleen Raine commented most appositely on this aspect of David Jones's poetry.[1]

> Such is the paradox of our time that the more a poet draws on an objective tradition, the less on subjective experiences, the more obscure he will seem. It is important to realise that neither *The Waste Land*, the *Cantos*, nor even *Finnegans Wake* is obscure to us chiefly because its author refers to some subjective and private world, but for the opposite reason. All these works assume a knowledge of a common fund of traditional culture, that few any longer in fact do possess.

David Jones's main sources of literary reference are such central figures as Chaucer, Malory, Dunbar, Shakespeare, Milton, Coleridge, Tennyson, Hopkins, Eliot and the Bible.

David Jones's reading in the field of English literature is that of the average man, not of a contemporary poet or man of letters. But outside this field his reading is wide and eclectic, as the acknowledgements in the last few pages of the Preface to *The Anathemata* indicate, ranging from Christopher Dawson and Sir James Frazer to Baron Friedrich von Hügel and the late Professor Eva Taylor. History and prehistory, archaeology and anthropology, mysticism, theology, the whole range of the visual arts, historical geography and the science of navigation, the myths of Greece, of pagan Scandinavia and of Arthur—all these and more form David Jones's scale of reference. His sense of history, his awareness of the precise detail that is important, stem from the conviction that our understanding of the particular place and moment of time in which we find ourselves depends on the total historical context. The past and the present are inseparably one. For David Jones the personal experience of the individual is too limited a basis for art or literature. It is perhaps for this reason (as well as for the accidents of parentage) that he is so attracted by the medieval Welsh tradition with its happy blend of personal and social elements and is something of an outsider to the great English tradition of personal poetry.[2] In this emphasis on the impersonal he goes even further

---

[1] *New Statesman and Nation*, vol. XLIV, 22 November 1952, p. 607.
[2] See Gwyn Williams, *An Introduction to Welsh Poetry* (Faber, 1953), pp. 1f.

than Eliot, who may be allowed the last words in this introduction:[1]

> One of the facts that might come to light in this process (*sc.* of criticism) is our tendency to insist, when we praise a poet, upon those aspects of his work in which he least resembles anyone else. In these aspects or parts of his work we pretend to find what is individual, what is the peculiar essence of the man. We dwell with satisfaction upon the poet's difference from his predecessors, especially his immediate predecessors; we endeavour to find something that can be isolated in order to be enjoyed. Whereas if we approach a poet without this prejudice we shall often find that not only the best, but the most individual parts of his work may be those in which the dead poets, his ancestors, assert their immortality most vigorously.

[1] 'Tradition and the Individual Talent' in *Selected Essays*.

2
Observations on art

In his *Life of Eric Gill* Robert Speaight relates an amusing episode from David Jones's first meeting with Gill (p. 111):

> It was a very wet day, and he found Eric in his workshop. Eric went on working and presently said: 'You don't have a very clear idea of the direction you're going in, do you?' Jones agreed that he did not. Then Eric took a piece of paper and drew a roughly triangular figure with the corners not meeting, followed by a second in which they nearly met but not quite, and finally a third where they met perfectly.
> 'Which of those do you think is a triangle?' he asked. Jones replied that he did not know, but that he liked one of them better than the others.
> 'It's not a question of being better', said Eric; 'the other two aren't triangles at all.'

This incident instructively epitomizes the difference between Eric Gill and David Jones, both as practising artists and as men who have attempted to put into words, in various ways, the theoretical basis of their experience as artists. Eric Gill was a man who saw things in terms of sharp contrasts: either the lines he had drawn made a triangle or they did not. And quite frequently his judgements on matters more complicated than that were based on the assumption that they were better treated as triangles or non-triangles. Furthermore he was totally estranged from the spirit of his time, and his remark that 'our whole civilization is wrong from top to bottom, and past remedy, too,'[1] is quite typical of his polemical essays. In seeing the Industrial Revolution as the origin of all man's woes he hankered after a falsely idealized pre-industrial society. By contrast David Jones did not and does not take such a black-and-white view of the world, nor did he agree with everything that Eric Gill said. As Robert Speaight says, 'What struck him was the clear method of his exposition. It was like talking to Socrates. He recognized the genius of the teacher, irrespective of the rightness of his teaching; and the gentle integrity of a man who knew exactly where he was going' (p. 111). It is entirely characteristic of David Jones that he should have been concerned with liking one of the 'triangles' better than the others, with the question of delight and beauty rather than categorizing and judging. At the time, however, it was necessary for him for his own development to sharpen his intellectual faculties and clarify his ideas, and the day-to-day contact with Gill over a number of years provided him with the needed stimulus.

Some twenty years elapsed after his first contact with Eric Gill and his friends and family before David Jones put pen to paper in the attempt to formulate in words the basis of his understanding of art. Like most of his work, these essays of 1941 onwards are the fruit of long ponderings. They are mainly concerned with the nature of art generally, though there are many passages which bear directly on his work as a painter and engraver. The Preface to *The Anathemata* deals, of course, specifically with the problem of writing poetry in our present stage of civilization. These essays, it should be insisted upon, represent the struggles of an artist and a poet to express in other terms something of the background and theory of his own artistic works. They are not the writings of a philosopher, and I think it would do David Jones a disservice if one tried to make out that they should be taken as philosophical essays. Although there are strenuous attempts to systematize and classify, there are often some gaps in the argument that either are not bridged or can only be bridged by some one sharing the same (Catholic) presumptions. The general character of the essays is determined by the association of ideas. When David Jones refers to his efforts as 'these

[1] Eric Gill, *Essays* (Cape, 1947), p. 54.

meanderings',[1] we should accept the image and discard the wish to interpret it as a conventional humility-formula. The rivers that wind their way through the plains have different delights from the swift mountain streams. Similarly, his essays pause to examine the ox-bows that the meanders often form, to look back up to the hills and again to the sea. Moreover, they are exploratory in mood rather than definitive. They outline the contemporary situation, analyse it with sympathy and discuss it with an enquiring mind. From this rather than any posited solution we derive our enlightenment.

The essays on problems relating to art collected in *Epoch and Artist* were written over a period of more than fifteen years and first published in a variety of books and journals. Some of them were written with a Catholic readership in view, as, for example, 'Religion and the Muses', first published in the *Tablet*, and 'Art and Sacrament', first published in a volume called *Catholic Approaches*, edited by Lady Pakenham. The other essays are also based, implicitly if not explicitly, on Catholic premises. Some readers may find this off-putting, but if they exercise tolerance they will probably find little that they can dismiss as merely sectarian in what David Jones has to say.

From the beginning of 1922 onwards David Jones was intimately associated with Eric Gill and the Ditchling community. It was in this setting that he became acquainted with the writings of the Catholic philosopher Jacques Maritain, whose thinking had a considerable influence on him and made its impact twenty years later in his essays. The book that was so significant was a quite small work called *Art et Scolastique*, which Eric Gill first read early in 1922.[2] He and his friends found it expressed so well their own aspirations that they persuaded Fr John O'Connor to make a translation of it, which they published in 1923 at St Dominic's Press under the title *The Philosophy of Art*. As this was a limited edition of 500 copies, its circulation was not very extensive, and a new translation by J. F. Scanlan was published in 1930, together with some new essays, under the title of *Art and Scholasticism*. Maritain's book

---

[1] 'Art and Sacrament', *E & A*, p. 147.
[2] Speaight, *op. cit.*, pp. 124ff.

17

has often a somewhat sermonizing tone, and the nature of his judgement in matters respecting the modern world and its art is apparent in his early dismissal of Stravinsky, which he corrected later in an extravagant footnote, and in his unclouded praise of Léon Bloy and Claudel. Maritain looks back to the Middle Ages for his models 'because the Middle Ages are relatively the most *spiritual* period to be found in history and offer us an example very nearly realized—I do not deny the vices and defects—of principles which the author believes to be true.'[1] That the Middle Ages may be a source of enlightenment on many topics is a fact that is nowadays all too likely to go by the board—the word 'medieval' is most frequently applied as a term of abuse—but the social, economic, political and religious conditions which made possible the medieval outlook on art have gone irrevocably. Nonetheless, the basis of much in modern government and religion was provided by the Middle Ages, and many of the intellectual problems confronting us today were quite clearly formulated by them too. Maritain's analysis of certain philosophical ideas proved a vital stimulus to both Eric Gill and David Jones, however much their attitudes varied, and this analysis is all the more important for being general and abstract.

'Art,' writes Maritain, tracing the views of the Scholastics, 'is a habit of the practical intellect' (p. 11). He contrasts the virtues of the practical intellect in terms of Prudence, which is concerned with action, and of Art, which is concerned with productive action or making. Both virtues are also called to judge and to command, though the primary function of Art is only to judge, whereas that of Prudence is to command. The course of Art is determined by following certain rules according to the end pursued (as, for example, in making a ship or a clock, which requires certain rules to be followed if the end-product is to be recognized as a ship or a clock). Since these rules belong to the sphere of the practical, and not the speculative, intellect, 'the naturally appropriate method of teaching it is education by apprenticeship, a working novitiate under a master and in face of reality, not lessons doled out by

---

[1] Jacques Maritain, *Art and Scholasticism* (Sheed & Ward, 1930), p. 105, in the additional essay entitled 'The Frontiers of Poetry'.

teachers' (p. 43). According to Aquinas, 'in every form of discipline and teaching the master merely gives assistance from outside to the principle of immanent activity within the pupil' (p. 45). These considerations were, as may easily be imagined, quickly assimilated by the Ditchling community. Indeed, they were simply a proper formulation of their own experience.

In discussing the concept of beauty Maritain starts from Aquinas's definition of the beautiful as *id quod visum placet*, 'what gives pleasure on sight', and relates this to the absolute beauty of God, concluding that beauty belongs to the transcendental and metaphysical order. Moreover, since art is 'fundamentally constructive and creative', the artist 'is as it were an associate of God in the making of works of beauty', though 'artistic creation does not copy God's creation, but continues it' (p. 63). In view of this significant relationship between God's work and that of the artist, and bearing in mind the fact that art can be exercised only as a habit, i.e. as a way of life and mode of vision, the Christian artist (by which the selector of religious subjects is *not* meant) must continually strive to realize what Fra Angelico said: 'Art demands great tranquillity, and to paint the things of Christ, the artist must live with Christ' (p. 71). This is not to reject great works of art that have proceeded from another culture, for Maritain says: 'Consider also that wherever art, Egyptian, Greek or Chinese, has attained a certain degree of grandeur and purity, it is already Christian, Christian in hope, because every spiritual splendour is a promise and a symbol of the divine harmonies of the Gospel' (p. 69). This view is, as we shall see later in greater detail, of fundamental importance for David Jones.

Beauty is related to order and logic, states Maritain, quoting Baudelaire:[1]

> Là, tout n'est qu'ordre et beauté,
> Luxe, calme et volupté.

The logic of art is not, however, the 'pseudo-logic of clear ideas' or 'the logic of knowledge and demonstration' but the working logic

---

[1] *Op. cit.*, p. 51. 'There all is ORDER (Maritain's capitals) and beauty, Richness, tranquillity and voluptuousness' (*L'Invitation au Voyage*).

of every day, eternally mysterious and disturbing, the logic of the structure of the living thing, and the intimate geometry of nature' (p. 52). Unfortunately for the reader Maritain does not explain in what this logic consists, apart from the tautology of being *per ordinem et conformitatem ad regulas artis* (p. 52), though he declares that Vergil, Racine, Poussin, Shakespeare, Baudelaire, Mallarmé, Claudel, Pierre Reverdy and Eluard are logical, while Chateaubriand, the only counter-example (though retracted in a later footnote), is not. In this discussion of the purity of art Maritain objects to what is unnecessary in art and what is a fake. The imitation of nature and the creation of an illusion are wrong. What the artist paints should look painted.

'Art is a fundamental necessity in the human state,' he writes. It 'teaches men the pleasures of the spirit, and because it is itself sensitive and adapted to their nature, it is better able to lead them to what is nobler than itself' (p. 80). And yet at the same time, though 'there cannot in fact be any absolutely "gratuitous" work of art—except the universe' (p. 77), there is something about a work of art which demands the application of the word 'gratuitous'. This is the case simply because the work of art is self-determined: '...in the actual production of the work the virtue of art has only one object, the good of the work to be done; to make matter resplendent with beauty, to create a thing in accordance with the laws of its being, independently of anything else.'[1] This concern with gratuitousness is highly characteristic of David Jones's writings on the nature of art.

The above remarks are merely a rough sketch of Maritain's views. There is much that I have left out, of course, but I hope there is no serious omission or distortion in what I have singled out. It is clear even from this brief resumé, how much Maritain spoke to the condition of Eric Gill and his friends. Here was a coherent philosophy of art grounded on the fundamentals of the Catholic faith and agreeing in all essentials with their own practical experience. It is small wonder, then, if we find time and again quotations and echoes from Maritain through the essays of both Eric Gill and David Jones. But there is a cardinal distinction between the two

[1] *Ibid.*, p. 127, in the additional essay entitled 'An Essay on Art'.

men's views which is perhaps illuminated by Gill's frequent citation of Ananda Coomaraswamy's dictum that 'art is not an aesthetic but a rhetorical activity'.[1] Though it has been said that Eric Gill rarely tried to influence anybody,[2] he was nonetheless a great pamphleteer, if not indeed a preacher, as most of his essays amply demonstrate. In his writings, lectures and talks on art the teacher in him will always out. David Jones's talent is much less vociferous. One reason for this is that he finds himself intricated in the perplexities of the present situation of civilization. They are part of himself, and he cannot withdraw from them or reject them in the way that Eric Gill tried (and only tried) to. As he says of his enquiry in one essay, 'It is not an indictment, it is a reconnaissance.'[3] He can see the beauty of an aeroplane and even its weapons.

> But when we glance from the airman's weapons to the airmen's mess—O what a fall is here, my countrymen! No one is to blame. We are born into civilization at this date. Certainly no one can afford to be superior, for we all, in one way or another, are involved, and all seek differing compensatory means as each is best able.[4]

This is not an isolated comment; it is at the back of most of what David Jones has to say. He sees the situation and the problem as much more complex, subtle and involved than Eric Gill could allow. It is hardly an accident that Eric Gill should have excelled in the black and white field of engraving and typography, whereas David Jones's best work is to be found in his extraordinarily refined watercolour drawings and his poetry.

The difficulties of the artist in the present situation are suggestively considered in the essay 'Religion and the Muses', from which the above passage has been quoted. The import of ideas cannot easily be summarized, and this is a strength in David Jones's writing. It is fed from a large number and variety of sources and touches, always quite properly and naturally, on such topics as the Pre-Raphaelites, James Joyce, Picasso, Leonardo, Cézanne, canon

---

[1] Cf. Eric Gill, *Essays*, pp. 9, 18.
[2] Speaight, *op. cit.*, p. 124.
[3] 'The Utile', *E & A*, p. 183.
[4] 'Religion and the Muses', *E & A*, p. 105.

law, the *Dies Irae*, and the decor of public houses, to mention only a selection. But the constant theme is the widespread breakdown of the validity of symbols in our present culture situation, which looks very little different now from what it did in 1941, when the essay was first published. Such solutions as there may be will most probably be individual ones, not valid for a whole community, but having a certain validity nonetheless. 'Instinct rather than rule will have to serve. There can be no operation orders, and our flanks have been in the air long since' (p. 105). The essay concludes with a pregnant quotation from W. P. Ker's literary history *The Dark Ages*, dealing with the gods of the pagan North: 'But the gods who are defeated, think that defeat no refutation.' Such a remark characterizes David Jones's open hopeful attitude in a situation that is perhaps only imperceptibly on the way to a more general solution. His approach to philosophical and theoretical questions is less analytical than gently intuitive. It is the indirect, tentative approach of the artist, not the critic.

This same approach marks the essay on 'Art and Democracy', written about a year later than the previous one, but not published until 1947. The key thought in these reflexions is that 'Men are equal in the sense that they are all equally judged to be men because all *behave* as artists.'[1] This emphasis on man as artist is a basic tenet of Eric Gill's, who constantly quotes Coomaraswamy on the subject to the effect that 'the artist is not a special kind of man, but every man is a special kind of artist'.[2] It is essential to realize, as David Jones points out, that the word 'artist' is used here in the very basic sense of 'maker' and that the discussion centres on the nature of *art*, not of the fine arts. These remarks on making lead to an instructive difference between man and the animal kingdom that is fundamental to the whole concept of art:

> But, you may say, animals too are makers; they too make things: the beaver, the ant and notably the spider, as the Scots king saw, and, of course, the bee, that 'teaches the act of order to a peopled kingdom'. But do we ever say: 'That honeycomb had something about it; it had real feeling'? We do not and never shall, except we use

[1] 'Art and Democracy', *E & A*, p. 86.
[2] Eric Gill, *Essays*, pp. 14, 54.

words and indulge in thoughts which have no regard for the nature and virtue of art. These 'beauties' and 'designs' of nature are all without conscious variety, neither is there in them anything of the gratuitous, which is the *sine qua non* of art (p. 87).

This concept of the gratuitous, which we noted particularly in Maritain, is pursued by David Jones, both here and elsewhere, as the distinguishing mark of man:

> If we could catch the beaver placing never so small a twig *gratuitously* we could make his dam into a font, he would be patient of baptism—the whole 'sign-world' would be open to him, he would know sacrament and have a true culture, for a culture is nothing but a sign, and the *anathemata* of a culture, 'the things set up', can be set up only to the gods (p. 88).

In this passage we have in a nutshell the essence of David Jones's thinking on the nature of art—the concept of the gratuitous, the idea of the 'sign', its relationship to 'sacrament', the characteristics of culture and the connexion with religion. These ideas are dealt with in greater detail in other writings, notably in the essay on 'Art and Sacrament' and in the Preface to *The Anathemata*.

The gratuitous nature of art is one with the notion of man's free will. Man, unlike the bee or the beaver, is not totally subject to the control of instinct and the formative powers of environment. He is capable of making decisions and especially of performing actions which are not *necessarily* required in order to keep himself alive. He is 'a creature which is not only capable of gratuitous acts but of which it can be said that such acts are this creature's hall-mark and sign-manual.'[1] There is a sense in which 'art is for art's sake' without the derogatoriness that this tag usually evokes. David Jones recalls another saying, which is less open to misinterpretation and means virtually the same thing: 'Art is the sole intransitive activity of man' (p. 149). He then goes on to say: 'It is the intransitivity and gratuitousness in man's art that is the sign of man's uniqueness; not merely that he makes things, nor yet that those things have beauty.' There is a certain difficulty here in trying to talk about art

---

[1] 'Art and Sacrament', *E & A*, p. 148.

in terms of intransitive activity, especially when two such disparate illustrations as a door-handle and the Venus of Melos are given. The question under discussion is concerned with the perfecting of a work. A door-handle, with its obvious functional end of providing a means to open the door, may quite reasonably achieve its perfection through an activity which has nothing in mind but the most convenient way of opening a door. Such activity as merely enables the door to be opened and nothing more may be denoted as transitive, but it is the accidental activity which produces, as a by-product, perfection in a door-handle such as to arouse our admiration which is to be called intransitive. The same is also true in the examples from playing cricket that David Jones adduces: 'It is then, in the last analysis, the intransitive activity of art that is the cause of such ejaculations as "A beautiful ball, sir!" or "Very pretty"' (p. 153). The difficulty is that in the examples of the door-handle and the game of cricket the obvious activity involved is transitive; it has a clear functional end in enabling the door to be opened and in getting the batsman out. In such cases the quality which makes us recognize them as art is additional to what would make them perfectly well serve their purpose, and as such it is gratuitous.

From this point we can move on to consider the idea of the 'sign' and the related term 'sacrament', for though an activity may be gratuitous, it is not meaningless. On the contrary, its very gratuitousness is significant in the etymological sense of the word. The argument starts, chronologically, from the fact that primitive man 'juxtaposed marks on surfaces not merely with utile, but with significant, intent; that is to say a "re-presenting", a "showing again under other forms", an "effective recalling" of something was intended' (p. 155). The cave paintings of Lascaux are the most obvious and readily recollected examples of this intent, but, as David Jones continues:

> The merest rough, bungled incision or the daubed on red ochre, the most elementary 'cup-markings' on the stone at the burial-site (and Homo Neanderthalis appears to have done this much) provide perhaps more foolproof examples of what I mean. For here, with the barest minimum of skill and without any, or much, shining out of

the *splendor formae*, we would appear already to be in the domain of sign (sacrament), of anamnesis, of anathemata. We are with beasts of a sort, but not, it would seem, perishing beasts (p. 156).

Basically, the sign is a representation under different conditions of something seen or experienced which is considered, however modestly, as important. It is a re-creation in other terms of something belonging to the realms of the intangible or the invisible that is nonetheless felt as real. It is a means of expressing an attitude towards life. David Jones believes that this concept of the sign is inseparable from the idea of the 'sacred', and for the following reasons: 'A sign then must be significant of something, hence of some "reality", so of something "good", so of something that is "sacred". That is why I think that the notion of sign implies the sacred' (p. 157). The steps from one of these realizations to the next depend on various arguments adumbrated in the paragraph preceding this conclusion, namely, that if something is real it has *esse*, and that *bonum et ens convertuntur*, 'good and being are interchangeable'. The argument in this essay is reduced to an absolute minimum because it was addressed to a Catholic audience. There are, in fact, a good many assumptions in the essay which it would be natural for Catholics to make. Other readers would no doubt require a reasoned justification of the case presented, which David Jones would probably have attempted if he had been directing his remarks in the first place at a wider public. As it is the ordinary reader must bear this in mind and make such allowances as may be necessary.

The use of such terms as 'sacred', 'sacrament' and 'religion' is apt to be problematic nowadays, as David Jones is well aware. They are liable to be interpreted (even by Catholics) in a much narrower sense than he intends, at least partly because they are held by many people to belong to that sideline piety of ecclesiastical practices widely considered to be irrelevant to modern daily life. Moreover, such terms often constitute a psychological barrier (arising, for example, from intellectual scruples, a non-Christian education, a revulsion from the disparity between Christian preaching and Christian practice, or a severely rationalist approach to life, to mention only a few of the possible reasons), and this barrier is difficult to break through. As a Catholic David Jones is committed to the conventional, ordinary understanding of the terms 'sacred', 'sacrament' and 'religion', but the nub of his argument is that these terms are of much wider relevance than their conventional connotations. At this point it is necessary to return to some remarks made at the beginning of 'Art and Sacrament'.

The essay opens with a discussion of the relationship between Ars and Prudentia, following closely in the footsteps of Maritain, from whom the use of the terminology is familiar. The term Prudentia is used to denote 'the tutelary genius who presides over the whole realm of faith, moral, religion, ethic; she is thought of as Holy Wisdom' (p. 145). (It is interesting to note how much of David Jones's thinking goes on in terms of personification of abstract concepts.) The import of the argument is that man, by virtue of his capacity for choice, i.e. by virtue of free will, and because of his being a social animal, is necessarily involved with questions of acceptable or unacceptable behaviour, i.e. with morals. Religion is, of course, especially concerned with morals (*prudentia*), but as David Jones points out:

> It is perhaps less often observed, though it requires observing, that those who reject the postulates of supernatural religion are no less bound than are the men of religion by the allurements of *a* Prudentia; indeed this binding is most marked....
>
> But if we abandon this Prudentia (*sc.* the original Prudentia) it is only to be committed to another. Her charms are substantial and unelusive. Her get-up is woven of the immediate and the contingent. She assures us that she is unconcerned with moral, yet there is about her a familiar tang, and no wonder, for she uses Black Market products, concocted of crude ethic and raw moral, certain important ingredients, suspending agents and solvents being omitted from the stolen prescriptions. She is full of does and don'ts. She is on intimate terms with a number of party-leaders, and before we know where we are she induces us to become party-members; and the party is of necessity a prudential society concerned with oughts and ought nots. So that, no less than the saints or the men of dogmatic religion or the men of ethic or the men of primitive cults or the enlightened inheritors of yesterday or their disillusioned inheritors of today we *all* are committed to a Prudentia of sorts (pp. 146ff.).

So far, so good. The argument is intelligible to those who would not go further with David Jones to assert that man 'because he is endowed with rationality (i.e. has a "rational" soul) must have a supernatural end' (p. 147). It is intelligible to anyone who sees some kind of order implicit in the universe, whether he considers it that of a self-organizing system or one directed by a supernatural orderer.

In the same way David Jones's use of the word 'religion' is not meant in the simple sense as referring to 'pieties, dispositions of the will, explicit acts of worship, states of mind or soul' (p. 161). It has a more general, inclusive sense derived from a common etymology of the word connecting it with binding (as also in 'obligation' and 'ligament'): 'It refers to a binding, a securing. Like the ligament, it secures a freedom to function. The binding makes possible the freedom. Cut the ligament and there is atrophy—corpse rather than *corpus*' (p. 158). In this sense art can be said to be a 'religious' activity, because it binds things together in a new form. David Jones then continues, using strategy as his example of an art:

> In so far as form is brought into being there is reality. 'Something' not 'nothing', moreover a new 'something', has come into existence. And if, as we aver, man's form-making has in itself the nature of a sign, then these formal realities, which the art of strategy creates, must, in some sense or other, be *signa*. But of what can they possibly be significant? What do they show forth, re-present, recall or, in any sense, reflect? It would seem that the forms which strategy shows forth can be typic only of that archetypal form-making and ordering implicit in the credal clause *per quem omnia facta sunt*. That is to say they partake in some sense, however difficult to posit, of that juxtaposing by which what was *inanis et vacua* became radiant with form and abhorrent of vacua by the action of the Artifex, the Logos, who is known to our tradition as the Pontifex who formed a bridge 'from nothing' and who then, like Brân in the *Mabinogion*, himself became the bridge by the Incarnation and Passion and subsequent Apotheoses (pp. 159f.).

But having gone so far in his argument about 'signs' David Jones then proceeds to ask why this art-form of the sign should have been used and converted into a sacrament. Why should an outward sign and a manual act have been made obligatory for the continuance of Christianity? David Jones believes that the sacraments of Christianity were instituted not as props for the spiritual support of the infirmity of the body, nor merely because man naturally delights in signs and commemorative acts, but because these things are 'natural to him in virtue of his being an artist' (p. 165). In this way we are led to see what may be meant by the statement that all art is religious. It is perhaps an unusual viewpoint to take in that it involves a somewhat different understanding of the terms 'art' and 'religious' from the conventional one. The word 'sacrament' is normally reserved to refer to a limited number of ritual acts almost universally observed in the various forms of Christianity. The number varies between denominations and has varied through the course of history, but the sacraments of baptism and communion are generally recognized. What David Jones is trying to say is that these well-known ritual acts are but the culmination of a type of behaviour which is universal:

> Some man known to the reader may indeed appear to escape from all that is commonly or vulgarly meant by the 'sacramental', but no sooner does he put a rose in his buttonhole but what he is already in the trip-wire of sign, and he is deep in an entanglement of signs if he sends that rose to his sweetheart, Flo; or puts it in a vase by her portrait; and he is hopelessly and up to his neck in that entanglement of Ars, sign, sacrament should he sit down and write a poem 'about' that sweetheart. Heavens knows what his poem will really be 'about'; for then the 'sacramental' will pile up by a positively geometrical progression. So that what was Miss Flora Smith may turn out to be Flora Dea and Venus too and the First Eve and the Second also and other and darker figures, among them no doubt Jocasta. One thing at least the psychologists make plain: there is always a recalling, a re-presenting again, anaphora, anamnesis (p. 167).

This pre-occupation with the 'sign' and the sacramental is a marked feature of David Jones's writings, and what he says in discursive essay form furnishes a helpful background to his poetry. But what he says here has a wider application for the peculiar difficulties which modern poets have to face generally, for the analogical, allusive procedure of thinking so fundamental to poetry is quite alien to many people in the modern world. As he commented in an interview with Peter Orr, 'there is something about technological science in the modern sense which doesn't easily accommodate itself to forms that are purely signs. It is utile, it is utilitarian, one thing follows from the other and that is that.'[1] David Jones has expressed these ideas also in a talk entitled 'Use and Sign' published in the *Listener* (24 May 1962).

The sign is the main subject of the essay on 'Art and Sacrament', but it also figures importantly in the Preface to *The Anathemata*, where the discussion centres more on its application in the arts of literature. The whole of life and experience is, for David Jones, sacramental in the sense outlined above, and everything is seen in the setting that is crowned by Christianity in the rite variously referred to as the mass, holy communion, the Lord's supper, or the breaking of bread. As we noted earlier in Maritain, 'every spiritual splendour is a promise and a symbol of the divine harmonies of the Gospel.' Especially important for David Jones's development of the ideas of sign and sacrament is the massive work of Maurice de la Taille, s.J., entitled *Mysterium Fidei*. This monumental discussion of 'the most august sacrament and sacrifice of the Body and Blood of Christ', completed in 1915 and published originally in Latin, was not published in English until 1941 (book I) and 1950 (book II), but an English resumé appeared in 1934, from which David Jones gained much illumination, as he several times mentions both in this essay and in the Preface to *The Anathemata*. The final sentence of 'Art and Sacrament' spells this out: 'As a postscript I venture to ask the reader to consider what Maurice de la Taille said was done on Maundy Thursday by Good Friday's Victim, I quote: "He placed Himself in the order of signs."' This same quotation serves as an epigraph to all the writings collected in *Epoch and Artist*.

It will be necessary to return to these considerations later when dealing with the Preface to *The Anathemata*, but since 'Art and Sacrament' is more concerned with the visual arts where it is not general, it is appropriate to continue this line of thought first. I do not think the word 'transubstantiation' is used by David Jones in the analogies he draws between the sacraments of the Church and

---

[1] *The Poet Speaks*, ed. Peter Orr (Routledge & Kegan Paul, 1966), p. 101.

the signs of art, but it surely lies behind his discussion of representational and abstract art (to use the commonly employed distinctions). The sacrament embodied in the mass was instituted by an intention which envisaged 'an abstract art *par excellence*; for nothing could be less "representational" or more "re-presentative" or further from "realism" or more near reality than what is intended and posited in this latter instance. (A non-Christian person) would note an extreme objectivity in the view that sign and thing signified are regarded as having a true identity.' Then, changing the object of his remarks, David Jones goes on to assert: '...the painter may say to himself: "This is not a representation of a mountain, it *is* 'mountain' under the form of paint." Indeed, unless he says this unconsciously or consciously he will not be a painter worth a candle. It is indeed the "pith and knot of the matter". This applies also to the poet' (p. 170). It is his contention that it is the abstract quality in a picture which gives it 'being', which makes it into a thing in its own right and not merely the impression of some other thing, but which at the same time enables the relationship between the reality or object that is the point of departure and the final product of the picture to be discerned. If this is the case, then the common distinction between the representational and the abstract in art is seen to be somewhat misconceived, for it becomes 'axiomatic that all art is "abstract" and that all art "re-presents"' (p. 173). In order to clarify what he means by 're-presents', David Jones undertakes a detailed analysis of Hogarth's *Shrimp Girl* and shows how very complex the relationship is between the painted 'thing' and the reality in Hogarth's mind that gave rise to it. In this way it becomes much more obvious how inadequate the simple idea of 're-presenting' is, even (or perhaps especially) with a picture that conforms so easily to what is conventionally considered representational.

These ideas on the abstract in art are propounded in a slightly different context in a letter David Jones wrote to the *Listener*, which is reproduced in *Epoch and Artist* under the heading 'Abstract Art'. The importance of this contribution to the general public discussion of the problems involved in art, especially in view of the current pre-occupation with the non-naturalistic or the non-representational, is indicated by the fact that Herbert Read, in the revised edition of his *Contemporary British Art* (1964), quotes most of it to illustrate the nature of reality in art. He himself writes: 'Reality is not the four walls of the room we are sitting in, or the trees and men we see out of our window; it is a mental construction, a stability of vision, and the next phase of human development may find such stability in an art that is anti-organic, absolute, and ideal' (p. 45). The fact that Sir Herbert quotes from this letter rather than from the essay, though the essence of the views expressed on the abstract in both places is the same, is perhaps due to the *generality* of the remarks in the letter in contrast to the specifically religious context of the essay. This underlines the fact that David Jones's views here, as in other places, receive a confirmation from the Christian religion rather than derive their justification from it. Since *Epoch and Artist* David Jones has published another article, 'Looking Back at the Thirties'[1] in which he substantially reiterates his ideas on the problems facing the artist.

The Preface to *The Anathemata* was designed as an introduction to that work in order to give some kind of background to the aims and techniques of the poem. It serves nonetheless as David Jones's *ars poetica* and as such has recently been included in a collection of essays called *Modern Poets on Modern Poetry*,[2] where it appears in the company of, *inter alios*, Yeats, Pound, Eliot and Auden. Like his essays on art in general, it is much less a theoretical account than a statement of findings relevant to the understanding of his own poetry. W. H. Auden has made some highly pertinent remarks about poets' theory:[3]

> I am always interested in hearing what a poet has to say about the nature of poetry, though I do not take it too seriously. As objective statements his definitions are never accurate, never complete and always one-sided. Not one would stand up under a rigorous analysis. In unkind moments one is almost tempted to think that all they are really saying is: 'Read me. Don't read the other fellows.' But, taken as critical admonitions addressed by his Censor to the poet himself, there is generally something to be learned from them.

[1] *London Magazine*, New Series, V, No. 1, April 1965, pp. 47–54.
[2] Ed. James Scully (Fontana Library, 1966).
[3] W. H. Auden, *Making, Knowing, and Judging* (Oxford, 1956), p. 25.

This is quite true of David Jones, though there are of course assertions which illuminate other people's poetry too. There is, moreover, a great deal that Auden has to say in his writings that agrees with David Jones's views.

Given the change of subject from the visual arts and art generally to poetry in particular, the basis of David Jones's remarks in the Preface to *The Anathemata* remains the same as in his other essays. But he is concerned here more with the problems arising from this rather than with the theory behind it, for we can take it as read that poetry is also a matter of dealing with signs and that the poet too is, to use Thomas Gilby's words, a *venator formarum*, 'a hunter of forms'. The question most deeply at issue is the validity of the signs used. In a world where the Christian religion was taken for granted and those who read poetry were educated in the classics and had some knowledge of foreign literature, the question of the validity or otherwise of signs hardly arose. But the world in which the literary setting of *Lycidas*, for example, was lucid, was a smaller world than ours, and it is gone. There is no longer that kind of literary cohesion, even among the educated. 'This presents,' writes David Jones, 'most complicated problems to the artist working outside a reasonably static culture-phase... It may be that the kind of thing I have been trying to make is no longer makeable in the kind of way in which I have tried to make it.'[1] The task of the poet is, in the midst of the geographical expansion and the historical contraction of our times, to discover what signs *are* valid.

Most poets find their valid signs in the data of individual psychology, in personal experience. But what happens here to tradition? What David Jones says about 'water' serves as an example of the problem:

> Water is called the 'matter' of the Sacrament of Baptism. Is 'two of hydrogen and one of oxygen' that 'matter'? I suppose so. But what concerns us here is where the poet can and does so juxtapose and condition within a context the formula H_2O as to evoke 'founts', 'that innocent creature', 'the womb of this devine font', 'the candidates', or for that matter 'the narrows' and 'the siluer sea,

---

[1] *The Anathemata*, p. 15. All references to the Preface are to the pages of the book and not to those of *Epoch and Artist*.

Which serues it in the office of a wall, Or as a Moat defensiue to a house'.

A knowledge of the chemical components of the material water should, normally, or if you prefer it, ideally, provide us with further deeper, and more exciting significances *vis-à-vis* the sacrament of water, and also, for us islanders, whose history is so much of water, with other significances relative to that. In Britain, 'water' is unavoidably very much part of the *materia poetica*. It may be felt that these examples are somewhat far-fetched, but I choose them as illustrations only. And if you consider how the men of some epochs have managed to wed widely separated ideas, and to make odd scraps of newly discovered data subserve immemorial themes (cf. the English Metaphysicals?) my examples may not appear all that strained (pp. 16f.).

These remarks make it clear that David Jones conceives of poetry as being concerned with much more than personal data. One could go so far as to suggest that poetry can only be poetry where such personal data are effectively incorporated into the total expression of a culture. Thus, David Jones writes: 'I believe that there is, in the principle that informs the poetic art, a something which cannot be disengaged from the mythus, deposits, *matière*, ethos, whole *res* of which the poet is himself a product' (p. 20). A poetry, therefore, which aims at an utterance of public significance, must of necessity be rooted in a tradition and not consist simply in the creation of a purely private world. David Jones's viewpoint is, in fact, a personal restatement of Eliot's:[1]

Tradition is a matter of much wider significance. It cannot be inherited, and if you want it you must obtain it by great labour. It involves, in the first place, the historical sense, which we may call nearly indispensable to anyone who would continue to be a poet beyond his twenty-fifth year; and the historical sense involves a perception, not only of the pastness of the past, but of its presence; the historical sense compels a man to write not merely with his own generation in his bones, but with a feeling that the whole of the literature of Europe from Homer and within it the whole of the literature of his own country has a simultaneous existence and composes a simultaneous order. The historical sense, which is a sense

[1] T. S. Eliot, 'Tradition and the Individual Talent', *Selected Essays*.

of the timeless as well as of the temporal and of the timeless and of the temporal together, is what makes a writer traditional. And it is at the same time what makes a writer most acutely conscious of his place in time, of his contemporaneity.

The poet, however, like other men, is incapable of knowing more than a fraction of this tradition. It is the particular fraction that he knows and that he can make into his own framework which gives him his individuality as a poet. He must, as David Jones says, 'work within the limits of his love. There must be no mugging-up, no "ought to know" or "try to feel"; for only what is actually loved and known can be seen *sub specie aeternitatis*' (p. 24).

The Preface to *The Anathemata* is largely a formulation of the problems confronting a poet in the late period of a civilization. Its significance for an understanding of the particular work which it prefaces will be examined later. In a way, the fact that it is connected like this with *The Anathemata* may have unfortunate consequences, since its observations, while having their own validity, may be regarded as invalid because the poem does not come over to the reader in the way the poet hoped, for whatever reasons. But the argument as to whether the poem is an 'effective recalling' or not is a different matter from whether a recalling as such is the purpose of poetry. Certain objections and queries raised by one reviewer of the whole book elicited a further statement by David Jones on the problematic position of the artist, but this consists chiefly in a reiteration of the points already put forward. It does, however, contain one brief paragraph that sums up the situation:[1]

> No one intimately and contactually involved in the making of works today would underestimate the almost insuperable difficulties of how to make the signs available for today. We can, in my opinion, assert little with confidence, but I think we can assert that the poet is a 'rememberer' and that it is a part of his business to keep open the lines of communication. One obvious way of doing this is by handing on such fragmented bits of our own inheritance as we have ourselves received. This is the way I myself attempt. There are, no doubt, other ways. The artist is not responsible *for* the future, but he is, in a certain sense, responsible *to* the future.

[1] 'Past and Present', *E & A*, p. 141.

3
The visual arts

I

Childhood possesses many attractive features—spontaneity, innocence of vision, naïve curiosity about the world, delight in animals and the simple things of nature. These qualities are easily recognizable in David Jones's work at many periods of his life, but it is characteristic that he should say in his note to the illustrations of the *Agenda* Special Number that there are few of his later works that he likes better than the *Dancing Bear* of 1903, done at the age of seven.[1] Together with his earliest preserved drawing, the *Leopard and Tiger* of 1902, the *Lion* of the same year,[2] and the watercolour of the *Wolf in the Snow* of 1906,[3] of which the original is now lost, it reveals a sense of sympathy with the animal world that is clear throughout his career. It finds expression in his engravings as well as in his later drawings and watercolours—especially in his splendid series of animals in the Regents Park Zoo of 1930–1. The very early works are chiefly interesting from an historical point of view, showing what considerable achievements a gifted child is capable of, but the drawings already provide evidence of that interest in line that has kept David Jones busy ever since.

The years of school and art college are largely unknown to us, and it is only from the period of his association with the Ditchling community that we can really trace the development of his powers

[1] Reproduced in Ironside, 2; Arts Council catalogue, I; *The Wind and the Rain. An Easter Book for 1962*, ed. Neville Braybrooke (London, 1962), 8.
[2] *The Wind and the Rain*, 7.
[3] Ironside, 4.

as an artist. Although he learnt various skills at Ditchling, including wood-carving and mural-painting, it was in the sphere of wood-engraving that he made his début as a professional artist. Not very much later he was painting watercolours of hillsides and seascapes and achieving a promising reputation here too. The two activities of painting and engraving ran side by side until about 1930–1, after which David Jones did no more engraving on either wood or copper because of eye trouble, but concentrated on drawings and watercolours. These again fell into second place as writing became his chief occupation. It is remarkable how the majority of his watercolours exclude any human figures in their preoccupation with landscape, windows and flowers, while the engravings most frequently depict intensely involved groups of figures. In the water-colour drawings of the late 1930s and after, these two tendencies are strikingly combined. But there are certain themes and motifs that cut across the divisions of material, boats and beasts being the most readily apparent.

The 1920s and 1930s were the heyday of British wood-engraving, and David Jones occupies a position of peculiar distinction in its annals. Not that he is recognized as a leader or as the technically most outstanding, but he is universally accorded praise for his accomplished work of the latter half of the 1920s, which is quite different in mood from what anyone else was doing. This is evident both in the choice of subject and in the composition, as well as in the actual technique of engraving. The prevailing tendency was to concentrate on themes from nature, whether in terms of pastoral landscape or the smaller, closely observed details of plants, birds and animals. Here one thinks immediately of Robert Gibbings, Eric Ravilious, Gwendolen Raverat, Joan Hassall, John Farleigh, Paul and John Nash, Gertrude Hermes, and so on. Among these artists there is a considerable variety of styles, ranging from the bold, simplified vision of Gibbings with strong contrasts of black and white to the more subtle gradations of tone achieved by such engravers as Gertrude Hermes and Agnes Miller Parker. Yet this vision of nature was never the whole of the story, and numerous artists put their talents to the illustration of incidents from narrative works, frequently of a period flavour and employing less straightforwardly naturalistic modes of portrayal and composition. In this connexion one thinks especially of the brilliant work of Blair Hughes-Stanton. There was also Eric Gill, devoting himself *inter alia* to Christian themes and decorations for Chaucer, eschewing all unnecessary flourish and detail and concentrating on the simple effectiveness of controlled, but sensuous line. Each of these artists explored the special problems of engraving differently. Questions of technique interested them as much as subject-matter—the acceptance and mastery of black as the expressive medium of the wood-block, the balancing of black and white, the gradation of tone, the creation of solid form and space, the use of line, whether white on black or vice versa, the control of the burin.

Many of the major talents of the period were assembled in the Society of Wood-Engravers, founded by Gibbings in 1920. A few years later there blossomed the English Wood-Engraving Society, which united the more sophisticated techniques—particularly the skilled use of the multiple tool—of such artists as Leon Underwood, Blair Hughes-Stanton and Gertrude Hermes. This whole enterprise of wood-engraving as a viable artistic mode went, of course, hand in hand with the development of the private presses, printing their limited editions of rare classics or unusual new works with the highest standards of book production. Among those that were prominent in the post-war period were the Golden Cockerel Press, founded in 1920 and directed from 1924 by Robert Gibbings; the Nonesuch Press, established in 1923; the Gregynog Press, founded in 1922 in Newtown, Montgomeryshire. But it was in the St Dominic's Press, which grew out of the small hand press that Hilary Pepler had set up at Ditchling as early as 1915, that David Jones's engravings were first published, though most of his best work was done later for the Golden Cockerel Press.

St Dominic's Press, with Eric Gill as its most illustrious collaborator, was probably the most eccentric of the many private presses of the time. Its publications, as one would expect from the aims of the Tertiaries of the Order of St Dominic, were essentially didactic in character, ranging from handbooks on vegetable dyes and diatribes against the iniquities of the factory system to editions of puppet plays, the first translation into English of Maritain's *Art et*

Scolastique, anthologies of humorous and satirical verse, and religious treatises. A quintessence of the interests which motivated it may be found in *The Game*, an occasional publication or magazine, of which the first number appeared in October 1916 and which continued to be published at irregular intervals over several years. *The Game* was, as Robert Speaight remarks, 'frolicsome as well as fundamental',[1] but the frolicsomeness is at times embarrassingly adolescent; it does not bear the test of time.

It was in *The Game* that David Jones's first published engravings appeared. He had learnt engraving from Desmond Chute, and volume V of *The Game* from January to December 1922 contains a series of twelve illustrations to the Ten Commandments that he did. Nowhere is there any indication of the artist, which is appropriate enough to the anonymity of the style of these early efforts. This omission of names was quite common in the publications of St Dominic's Press. The authors are normally mentioned by name, occasionally by initials, but illustrators are often anonymous by negligence rather than design. Hilary Pepler made good this omission by referring to the Ten Commandments in his book on *The Hand Press*, where he is swift to recognize that David Jones was handicapped in his engravings by the idea of propaganda imposed on him.[2] These engravings are unremarkable; they lack any real feeling, whether primitive socialist or Christian, and are understandably omitted from the list of illustrated books in the catalogue to the Arts Council retrospective exhibition of 1954.

The simple didacticism of *The Game* is continued in the first book that David Jones did a number of engravings for. This was a very slim volume of verses by Gill and Pepler called *In Petra*—the allusion is to Psalm xxvii. 6 in the Vulgate—published in 1923. The verses are didactic, semi-humorous and religious, and none of them better than doggerel. David Jones's anonymous decorations are similarly unpretentious. The eight tiny engravings are much smaller in scope than the Ten Commandments. Two are simply decorated initials, while the others basically contain a single motif. They are very similar to the kind of thing that Eric Gill himself did

[1] *Op. cit.*, p. 86.
[2] H. D. C. Pepler, *The Hand Press* (Ditchling: St Dominic's Press, 1934), p. 33.

a great deal of at the same period or earlier.[1] They are perfectly suited to the verses they accompany and tend to increase in decorative charm as their didacticism becomes less obtrusive.

The boyish mixture of *In Petra* was succeeded in 1924 by another collection of verses by Hilary Pepler called *Libellus Lapidum*, for which David Jones did a further series of engravings. The book consisted of a number of pot shots at prominent public figures and fashions—John Drinkwater, Epstein and Augustus John, Beatrice and Sidney Webb, Ronald Knox and Bernard Shaw. The verses, for all the social criticism they contain, are more bubble-pricking than serious. The illustrations are larger than those of the previous volume and tend to be more complex. One is repeated from *In Petra*, while that used to guy the Webbs is made further use of in a later anthology called *Pertinent and Impertinent* (1926). This volume follows the same pattern as the preceding ones, but has three illustrators—Desmond Chute, David Jones and Harold Purney—who are all named for once. The four engravings by David Jones are quite undistinguished—two landscapes in addition to 'England Webbed', and a rather forcedly religious one illustrating some folksy verses beginning:

> Our Lady was a Milkmaid,
> a peasant girl, and poor,
> She whom Almighty God obeyed
> would scrub her dairy floor.

In addition to this mixed bunch of illustrations for the verse anthologies David Jones engraved a further series for *A Child's Rosary Book*, published in 1924. These fifteen illustrations for the Joyful, Sorrowful and Glorious Mysteries range from the Annunciation to the Coronation of the Virgin and are stiffly medieval in conception, again in the wake of Eric Gill. They were all reprinted in a Rosary Calendar for 1931. Up to this point there is little of an individual style in David Jones's engravings. They are hardly distinguishable from those of the rest of the Ditchling community, and although in many cases they are close to Gill's illustrations of Christian themes and his vignettes, they do not have his fluid lines.

[1] See, for example, *The Engraved Work of Eric Gill* (Victoria and Albert Museum, H.M.S.O., 1969), pp. 21 and 40.

But the sympathy that each had for the other is demonstrated by the number of engravings that Gill did after designs of David Jones.[1]

All the engravings mentioned so far were done for St Dominic's Press, but in 1924 David Jones had begun to branch out by illustrating Eleanor Farjeon's verses for *The Town Child's Alphabet*, published by the Poetry Bookshop. These lightly coloured, pen-and-ink designs are stylistically linked with the Octavia Hill engraving from the *Libellus Lapidum* by a sense of controlled movement apparent in the composition of the pictures. The decorations for *In Petra* had been mainly static and of things, whereas in these later illustrations the human, present-day element has a more important place. David Jones still continued to do engravings for the productions of the St Dominic's Press after this, but it was through the better-known private presses that his mature work won recognition.

His first major breakthrough came with Robert Gibbings's commission for some forty engravings for the Golden Cockerel Press two-volume edition of *Gulliver's Travels*, published in 1925. These, together with the two delightful engravings for Sir Francis Coventry's *History of Pompey the Little, or, The Life and Adventures of a Lap-dog* (Golden Cockerel Press, 1926), represent the transition from learning the technique of a new medium to mastery in it. The forced, often jumbled didacticism of the early efforts, so frequently lacking in any real feeling, now yields to more sympathetic fields of expression. The jaunty little dog at the end of *Pompey* breathes a freer air than anything that David Jones had done earlier. It appears as a release from the pedagogic intent of St Dominic's Press. Swift's mordant satire is directed at a whole world of constant human foibles and failings, and this provides a broader basis of artistic expression. Four of David Jones's engravings are full-page maps, in which the prominence of the lettering amidst the decorative monsters, ships and animals perhaps anticipates the inscriptions, which form such an idiosyncratic part of his later work. The other engravings vary considerably in size from small two-and-a-quarter-inch squares to vertical and horizontal rectangles of about double that size, but all of which are appropriately incorporated into the

---

[1] *The Engraved Work of Eric Gill*, nos. 63, 67, 73.

PLATE ONE

'The Oblation of Noah' (1927)

'I shot the ALBATROSS' (1929)

typographical structure of the page. A considerable number of them are coloured by hand in red, blue, yellow, green, brown and purple, especially where the engraving would otherwise have shown large areas of white. The composition of these illustrations is strong and simple, but not too simple, and makes a more extensive use of contrasts between shaded black and clean white than in many of his earlier pieces. Most of the engravings, in keeping with Swift's skilful combination of fantasy and naturalistic detail, are beautifully stylized and full of primitive clarity. There is no attempt to disguise the nature of the medium in which the artist is working. Its obvious 'woodenness', in the literal sense of the word, is part of its charm. Especially attractive are Gulliver wading from his shipwreck to the shore of Lilliput (I, 19), his fight with the wasp in Brobdingnag (I, 101), and his resistance to being embraced by an odious female Yahoo after bathing (II, 109). The book gave David Jones ample scope for choice in illustration, and it is worth a brief note that he found the opportunity for six pictures of the sea and ships, a subject which is one of his favourites and which appears here for the first time. These engravings show him as now quite clearly inhabiting the same world as Derrick Harris, Eric Ravilious and Robert Gibbings.

After the entertaining secularism of *Gulliver* David Jones returned to a religious theme and did thirteen engravings for another Golden Cockerel book, the *Book of Jonah* (1926). These illustrations belong to a different realm altogether from *Gulliver*, as well as being quite different from the other traditional religious subjects that he had engraved a couple of years or so earlier. Yet they are still stylized, a little stiff, and not at all indebted to the naturalistic mode of expression which is general among other engravers of the same period. As in some of the *Gulliver* pictures, there is a liberal scooping away of the wood to produce largish white areas and to depict figures with black outlines as a contrast to others where the more usual technique of white on black is used. The cuts are strong and clear, the outlines definite and simplified, and as the engraver's mastery over his medium has grown, his subjects become more moving and evince a deeper sense of rhythm and movement. The whole series has a pronounced medieval and liturgical quality about it, reminiscent of early fifteenth century German woodcuts as well as being related to Eric Gill's engravings on Christian themes. Yet, although one may assert the medieval mood of these illustrations, there is nothing conventional about them, for they are infused with a personal vitality that illuminates the traditional material. Above all, there is a pervading sense of significance and movement about them, whether in the dominating, heaven-sent figure of Gabriel (p. 3), the hurried attempted escape of Jonah down the steps to the boat for Tarshish (p. 4), the storm, the terror of the sailors and their casting of Jonah into the raging sea (pp. 5–7), or the despair of Jonah under the burning sun of Nineveh (p. 14). But there are also calmer moments as when the sea grows still and the whale spouts in the foreground (p. 8), or when Jonah is compassed about with fishes and weeds in the murky depths of the sea and prays for deliverance (p. 9). The whole book is a fine example of typography and engraving fittingly complementary and unified.

Though the *Book of Jonah* is no mean achievement, it is surpassed in excellence of technique and depth of vision by the illustrations to three books—the *Llyfr y Pregeth-wr* (the Welsh translation of Ecclesiastes), published by the Gregynog Press; Eric Gill's *Christianity and Art*, published by Francis Walterson at Capel-y-ffin; and the *Chester Play of the Deluge*, the last work that David Jones illustrated for the Golden Cockerel Press. All these books appeared in 1927.

The *Llyfr y Pregeth-wr* contains two engravings—a very small square decoration on the title-page and a full-page frontispiece on the *vanitas vanitatum* theme. This frontispiece is a good deal more complex than anything David Jones had hitherto attempted and marks a definite advance on the *Book of Jonah*. Almost the first thing that strikes one about it (and the *Deluge* engravings too) is the relative blackness of the total design: there is very little scooped away to form white contrasting blocks or backgrounds. All the time David Jones is avoiding the contrast of pure black against stark white. His designs are becoming more intricate, every corner filled with detail, and his technique and all-over effect seem to be inclining to that of the English Wood-Engraving Society, though without their virtuoso appeal. This reduction of contrast is related to the fact that, as the designs are for books, they have to be looked at closely and thus complexity and subtlety of shading is feasible. The figures and shapes have a now thinner, now thicker white outline to detach them from their surroundings, but the spaces around them are hatched with a myriad tiny criss-cross lines, and the figures themselves are moulded and rounded into solidity by the same technique. The central position in the engraving is taken by Christ on the cross, surrounded by a group of mourners, who, in true medieval fashion, are smaller in size because less in importance. But despite his centrality the figure of Christ does not dominate the picture; there are too many other elements attracting our attention for this to be possible. On one side lovers embrace, on the other two naked men struggle, trying to stab each other in the back, while the foot of the picture is occupied by curious monsters devouring their victims among the flames of hell. A cupid seems to walk in the sky, armed with bow and quiver, above the eclipsed sun. There is even a little house collapsing among flames, and, slightly incongruously, a sailing ship on the sea (David Jones finds it hard to resist including a boat where the opportunity for one is offered or space permits). Altogether this is a bewildering picture, which, with the multiplicity of the motifs grouped around a central figure, anticipates the complex watercolour drawings of a dozen years later. In these later drawings, however, the spatial relationships of the various figures and motifs are more consistently realized, whereas in the engraving there is a not completely satisfactory juxtaposition of elements that are meant to be interconnected. But it is hardly surprising that this first essay in a much more subtle technique and ambitious theme is not the most successful.

    The frontispiece to Gill's *Christianity and Art* is a smaller piece of work, but its composition round a central figure is very similar to that of the *Llyfr y Pregeth-wr*. The posture of the Christian artist sitting in his cell, poised over his picture of a fish and surrounded by animals, birds and flowers and the tools of his trade, is strongly reminiscent of medieval miniatures of the Gospel writers at work. The fluidity and movement of the whole design recalls such pictures as that of the quivering St Matthew from the Gospel Book of Archbishop Ebbo of Reims. Not that there is any conscious influence exerted here, for this type of composition results quite freely from the nature of the subject depicted.

All of this leads splendidly up to the ten large engravings for the *Chester Play of the Deluge*, one of the finest productions of the Golden Cockerel Press. It is certainly the best known of David Jones's wood-engravings, since several individual pictures have been reproduced in a number of publications and thus contributed to their fame. The first engraving, which depicts the world with the 'people in deede and thoughte...sette fowle in synne', is remarkably close in conception to the *Llyfr y Pregeth-wr*, but with a greater degree of relatedness in the distribution of the various groups of pleasure-bent mortals clustered about the central cell of the devout and the Lamb in heaven. Each of the full-page engravings reveals an extraordinarily complex composition with strong rhythmic qualities. Attention has often been focussed on the entry of the animals into the ark with a proud array of beasts and birds proceeding in a most orderly fashion across the facing pages from left to right (Ironside, 8; Ede, 4). The anonymous poet of the *Deluge* at this point mentions some forty different birds and beasts, of which David Jones includes a very fair number. They are extremely skilfully distributed over the pages, for the doubling of each kind is presented with delicate variations, some walking in identical gait side by side, some running or flying ahead. Some point their heads deliberately forwards, others glance inquisitively backwards or sideways, while the marmosets scurry nimbly down medieval trees and across the ground. These two pictures are a fine example in his mature work of that sympathy for animals which Robin Ironside felicitously characterizes as Franciscan.[1]

By common consent the ninth engraving, of the dove, is reckoned the masterpiece of the series and has been reproduced many times.[2] The ark has just come to rest on the top of Mount

---

[1] Ironside, *op. cit.*, p. 15.

[2] Arts Council catalogue, IV; Clare Leighton, *Wood-Engravings and Woodcuts* (London: The Studio Ltd., 1932), p. 69; Nicolete Gray, 'David Jones', *Signature*, no. 8, 1949, p. 51; René Hague, 'David Jones at the Tate Gallery', *Studio*, vol. CXLIX, no. 745, April 1955, p. 109.

Ararat, the vague shape of which is just visible through a vast, calm expanse of water. The sun is about to rise over the horizon, and a tree emerges from the gentle waves with little branches of new leaves and life, while the dove wings its way downwards on its mission from the ark. The whole picture displays a beautiful shimmering quality of light on the water,[1] an atmosphere of immense peace and calm. In its subject-matter it is much simpler than the other illustrations, but the technique which goes to make its success is of an equally high order. The final engraving (Plate 1), constructed around the central figure of Noah, depicts the oblation of Noah:

> Lord I thanke the through thy mighte
> Thy byddyng shall be done in height,
> And as fast as I may dight,
>   I will doe the honoure
> And to thee offer sacrifice,
> Therfore comes in all wise,
> For of these beastes that bene hise
>   Offer I will this stower.

The picture[2] forms a lively contrast to that of the dove, for here every corner is filled with tokens of rejoicing. As Noah's family kneels at his feet, together with the animals, while the birds of the air flutter gaily about, even the little hills in the background seem to be jumping up and down for joy. Like so much of David Jones's work, this is a *Benedicite, omnia opera, Dominum*.

Among the other wood-engravings, several of which were occasional productions for book-plates or Christmas cards, mention must be made of three in particular. The first, from 1929, was done for a projected edition of *Everyman* which was never published, and depicts the meeting of Everyman, a gay young man wearing a plumed hat, who is dallying with two delightful maidens, with Death, a black skeleton, playing a violin.[3] This is the most

---

[1] Clare Leighton, *op. cit.*, p. 68.
[2] Reproduced in Thomas Balston, *English Wood-Engraving 1900–1950* (London: Art & Technics, 1951), p. 40; Douglas Percy Bliss, *A History of Wood-Engraving* (London: Dent, 1928), p. 215.
[3] Reproduced in Clare Leighton, *Wood-Engravings and Woodcuts*, new edition, 1944, 1948, p. 69.

attractive of the three in the vigour of its flowing lines. Like the *Deluge* it demands careful observation before it yields its full beauty. These post-*Jonah* engravings do not make an immediately realized impact on the viewer; they do not form a unified whole that is directly perceivable and may then be explored for detail. The viewer must allow his eye to rove over the whole surface of the engraving and thus gradually appreciate the subtlety of the design.

The second, in a similar style, is a frontispiece to W. H. Shewring's *Hermia and some other poems* (St Dominic's Press, 1930). Although these verses on religious, classical and pastoral themes are of indifferent quality, David Jones's engraving, entitled elsewhere *The Bride*, has enjoyed considerable popularity.[1] It is an allusive picture, rich in signs and symbols, like *Everyman*, and full of decorative detail. Like most of David Jones's later work it is deeply concerned with the reality of the interrelationships of what it is trying to depict. Formal and technical interest subserves the spiritual, in particular the Christian vision of the world in which we live. The bride lighting her candle at the crucifix seems already to be inhabiting the world that lies between palpable everyday things and aetherial truth.

Finally, an unfinished wood-engraving of 1931 was used with the title *He Frees the Waters* as an illustration for *The Anathemata*. This is David Jones's only excursion, in the field of wood-engraving, into the mysterious world of Arthurian romance. Here, more than anywhere else so far observed, we can feel the creation of a landscape of fantasy where creatures move, stars gleam and trees wave their branches in the half-light of a dream that is only dimly understood. The allusion in the title is to the role of Peredur in the story from the medieval Welsh collection of tales known as the *Mabinogion*, but the engraving seems more concerned with depiction of the Waste Land with its broken trees and chaotic movement than with the freeing as such. Though this is an illustration of a theme that is not primarily Christian, it has much fundamentally in common with the frontispiece to the *Llyfr y Pregeth-wr* and the first

---

[1] Reproduced in Basil Gray, *The English Print* (London: Black, 1937; reprinted University Microfilms Ltd., 1969), XVIII; Nicolete Gray, 'David Jones', p. 53; Harman Grisewood, *David Jones. Writer and Artist* (BBC, 1966), frontispiece.

illustration in the *Deluge*. In each picture a world of dissolution and sin is shown grouped around a central symbol of salvation—the crucified Christ, the eternal Lamb, and the lance and chalice of the Grail story.

The engraving from *The Anathemata* provides the clearest link between David Jones's work as both an artist and a poet, for a powerful literary theme stimulated him to his own personal reaction in the two media of wood-engraving and poetry. Literature and art further join in his involvement with the Ancient Mariner theme, for in addition to making a series of copper-engravings for Coleridge's poem David Jones incorporated the subject-matter into his own *In Parenthesis* as part of his *materia poetica* and wrote a lengthy essay on his understanding of the work. Curiously enough, while there has been general agreement on the extraordinarily quality of the wood-engravings for the *Deluge*, there has been a wide range of contradictory opinion about the copper-engravings for the *Ancient Mariner*. Eric Gill declared that 'Coleridge's poem has for the first time found adequate pictorial accompaniment'[1] and that sentiment is shared by both H. S. Ede and Nicolete Gray.[2] On the other hand, Sir John Rothenstein, who is usually so persuasive in his judgements, dissents strongly from this view. He finds 'little of the imaginative force of the earlier [series]' in it and would regard it as probably the only failure in this period of David Jones's creative life.[3] These ten engravings, done for Douglas Cleverdon's beautiful edition of 1929,[4] mark the culmination of his engraving on copper, a technique which he had embarked on in about 1926 with a number of animal pictures and nativity scenes. This new departure saw the publication in 1928 of *Aisopou tou muthopoiou logoi hepta* by the Lanston Monotype Corporation, consisting of seven fables of Aesop in the original Greek, with translations by W. H. Shewring and seven engravings on copper by David Jones, an attractive little volume dedicated to Desmond Chute.

[1] Eric Gill, *Essays*, p. 151.
[2] H. S. Ede, *op. cit.*, pp. 131f.; Nicolete Gray, *op. cit.*, pp. 46ff.
[3] Rothenstein, *op. cit.*, pp. 301f.
[4] The engravings were republished in a second limited edition, together with a foreword by David Jones, by the Chilmark Press, New York, in 1964.

Coleridge's poem is one of the most appealing and evocative poems in the English language. Although it speaks with simple words and appears so direct in expression, it is more elusive in its meaning than any other poem of comparable length. Maud Bodkin, I think rightly, sees its fascination and power as lying in its use of primordial images to give more than personal substance to the Mariner's essentially interior voyage, the voyage into his own soul.[1] It is this archetypal quality in the *Ancient Mariner* which brought out once more in pictorial form David Jones's profound consciousness of the interrelatedness of things, found here as well as in *Jonah* and the *Deluge*. There are eight full-page engravings, together with a smaller headpiece depicting a ship in the harbour and a tailpiece. The tailpiece with its traditional pelican symbolizing Christ spilling His blood for the love of mankind is a clear example of the typological mode of interpretation; and the power of much explicit Christian symbolism is as good a confirmation as any of Jung's theory of archetypes from the collective unconscious. David Jones extends this image of Christ's self-sacrifice to what Maud Bodkin calls the Rebirth archetype[2] by depicting the albatross impaled by the Mariner's arrow against the cross-shaped mast (no. 2) (Plate 2) and later the Mariner, arms outstretched like the crucified Christ, with the dead bird hung about his neck (no. 5):[3]

> Instead of the cross, the Albatross
> About my neck was hung.

This double identification of both the Albatross and the Mariner with Christ brilliantly illuminates the horror of the Mariner's crime and the way in which the bird may be seen as the Mariner's own 'Christian soul'. How clear this was in Coleridge's mind is perhaps debatable, but the constant repetition of the rhyme 'cross – Albatross' (Pt. I, st. 16, 20; Pt. II, st. 14; Pt. V, st. 24) provides a most plausible support for David Jones's interpretation.

The series of full-page engravings begins with a carefree illustration (no. 1) for 'The Bridegroom's doors are open'd wide'. The

---

[1] Maud Bodkin, *Archetypal Patterns in Poetry. Psychological Studies of Imagination* (Oxford University Press, 1934, 1963), pp. 26–89.
[2] Bodkin, *op. cit.*, p. 54. The *Book of Jonah* also contains a version of the closely related Night-Journey archetype.
[3] Nicolete Gray, *op. cit.*, p. 48.

THE VISUAL ARTS

wedding guests are hastening to the banquet, holding flowers in their hands, the background shows the sea with little ships, and the whole picture is full of light and movement. After the shooting of the Albatross there follows a memorable picture (no. 3) of the 'slimy things' that 'did crawl with legs/Upon the slimy sea'; but these monsters of the deep do not have quite the evil repulsiveness that the words of the poem conjure up. The 'terror' of the picture is created by the lurid shadows around sun, moon and stars. The picture of the Woman and Death (no. 4) playing their game of dice has more diabolical fascination. The sloping horizon and the desperate action and movement of the two figures create an awareness of the rocking of the boat and of violent emotion, which contrasts with the more static feeling of the dead men rising to do their work. The depiction of the walk to church (no. 8) is a happy parallel to the wedding-feast and includes many more individually observed figures (the sailors are sketched in a more or less impersonal fashion). Inside the church an acolyte swings a censer while another tolls a bell, a child dips its hands in the holy water stoup, a woman carries fishes in a basket, and a man is just about to remove his hat on going into church. Houses, boats and the sea make the necessary background. This is a most sensitive piece of observation and a fitting conclusion to the story.

In these copper engravings David Jones's interest in line is strongly evident. We can perhaps again see something of the influence of Gill in his mastery of creating a solid shape through simple outline. Distance and space in the *Ancient Mariner* pictures are created by the finely hatched, vibrant short lines that seem randomly scattered in the gaps between the human forms.[1] But the feeling of space, here as in the whole of David Jones's work, is related to the logic of the particular picture and is not a mere transposition of the observed relationships of the ordinary world. The range of mood attempted in these illustrations to the *Ancient Mariner* is rather wider than that of the *Deluge*, but they are not equal in their intensity, whether of joy or of despair and pain, to those of *Jonah* and the *Deluge*. David Jones seems to do better in those engravings where he attempts more, both in detail and in

[1] See Nicolete Gray's perceptive comments, *op. cit.*, pp. 47f.

emotion, and I think this is why the *Ancient Mariner* is not as satisfying as the *Deluge*. These illustrations form David Jones's last considerable body of engravings. They link up easily with his drawings of the same period, some of which were used as book-illustrations for his own work—notably *In Parenthesis*—as well as for that of other writers. At this point, however, we must revert to his early paintings.

II

Acquaintance with David Jones's engravings is not widespread, partly because of the limited editions in which they appeared and partly because galleries tend not to display many prints and few visitors tend to look carefully at them. David Jones also suffers from a lack of public awareness of his watercolours and drawings, as so few of them are owned by public galleries. Of the ninety paintings and drawings shown in the 1954 Arts Council retrospective exhibition only seventeen were from public collections (the three formerly belonging to H. S. Ede are now to be seen in the Kettle's Yard Collection that Mr Ede so generously donated to the University of Cambridge). Despite all this he is probably better known as a watercolourist, a painter of idiosyncratic landscapes, of coastal scenes and boats, of window-scenes and delicately spreading bowls of flowers that seem to be half-glimpsed visions of a transcendental reality. Yet even this idea of his work, derived chiefly from his paintings from the very late 1920s and early '30s, is only relatively true, for his early paintings are very different in style and feeling, and his later productions are different again. Despite his marked individuality of style, recognizable everywhere once he has served his apprenticeship, David Jones has worked in an extraordinarily wide range of media, even discounting his literary achievements, and he is in none an amateur. In all of his work there is a strong feeling of unity with nature, which is expressed in a multiplicity of ways. We have already seen how lovingly and joyfully the animals are depicted in the *Deluge*, for example, and in *Gulliver* too. This delight continues from the early paintings right through to the latest enormously complicated watercolour drawings. But the sense of community with the natural world really begins and ends for David Jones in the more generalized sphere of landscape.

English painting has a rich tradition in landscape painting, and David Jones is assured of a distinguished, if minor, position in it. But once this is said, it is unusually difficult to know how to situate him without making a series of totally misleading judgements or comparisons. For one thing, he does not derive his inspiration from any one well-loved corner of the British Isles. Though we may associate Ivon Hitchens with the leafy woods of Sussex, John Nash with Buckinghamshire or Edward Bawden with the Essex countryside, it is not possible to make the same kind of equation—facile though it may be in reality—for David Jones. To be sure, he has his connexions with South Wales, with the Pyrenees and Northumberland, but in a sense these are accidental. He did not discover himself more truly through any one of these than through anything else. Most frequently it seems that a particular regional setting is merely a point of departure for the evocation of something much more universal.

David Jones is perhaps most satisfactorily 'placed' among the artists who formed the Seven and Five Society, which he joined in 1928 at about the mid-point of its life. The Seven and Five was actually founded in 1919, but it was only with Ben Nicholson's introduction into the group by Ivon Hitchens in 1924 that it began to achieve real importance. Winifred Nicholson joined in 1925, Ben Nicholson became Chairman in 1926, introducing Christopher Wood in that same year, and Frances Hodgkins joined in 1929. David Jones exhibited with them until 1933, that is, until ill-health changed the direction of his career, though with Ben Nicholson's insistence on non-representational art from 1934 onwards, it is unlikely that David Jones would have continued to exhibit with them. Already in the late twenties Ben Nicholson's work shows an involvement with Cubism, Cézanne, Braque and Picasso, with the vital currents of European art. This kind of development seems to have passed David Jones by, and his later work—i.e. post 1932—is a logical elaboration of what he had in essence worked out before then. He remains within the English tradition.

An interest in the naïve, the innocent and the childlike vision seems to have been almost a mark of the times. In Paris the work of the Douanier Rousseau was particularly admired and influential. Among the Seven and Five one notices it perhaps especially in Ben Nicholson and Christopher Wood, and it was this that led them to the discovery of the Cornish primitive Alfred Wallis in 1928. It was probably the recognition of this element in David Jones's early work that led Ben Nicholson to invite him to join the Seven and Five. There was also among most of the group a distinct preference for muted colours. If at first there were sympathies and similarities between Nicholson and Jones, both in their choice of subject and approach to it, the differences soon became apparent. It can be seen as much as anything in the choice of oils as against watercolour—David Jones did only the occasional oil-painting. His colour is more tentative, softer, translucent, and altogether less solid and even than Nicholson's or Wood's. Both of them were far more interested in the solidity of the objects they depicted, whereas David Jones, while interested in the physical characteristics of his subjects, was also trying to capture something of their more spiritual, intangible qualities. There is a gentle romanticism about his paintings that contrasts strongly with the capacity for surprise and the slightly jarring quality that much of Nicholson's and Wood's painting of this period has. It is a quieter form of art, dreamier and altogether more insubstantial.

Every painter attempting the art of landscape painting has to start with a decision as to where he will delimit his subject-matter. It is a question in the first place of choice and order out of the vast expanses of the natural world: the landscape has to be made tractable before it can reveal its mysteries. One can almost feel this attempt to tame the landscape in a number of David Jones's very early paintings, notably in *Tir y Blaenau* (1925)[1] and *Hill Pastures— Capel-y-ffin* (1926),[2] where the landscape is controlled by a strictness of outline and a strongly stylized depiction of trees and flowers especially. There is a clear demarcation of shapes everywhere, both of horses and trees against the hillside and of the hills

---

[1] Private collection; reproduced in the *Agenda* Special Number opposite p. 32.
[2] Coll. the late Miss Helen Sutherland; Ironside, 1.

against the sky. One might expect that with this degree of stylization the resultant picture would be stiff and unnatural, but there is on the contrary a sweeping movement about the naked branches of the trees, and although the horses are quietly cropping the grass, one feels with the Psalmist that the mountains are skipping like rams and the little hills like lambs. The colouring of the latter picture is a subtle combination of thin yellows and greens with the odd hints of blue and pink, darkened and given varied tones by cross-hatching with pencil. Already the extensive use of pencil with watercolour that we find in the later 1930s is here foreshadowed. This clarity in the distinction of form is also strongly apparent in a number of seascapes, where the colour is evenly applied—a bluey grey over the sea and a deep terra cotta for the cliffs. The interest of the pictures is thus deflected into the curving shapes of the cliffs and the effect of colour masses against each other. With *Tenby from Caldy Island* (1925)[1] we have a picture which avoids these strong contrasts, though close in subject-matter. The scope of the painting is larger: there is room for houses near and far, for trees and grass, as well as ships. This wider vision is apparent too in *Montes et Omnes Colles* (1928),[2] which dates from the time that David Jones spent with the Gills at Salies de Béarn. Though we have gone from the quiet valley in the Black Mountains to the Pyrenees, the joyful movement of the picture (indicated in the title from Psalm cxlviii. 9) and the dancing shape of the trees and hills links up with *Hill Pastures*. The predominant colouring, however, has changed from a yellow green to reddish browns and blues. The feeling of openness that this picture gives is also found in *Roman Land* (1928),[3] which dates from this same visit to the south of France and creates a remarkable awareness of the whole agricultural way of life of that region. These early paintings move easily from mountains to the sea and back again. In various ways these two subjects form recurrent themes in David Jones's work, whether as the ostensible subject of a picture or as what might in another artist be thought of as part of the background. Mountains are certainly the less

[1] National Museum of Wales, Cardiff; Arts Council catalogue, II.
[2] Whitworth Art Gallery, Manchester; Ironside, 10.
[3] National Museum of Wales, Cardiff; Arts Council catalogue, VI; Decade 1920–30, no. 84.

important of the two, but the *Vexilla Regis* (1947) (Plate 6)[1] retains something of the movement of the hills in the background, while *The Hoggot, Cumbria* (1946)[2], painted during a stay at Miss Helen Sutherland's home in the Lake District, gives a very delicate apprehension of the muted colours and wide-stretching fells.

The sea and ships are a much more fundamental element in David Jones's whole *oeuvre*. Not only in the paintings and engravings, but also in extended sections of *The Anathemata* they find a place of affection. In part this may be traced to his early childhood experiences of the massed ships in the Thames at Rotherhithe with his beloved grandfather, Eb Bradshaw, about whom he still talks with undimmed memories. Ebenezer Bradshaw's working life was bound up with ships—he was a mast-and-block maker—and through him David Jones gained a lasting interest in their construction, which is apparent especially in such pictures as the engraving of the building of the ark in the *Deluge*, the immensely detailed watercolour drawing of *Trystan ac Essyllt* (c. 1962),[3] and in various passages in *The Anathemata*. The sea, however, might be held to feature so strongly in David Jones's work not simply because of childhood associations, however dear and deeply implanted they may be, but because the sea is, for all of us, perhaps the most powerful image of the great unknown. For the small child especially, catching his first glimpse of the sea so frequently as a strange new horizon between or beyond the ordered rows of boarding houses at a seaside resort, the sea is so completely other and so fascinating that it almost inevitably begins to symbolize the regions of spiritual as well as terrestrial exploration. There are the slightest hints of melancholy in a small number of David Jones's sea paintings, in, for example, *Out Tide* (c. 1931)[4] and *Factory Coast* (1936).[5] Both of these paintings are in oils, and as such they are untypical of the main body of his work. Moreover, they tend to give the impression from a distance of being watercolours, so light

[1] Kettle's Yard Collection, Cambridge; Rothenstein, opposite p. 297 (not in the Grey Arrow edition).
[2] Coll. the late Miss Helen Sutherland.
[3] Private collection; see Kenneth Clark's essay in the *Agenda* Special Number, pp. 97–8.
[4] City Art Galleries, Manchester.
[5] Coll. the late Miss Helen Sutherland.

in tone is the general effect and so thinly applied are the oils. But the bluish grey of the sea and the black of pier and factory in each picture have a tinge of sombreness about them that is absent in the watercolours.

In *Out Tide* we find one of the common characteristics of many of these sea pictures—the view from a room out on to the sea, which is shared by *The Terrace* (Plate 4),[1] *The Verandah* (both 1929),[2] and *Manawydan's Glass Door* (1931),[3] as well as a number of others. Of these *The Verandah* is the simplest in composition and colouring, showing only the sea beyond the slight framework of the verandah, but a sea with a beautifully subtle sheen on it, one small ship on the horizon and birds swooping through the air. Like the other two pictures mentioned this has the extremely pale, transparent hues which are the hallmark of David Jones's watercolour technique. His preoccupation with light tends to result in a blurring of outline as the objects depicted become absorbed in a kind of mazy visionariness.

The sea in these pictures is not experienced as essentially different from the room or terrace from which the painting is done. In such a picture as *The Terrace* the open door, the vase of flowers on the table, the terrace itself, and the sea seem to be made of the same element. The colour is washed on in small strokes and patches, and nowhere are there large areas of one colour unmixed with others. Everything merges into everything else, but yet there is a distinction of inside and outside, stone terrace and shining sea, the warmth of the day and the cool of the breeze wafting the curtains. We are made to feel that the natural world has been captured in a fleeting moment and that somehow the supernatural world is revealed in it and through it. Not only in this picture, but in many others, objects are not distinguished by different colours or by a coincidence of outline with colour. This forms part of a tendency for objects to lose their separateness—they merge into a continuum of sensory experience in which the space in between is as real and almost as tangible as the things that breathe or exist in it.

[1] The Tate Gallery, London.
[2] Kettle's Yard Collection, Cambridge.
[3] Coll. Mr Arthur Giardelli; Ironside, 23.

The presence of the supernatural world is made explicit in the title of *Manawydan's Glass Door*, where a restless green sea is seen through a closed curtained window. We might suspect, even without the allusive title, that there is more in this than mere physical appearances. The reference is to the Second Branch of the *Mabinogion*, the story of Branwen, daugher of Llyr (identifiable in a roundabout sort of way with Shakespeare's Lear). On the journey to London of the seven men who have escaped from the Irish and are taking the head of Bendigeidfran (Brân the Blessed) in order to protect the island from invasion, they stay for eighty years at Gwales in Penfro:

> And there was for them there a fair royal palace overlooking the sea, and a great hall it was. And they went into the hall, and two doors they saw open; the third door was closed, that towards Cornwall. 'See yonder,' said Manawydan, 'the door we must not open.' And that night they were there without stint, and were joyful. And notwithstanding that they had themselves suffered, there came to them no remembrance either of that or of any sorrow in the world. And there they passed the fourscore years so that they were not aware of having ever spent a time more joyous and delightful than that. It was not more irksome than when they came there, nor could any tell by his fellow that it was so long a time. . . .
> This is what Heilyn son of Gwyn did one day. 'Shame on my beard,' said he, 'if I do not open the door to know if that is true concerning it.' He opened the door and looked on Cornwall and Aber Henfelen. And when he looked, they were as conscious of every loss they had ever sustained, and of every kinsman and friend they had missed, and of every ill that had come upon them, as if it were even then it had befallen them; and above all else because of their lord. And from that same moment they could not rest, save they set out with the head towards London.[1]

The linking of this passage from the *Mabinogion* and what appears at first sight to be a fairly straightforward picture of a window with the sea beyond is typical of the way in which David Jones's mind works. He does not paint mere physical objects, or objects for their own sake, but tries to evoke as well the multifarious associations that

---

[1] *The Mabinogion*, tr. Gwyn Jones and Thomas Jones, pp. 39f.

PLATE THREE

Portrait of a Boy (1928)

PLATE FOUR

The Terrace (1929)

THE VISUAL ARTS

they have in his own consciousness. But *Manawydan's Glass Door* is only going one step forward from such comparable titles as *Montes et Omnes Colles* and *Roland's Tree* (1928).[1]

A number of other sea scenes go right out of the shelter of a house, from the between-world, into the open air. *Mare terraque* (1927)[2] is full of warm browns and an almost Mediterranean air, though it was painted during the time that David Jones was based at Capel-y-ffin. *The Reefed Place* (1931)[3] forms a beautiful contrast with its cool washes of blue, while *Surf* (1929)[4] and *Trade Ship passes Ynys Byr* (1931)[5] are similar essays in broader ranges of colour, though still exhibiting the characteristic lightness of tone. The themes of these pictures are very close to each other, even the composition is very similar, but each has an atmosphere about it that is all its own, despite the near-repetition of subject.

With these open seascapes we can approximately link a variety of landscapes with houses and churches. *The Fens* (c. 1929)[6] transports us into unfamiliar territory, where a lonely group of houses is conjured, floating, out of the seemingly endless vistas of light and space that mark that strange countryside. Eric Gill's Buckinghamshire home also provided subjects for David Jones's tireless brush. *Pigotts* (c. 1930)[7] and *Pigotts under Storm* (1930)[8] are two essays in somewhat stronger colour, applied rather blotchily in the second picture so as to produce the uncertain dark patchwork of the storm. Quite a number of other paintings were done about the same time or a little later at Rock Hall, Miss Helen Sutherland's home in Northumberland. Two of them, both painted from the room that David Jones used to occupy at the front of the house, are almost identical in the selection of the natural objects depicted, yet one is called quite simply *Chapel in the Park*,[9] while the other is mysteriously enveloped with associations from Malory in its title

[1] Coll. the late Miss Helen Sutherland.
[2] Coll. the late Miss Helen Sutherland.
[3] Coll. Miss Margaret Pilkington.
[4] Whitworth Art Gallery, Manchester.
[5] Coll. A. J. McNeil Reid; Ironside, 5.
[6] Coll. the late Miss Helen Sutherland.
[7] Coll. the late Miss Helen Sutherland.
[8] Coll. Mrs Christine Mocatta; Ironside, 19.
[9] The Tate Gallery, London; Ironside, 31.

of *The Chapel Perilous*[1] (both 1932). As with *Manawydan's Glass Door* the literary allusion makes explicit some of the manifold associations which David Jones works with in his pictures and indicates the kind of world he is trying to portray. It is something like a combination of Lord Clark's idea of 'the natural vision' and 'the landscape of symbols', the former applied by him to the main current of nineteenth century landscape painting, the latter predominantly to the art of the Middle Ages.[2] For in these two pictures we are presented with the here and now of an intimately observed Northumberland scene, which at the same time is intended to evoke the brooding atmosphere of a late medieval romance, of which the twentieth century landscape is perhaps only one temporary manifestation. The sheep are grazing, the birds flying in a park untrammelled by time. The ghost of Sir Lancelot is riding through the trees to perform the task which will heal the wounds of the knights who will otherwise surely die:

> and whan he com to the Chapell Perelus he alyght downe and tyed his horse unto a lytyll gate. And as sone as he was within the chyrcheyerde he sawe on the frunte of the chapel many fayre ryche shyldis turned up-so-downe, and many of the shyldis sir Launcelot had sene knyghtes bere byforehande. With that he sawe by hym there stonde a thirty grete knyghtes, more by a yerde than any man that ever he had sene, and all they grenned and gnasted at sir Launcelot. And when he sawe their countenaunce he dredde hym sore, and so put his shylde before him and toke his swerde in his honde redy unto batayle.[3]

Robin Ironside has called this kind of landscape with literary associations a *Stimmungslandschaft*,[4] a landscape of mood, and it is one that comes increasingly to the fore in David Jones's work, culminating in the detailed Arthurian and mythological watercolour drawings of c. 1940 and later. The transition between what is still a more or less naturalistically conceived landscape and these later drawings, where landscape and figures are fused into a new whole, is well represented by such a painting as *Window at Rock*

[1] Coll. the late Miss Helen Sutherland; Ironside, 26.
[2] Kenneth Clark, *Landscape into Art* (latest edition: Penguin, 1966), chapters 1 and 5.
[3] *The Works of Sir Thomas Malory*, ed. E. Vinaver (Oxford, 1959), VI, 15.
[4] Ironside, *op. cit.*, p. 16.

(1936).[1] The viewpoint is essentially the same as that of the other two, but their broadly applied colour has changed to a misty delicacy of light touches over pencil and brush outlines. The little bridge over the stream, the gravestones in the churchyard, the animals in the field among the trees are still there, but they have been absorbed into the mazy lines of a dream. Even the distinction between outside and inside has disappeared, and although the latch on the windowframe is in the very centre of the picture, we are hardly aware of it as a barrier. Many of these watercolours of the early 1930s are covered with a tracery of fine lines, in both paint and pencil, that links the various corners and details of the picture into a delicate kind of tapestry. This increasing subtlety of line is something we have already noted in his later engravings, and the technique becomes ever more important with the result that his later work consists almost exclusively of the most detailed and intricate pencil drawing heightened by the use of touches and patches of the softest colour.

This kind of filigree approach is apparent in several other window pictures that David Jones did about the same time. *English Window* (1931)[2] with its clavichord, bowls and jugs of flowers, has perhaps more interest in the interior of the room than the actual view outside, but in *Curtained Outlook* (1932)[3] the house in the garden is of as much importance as the worktable strewn with jars, bottles and a hundred other little objects. In some notes written for Mr H. S. Ede, David Jones said: 'I always work from the window of a house if it is at all possible. I like looking out on to the world from a reasonably sheltered position. I can't paint in the wind, and I like the indoors outdoors, contained yet limitless feeling of windows and doors. A man should be in a house; a beast should be in a field and all that.'[4] This discovery of the potentialities of the window scene for both uniting and separating, for keeping the terms of the natural order while simultaneously showing their intertwined relationships, is one of the keys to understanding the significance of the whole range of David Jones's work. For he is

[1] Coll. the late Miss Helen Sutherland; Ironside, 27.
[2] Coll. Arthur H. Wheen, Esq.; Ironside, 29; Arts Council catalogue, frontispiece.
[3] Coll. T. F. Burns, Esq.; Ironside, 11.
[4] Quoted in H. S. Ede, *op. cit.*, p. 131.

concerned above all with connexions and interrelations, both in painting and in imaginative literature, and certainly in the cross-connexions between them, and the window is a powerful symbol of such a mode of vision.

'If one is making a painting of daffodils,' writes David Jones in the Preface to *The Anathemata* (p. 10), 'what is *not* instantly involved? Will it make any difference whether or no we have heard of Persephone or Flora or Blodeuedd?' And when we see such a painting of his as *Gwyl Ddewi* (1950),[1] which is a painting of daffodils, we can sense that here is an artist who does invoke the goddess of flowers through the mere hints of colour that he allows to grace the mutability he has caught in his pencilled lines. But these daffodils invoke not only Flora Dea, pagan perhaps but universal, but also the Wales of St David, on whose feast day they become a national and Christian symbol.

Flowers are a constant subject for David Jones's brush. They figure in a number of the window pictures as well as forming the focus of such pictures as *Thorn Cup* (1932) (Plate 5)[2] and the much later *Flora in Calix-Light* (1950).[3] Both these watercolours, though separated by nearly twenty years, express similar moods of wonder at their fragile beauty. Such a mood is not especially common in flower painting, and indeed the famous flower pictures which immediately spring to mind—Van Gogh's *Sunflowers*, and the immensely detailed, photographically exact compositions of Dutch seventeenth century painters—seem to be much more concerned with capturing a riotous brilliance of colours. Sometimes David Jones uses flowers decoratively—especially in his engravings, where they often fill the spaces between figures—but everywhere they point to the precariousness of beauty in the natural world. They reflect a momentary balance that can be disturbed almost by a breath of air, but which, in the moment of its apprehension, shares in eternity. It is only in the explicitness of its title that *Flora in Calix-Light* differs from the earlier paintings of the '30s.

[1] Coll. the late Miss Helen Sutherland. The meaning of the title in English is 'Feast of St David'.
[2] Coll. the late Miss Helen Sutherland; Ironside, 17, with the title *Briar-Cup*.
[3] Kettle's Yard Collection, Cambridge.

THE VISUAL ARTS

In addition to these flower pictures David Jones has painted several still-lifes, though the inappropriateness of the name borders on the ludicrous when one looks at these vibrant compositions—*Hierarchy—Still Life* (1932),[1] *Martha's Cup* (1932),[2] *Violin* (1932),[3] *The Queen's Dish* (1932),[4] *Hague's Press* (1930).[5] Even these ordinary objects are made to partake of the same nature as the leaves and flowers that so characteristically surround them. The discontinuous strokes of colour, all typically pale, though nonetheless varied in hue, produce an effect that is frequently as restless as it is vital. Despite their subtle tones and seemingly innocuous subjects these paintings can be extremely disturbing.

Landscapes and flowers form a considerable part of David Jones's output, but he has also done several very fine animal drawings. With a splendid economy of line and little colour he has depicted *Lynx* (1931),[6] *Jaguar* (1931),[7] *Panthers* (1931),[8] *The Old Animal from Tibet* (1930),[9] and the cervil cat under the title of *Agag* (1930).[10] There is a curious allusion here to the king of the Amalekites, who 'came unto Samuel delicately' (1 Samuel xv, 32). These drawings are much smaller in size than the watercolours and less ambitious, but they are remarkable for the graceful way in which they present the animals to us 'as God's creatures and not at all as man's possible enemies, and though we see they have a dark side, it is not the darkness of rapacious instincts, but the portentous obscurity of some mythological role, their relation with the unicorn or the albatross.'[11] These animal studies were chiefly done at the Regents Park Zoo, but there are numerous engravings and watercolours, such as *Cows*[12] or *Cath Gartref* (1930),[13] in which a larger setting is

[1] Coll. the late Miss Helen Sutherland; Ironside, 13.
[2] Coll. E. C. Gregory, Esq.; Ironside, 25.
[3] Victoria and Albert Museum, London; Ironside, 9.
[4] Coll. N. B. C. Lucas, Esq.; Arts Council catalogue, XI.
[5] Coll. the late Miss Helen Sutherland; Ironside, 15.
[6] Coll. the late Miss Helen Sutherland; Ironside, 22.
[7] Cooper Art Gallery, Barnsley.
[8] Walker Art Gallery, Liverpool. There is another of the same title and date, reproduced in the *Agenda* Special Number, opposite p. 64.
[9] Coll. the late Miss Helen Sutherland; *Agenda* Special Number, opposite p. 81.
[10] Coll. Harman Grisewood, Esq.; Ironside, 24; Arts Council catalogue, III.
[11] Ironside, *op. cit.*, p. 15.
[12] Kettle's Yard Collection, Cambridge; reproduced by Ede in *Horizon*.
[13] Coll. Miss M. L. Graham; Arts Council catalogue, VII.

depicted. The animal world, like that of the sea and ships, is part and parcel of the visual furniture of David Jones's mind so that, even where it is not the primary subject of his undertaking, it may find a place as an integral part of a unified whole.

Everyone would agree in liking David Jones's animals, but when it comes to his portraits, done again during this hectically productive period from about 1928 to 1932, divergent views are common. For one thing, they are not 'academic' portraits; and when we note what considerations go into his other paintings, we may well wonder how they could possibly be so, for these portraits and pictures of human beings are not painted in any essentially different way. They are not really anchored sufficiently in the individual and the particular to be properly successful portraits. The titles of the paintings frequently indicate as much. The *Portrait of a Boy* (1928) (Plate 3)[1] with its dark, animal-like eyes and a distance or detachment in the expression on the boy's face does not seem quite concrete enough to be real. Yet by contrast with the Petra portraits there is a firm dominance of line, which the use of colour simply supports rather than competes with. The same feeling of the not quite real is apparent in one of David Jones's rare oil-paintings—*Human Being* (1931),[2] which is in fact a self-portrait, though it was not intended as a conventional essay in the genre. Though the oils do convey a solidity beyond that of his watercolours, the human being seems to be only tentatively an identifiable man. As Robin Ironside writes, 'His feeling for any special "genius" in his fellow being does not take in the complexities of personality, but attaches rather to their function in a pattern of creation.'[3] These two paintings, together with the inchoate and neurotically disturbing *Portrait of a Maker* (1932),[4] are not meant as portraits in the conventional sense. The picture of *Eric Gill* (1930)[5] is, by contrast, a successful likeness and shows us more of the affectionate humanity of the man than do, for example, the photo-

---

[1] Whitworth Art Gallery, Manchester.
[2] Coll. the late Miss Helen Sutherland; Ironside, 20; Arts Council catalogue, VIII.
[3] *Op. cit.*, p. 15.
[4] Coll. T. Clutterbuck, Esq.; Ironside, 7.
[5] Private collection; Ironside, 14; Arts Council catalogue, XIII; Speaight, *op. cit.*, p. 78.

graphs in Robert Speaight's *Life*. Two other portraits—*Petra im Rosenhag* (1930–31)[1] and *Petra* (1932)[2] have closer affinities with the mood of the flower paintings than with the other pictures of human beings, and in this combination anticipate the mythological and religious drawings such as *The Annunciation* (c. 1963). 'Petra' was Eric Gill's second daughter, to whom David Jones was for some time engaged to be married. The second, later picture is the more orthodox portrait, but *Petra im Rosenhag*, though we are assured by Sir John Rothenstein that it shows her just as he remembered her,[3] is even more reminiscent of Flora in Botticelli's *Primavera* than of the medieval paintings of the Virgin Mary in a rose arbour to which the adjunct of the title alludes. This picture will not be remembered as a portrait, however close a likeness it may be, but as a kind of twentieth century representation of that idealization of woman that the Middle Ages experienced in courtly love and that in various mutations has been with us ever since. It becomes especially clear that colour is used more to suggest a mood than to render any precise physical tone or shape. We do not find large, continuous areas of a single colour, but rather a few strokes here and there, reflected in other sections of the painting too, and all pale or muted, connecting the whole of the picture and what goes on in it with the central figure, which is rarely completely dominant. The periphery is as important as the centre.

III

The years from about 1925 to 1932 were the most prolific period in David Jones's career, during which time he did his best engravings and the watercolours through which he is probably most widely known. He had also begun work on what was to be his first book, *In Parenthesis*. Soon after this, however, he suffered a breakdown in health, and when he started to work again a few years later it was chiefly through the medium of detailed pencil drawings heightened by the use of very delicate watercolour. The subjects which attracted his imagination—and we should never forget the impor-

---

[1] Coll. Lord Clark; Ironside, 16; Arts Council catalogue, XII.
[2] Coll. the late Miss Helen Sutherland; Ironside, 21.
[3] Rothenstein, *op. cit.*, p. 303.

tance of subject for him—were drawn largely from Arthurian legend and Christian and classical tradition. This was far from being a new departure, as the titles of some of his earlier watercolours amply testify. Nor is the technique a radical innovation, for the use of pencil is frequent enough from *Hill Pastures* onwards, and a more or less continuous line of development can be traced through from the copper engravings of *Aesop* and *The Ancient Mariner* to *Guenever* (1940)[1] and beyond. The links are also in the field of book illustrations. In 1931 David Jones did a drawing for John O'Connor's translation of Claudel's *Satin Slipper*, a work which, by the sheer complexity and symbolism of its themes, one might have thought to be very close to David Jones's own way of thinking. 'THE ARGUMENT is that all things minister to a Divine Purpose and so to one another, be it events or personalities. Even the falterings of circumstance and the patternings of personality, sin and falsehood, are made to serve truth and justice, and above all, salvation in the long run.'[2] Be this as it may, David Jones confesses that for this drawing, which has elicited much praise from both art critics and reviewers of the book for its interpretative qualities, he read no more than the first few pages of the play, finding it too obscurely complicated for his liking. Nonetheless, the illustration is complicated too and very close in style to the large Arthurian drawings.

Another watercolour drawing was reproduced by collotype as the frontispiece for R. H. J. Steuart's most readable account of his experiences as an army chaplain with the Highland Light Infantry in the First World War, published under the title *March, Kind Comrade*.[3] This is probably David Jones's first war picture, giving a realistic impression of the day-to-day battle scene—of trenches and duckboards, a few soldiers going about their routine business among the blasted trees and the barbed wire. The two drawings which he did for *In Parenthesis* in 1937 and which were conceived originally as designs for engravings are both part of the process of remythologizing the War, as Bernard Bergonzi has aptly described

[1] The Tate Gallery, London; Ironside, 30.
[2] Paul Claudel, *The Satin Slipper* (Sheed & Ward, 1931), p. xi.
[3] R. H. J. Steuart, S.J., *March, Kind Comrade* (Sheed & Ward, 1931).

David Jones's account of his own experiences.[1] The soldier's semi-nakedness amid the rats and the barbed wire is but the other side of the sacrificial lamb with all its intertwined relationships.

Guenever and *The Four Queens* (1941),[2] together with *Trystan ac Essyllt* are the most important of David Jones's pictures arising from his intimate involvement over a lifetime with the Matter of Britain. They were preceded, however, by a drawing of 1930–31, originally entitled *Merlin appears in the Form of a Young Child to Arthur Sleeping*,[3] but called, when used some twenty years later as an illustration to *The Anathemata*, by the more concise, but less explicit, title *Merlin-Land*. The three earlier pictures are all marked by a strange dream-like quality, which has caused one critic to refer disparagingly to them as escapist,[4] though one may doubt whether he would think of Chagall or Klee in the same terms for doing analogous things. The figures and animals in *Merlin-Land* inhabit a kind of starry space; they seem to float through the heavens with only a gossamer anchor to hold them to earth. The picture is full of movement: the horses, deer and hounds wander restlessly over the scene, even the trees are animated by an almost human vitality. Over everything lies an air of mystery and twilight that is the essence of what is depicted. The theme of the picture is derived from Malory's *Tale of King Arthur* (I, 19 f.), where Arthur has fallen asleep after the departure of the Questing Beast and Merlin appears to him 'lyke a chylde of fourtene yere of ayge' and informs him of his extraordinary parentage, thus making him aware of both his heritage and his calling. The other two drawings also take their subjects from Malory, but are vastly more complex in both scope and technique.

The love of Lancelot and Guinevere is one of Malory's most important themes, and *Guenever* illustrates that episode in it where Sir Lancelot comes to the queen at night in the castle of Sir Meliagaunce (XIX, 6). Guinevere had been surprised by Meliagaunce while out on a maying expedition and imprisoned along with the

---

[1] Bernard Bergonzi, *Heroes' Twilight. A Study of the Literature of the Great War* (Constable, 1965), p. 198.
[2] The Tate Gallery, London; Ironside, 32.
[3] Coll. M. W. Richey, Esq.
[4] R. H. Wilenski, *English Painting*, 4th edition (Faber, 1964), p. 288.

ten knights of the Round Table who had been accompanying her. Sir Lancelot, however, is brought news of the disaster and comes to their rescue. His mere arrival is sufficient for Meliagaunce to put himself at the queen's mercy, and Guinevere takes control of the situation. Sir Lancelot promises to come to her in the night when all are sleeping, finds a ladder to climb to her window and breaks the iron bars asunder with his bare hands, cutting them through to the bone.[1] This is the very moment that the picture captures, for Lancelot is just springing down from the window to keep his tryst with Guinevere as she lies magnificently naked on her bed, raising her right arm to wipe the sleep from her eyes. The wounded knights that she has been carefully tending lie on their pallets around her asleep in a variety of postures, one still even wearing his spurs. The drawing is far more complex than anything David Jones had hitherto attempted; one is continually finding fresh details— the dog curled up at the foot of the queen's bed, the cat jumping on the bed, the bats high under the vaulted roof. The composition of the picture focusses attention of course first on Guinevere, but then the shape of the vault and the angle of the queen's raised arm lead us to the far end of the prison where the reserved sacrament is kept. And as Lancelot leaps in through the window, bleeding, on the right, so on the left a small crucifix hangs on the column above Guinevere's head. This counterbalancing of secular and religious themes, which is also Malory's since the love of Lancelot for Guinevere, although adulterous, is seen in terms of an analogy to the Christian's devotion to the eucharist, forms an essential part of David Jones's vision of the coherence of all things, that vision of which *The Anathemata* is his most ambitious realization.

The Four Queens deals once more with Lancelot, but with an earlier adventure in his variegated career. While out on an expedition with his nephew Sir Lionel, he has fallen asleep under a little apple tree and is an object of great desire to the 'four queenys of a grete astate' (VI, 3) who have just come by—the queens of the Out Isles and Eastland, Arthur's sister Morgan le Fay, and the queen of North Wales. Morgan le Fay, the most dangerous of

[1] The details given by Ironside, *op. cit.*, pp. 16–17, do not quite square with Malory's account.

Malory's enchantresses, stands a little to the front of the other queens, seductively revealing her jewelled garter, and in the process of casting a spell over Lancelot that will keep him unconscious for seven hours. Lancelot, however, remains unflinchingly constant to Guinevere, who appears at his side in the guise of a fluttering swan. The whole atmosphere of the picture with its trailing, sinuous lines is like that of a dream, for the four queens seem barely to touch the earth with their delicate feet and diaphanous gowns as they hover around their prey. Behind them is the agitated figure of the 'grete horse' that they heard 'grymly nyghe' and that caused them to stop and notice Sir Lancelot. In the background—never unimportant in David Jones's work—there stands amid ruined pillars and gravestones what can only be the Chapel Perilous, while chalk horses are carved on the hillsides and cromlechs cast their prehistoric shadows. Both *Guenever* and *The Four Queens* are pictures which demand some intimate knowledge of the Arthurian legend for an adequate interpretation, though even those ignorant of the details of Malory must find pleasure in the extraordinary skill of the composition, in which every minute detail is carefully related to the whole conception. The colouring of the two pictures consists of the merest touches of very pale tints—a little blue, green or pink to offset the prevailing grey of the pencil —but their effect as a whole rests of the subtlety of line and shading rather than on the use of colour. With these later drawings in particular the whole surface of the picture presents a ramification of the most intricate lines meandering from corner to corner and linking the entire design. As in much of David Jones's work, it is an idiosyncratic sort of space that they create, for although he is constantly drawings objects and figures that ostensibly belong to a solid, three-dimensional world in terms of perspective and individuality, yet his pencil lines and colours overlap and cross to such a degree that things are perceived through and beyond each other in a manner which suggests that space is transcended.

The background details of *The Four Queens* in extending the scope and relevance of the Arthurian subject-matter point the way to the more symbolic *Aphrodite in Aulis* (1941)[1] and *Vexilla Regis*

[1] Private collection; Rothenstein, facing p. 293.

(1947).¹ The first of these, in pen, ink and watercolour, appears as a synthesis of almost everything that has gone before; pretty well every theme that David Jones has ever touched before is included in it. Not only is there the sea with ships of all kinds sailing about, but there are soldiers and a monk, three horses, countless birds, antique columns, a sacrificial lamb, and hills and trees in the background, all grouped around the central figure of Aphrodite. The key to this elaborate drawing lies in the identification of love with sacrifice and the combination of Christian with non-Christian elements, for it is David Jones's belief that myths and archetypes from all periods of the world's history may find their true fulfilment in the symbolism of Christianity. Thus, Aphrodite is also the Iphigeneia who was sacrificed—hence the shackle on her foot—by her father Agamemnon to the goddess Artemis in fulfilment of a vow made twelve years before he and the Greek fleet were becalmed in Aulis while en route for Troy. But this female figure bears also certain marks—the wounds of hand and foot—that make her a female counterpart of the crucified Christ. A British soldier bearing a lance at her side recalls the centurion Longinus, who pierced the side of Christ, and the blood of the ram carved on the pediment beneath her feet spurts into a chalice. Moreover, a monk at her left swings a censer as he would for the eucharist, and a soldier behind him bears a shield with the emblem PX. As Sir John Rothenstein observes, 'For David Jones it is the Eucharist that redeems the historical process; accordingly, around Aphrodite are ranged soldiers of those times and places that interest him most, Greek, Etruscan, Roman, Arthurian, British, German; columns and pediments are broken, but around this sign all the orders of architecture retain their validity. Around her neck Aphrodite wears a necklace that carries a cross, and indeed there are stars in her hair with a crescent moon above, as if she were after all the Madonna and the Mother of all the Living (as in Hopkins's 'May Magnificat'), while around her head fly doves, the effulgence of one of which radiates her body. In the eucharistic sign, then, is she seen for what after all she is—even if in aspect she be Phryne or Lesbia.'²

[1] Kettle's Yard Collection, Cambridge; Rothenstein, facing p. 297.
[2] Rothenstein, *op. cit.*, p. 306.

PLATE FIVE

Thorn Cup (1932)

PLATE SIX

Vexilla Regis (1947)

THE VISUAL ARTS

The depiction of Aphrodite is, despite the symbolism of sacrifice, one of a goddess of love, of physical beauty, and a detail on the hillside to the left of the Agelastos Petra, the cleft rock at Eleusis, with its cult-object representing the female generative organs, is a further minor indication of this aspect of her nature.[1] This picture is in many ways a visual counterpart to *The Anathemata*.

During 1947 and 1948 David Jones did a number of pictures of trees—among them *Leafless Tree* (1948)[2] and *The Storm Tree* (1948)[3] —in which he seems chiefly concerned with their skeletal structure. Foliage, as in most of his drawings of trees, appears to be either lacking or unimportant because it is the basic, unadorned shape or form that is the centre of interest. This attitude has a bearing on the *Vexilla Regis*, completed some six years after the *Aphrodite*, for here the bareness of the trees identifies them all the more closely with the three crosses of Golgotha. The title of the picture is taken from the famous hymn of Venantius Fortunatus, which was written for the reception of a fragment of the True Cross sent by the Emperor Justin II from Constantinople to Queen Radegund, Abbess of the convent of the Holy Cross at Poitiers, in 569. At first glance the relationship with the Crucifixion may not be clearly evident, but a closer look soon shows that the central tree is marked with the four nails, above which we see a 'garland' round a branch, while the one on the right bears a Roman eagle and is driven into the earth like a stake (the unrepentant sinner), and the one on the left has a pelican, a common symbol of Christ, nesting in its branches (the repentant sinner). But amidst the other trees we glimpse a Greek temple, a prehistoric stone circle, and various other shrines of gods and goddesses. Like the *Aphrodite* this is a further depiction of truths subsumed in the Christian truth, but beginning this time with the natural world and extending it through time and place. It is a landscape of symbols that David Jones portrays, but it never loses touch with the primary reality of nature. The hills and trees with their mysteriously wandering horses are not stylized into other shapes, but through their natural forms evoke the associations of another, usually hidden world.

[1] See *The Anathemata*, p. 56.
[2] City Art Galleries, Manchester.   [3] The British Council.

These later drawings represent the culmination of a lifetime's striving to put into visual form a conviction of order and relationship in the phenomena of the universe, of 'all things visible and invisible'. During the time that they were made David Jones was also working on The Anathemata, and indeed writing has now become a more demanding vehicle of communication. Such pictures as the Annunciation to Shepherds (1942) and Lamb (c. 1950),[1] which was originally conceived as an illustration to The Anathemata, but which turned out too complex for reproduction, prepare the way for the latest of his drawings—The Annunciation (c. 1963) and Trystan ac Essyllt.[2] The picture of Trystan and Essyllt is probably the most straightforward of David Jones's illustrations of the Matter of Britain, not being ramified with extensive symbolism like Guenever and The Four Queens, but nonetheless full of copious detail in the depiction of the drinking of the love-potion on the ship sailing from Ireland to Cornwall, especially of the dismay of Brangwaine below deck when she glimpses what is taking place. And again unlike the other pictures, this is characterized by a strong use of large areas of colour, particularly of blue. The Annunciation is once more in the vein of the Aphrodite and Vexilla Regis, though the Christian theme is more patent than in either of the other two. In mood and to a certain degree in composition it is reminiscent of Dürer's Virgin and Child with Animals, one of his most attractive watercolours. Among other pictures done during this latter period mention should be made of an illustration done for T. S. Eliot's Ariel Poem The Cultivation of Christmas Trees,[3] an unimportant poem, but a beautiful fairy-like picture; a Christmas card of an angel playing a violin, designed for Faber and Faber in 1961; and a drawing in pencil and chalk entitled La Belle endormie (1958).[4] Elegant though these smaller pictures are, they are hardly comparable in scope with The Annunciation. But we should not be blind to their delicacy and skill, for they are every bit as refined in line and colour as these more ambitious works.

[1] Both Coll. the late Miss Helen Sutherland.
[2] Both private collection. For a detailed discussion of these two pictures see Kenneth Clark, 'Some Recent Paintings of David Jones', Agenda Special Number, pp. 97–100.
[3] Faber and Faber, 1954.
[4] Coll. the late Miss Helen Sutherland.

IV

So far in this outline of David Jones's career as a painter and engraver I have barely referred to one sphere in which he has created a unique place for himself—that of calligraphy. Since about 1948 he has done a considerable number of inscriptions, lettered in a personal modification of Roman capitals, generally on paper prepared with a background of Chinese white, and coloured in black, red, yellow, purple, what have you. Several of them have been reproduced in *The Anathemata*; others have appeared in *Epoch and Artist*. One was done specially for the symposium edited by Neville Braybrooke for T. S. Eliot's seventieth birthday;[1] another has appeared in Peter Levi's *Fresh Water, Sea Water*,[2] which is in fact dedicated to David Jones; one was included in the decorations for *The Cultivation of Christmas Trees*, where it suffered through being reproduced in uniform black, whereas the original was designed for a number of colours. A further inscription was done for the 1961 Faber and Faber Christmas card, where it was given the full colour treatment. Moreover, quite a few other designs have been made for book covers—not only for David Jones's own works (*The Anathemata* and *Epoch and Artist* for Faber and Faber, *The Tribune's Visitation* for the Fulcrum Press), but also for such books as Frank Morley's *The Great North Road*.[3] In addition to this, several of David Jones's friends have been privileged recipients of this unusual art form at the celebration of some important occasion in their lives. Most frequently the inscriptions are quotations in Latin, Welsh and English, sometimes singly, more often in combination. Usually one or part of one of the quotations will be arranged as a kind of frame round the main portion of the text, giving the words a physical as well as a semantic significance.

It is curious to note that while Chinese and Japanese calligraphers have always emphasized the arduous training which must precede the then unstudied execution of their characters, David Jones works at and modifies his letters and shapes as he goes along, altering the form of a letter here and there to achieve the kind of

---

[1] Rupert Hart-Davies, 1958.
[2] Black Raven Press, 1966.
[3] Hutchinson, 1961.

balance and freshness he is seeking. He paints with immense care on the Chinese white that allows him this freedom of modification. Yet the final result does not appear laboured; on the contrary, it exhibits a living tension similar to what the best Eastern calligraphers accomplish. The use of colour is vital to this movement for him, and the reproduction of his work in monotone thus fails to do justice to his vision and deadens it.

When Saunders Lewis spoke on the Welsh Home Service on a programme devoted to David Jones in connexion with the Arts Council retrospective exhibition in Wales,[1] he saw the inscriptions as 'a key to the understanding of the whole exhibition' and declared that in them 'poet and painter join to state, to proclaim the mystery, the annunciation, the charged sign, that words sometimes carry like an aura around them, just like a human body.' He went on to emphasize the physical shape of the words on the page, the subtlety of their arrangement and spacing and colouring. The words of course have their meaning, though this is not the primary thing. David Jones himself has said: 'It seems to me that Latin and Welsh are the languages in which to make inscriptions. In English the words and their meanings are too close to me. They *interfere*.'[2] It is significant that when English words are used they are frequently medieval or archaic in form. For this reason it is true to say, with Nicolete Gray, that these inscriptions are 'like pictures designed in a peculiarly formal medium... his aesthetic intention is conveyed purely in the things drawn, not in the extraneously recognized sense of the words which the spectator may read.'[3] At the same time one can perceive them as a kind of poetry related to the methods of *The Anathemata*, following them on a different and perhaps not wholly congruent level of awareness.

In one way it is possible to regard David Jones's last drawings such as *The Annunciation* or *The Four Queens* as the summit of his career. They represent his most ambitious attempts at synthesizing profundity of theme with mastery of a complex idiom and are

[1] 29 October 1954; quotation from transcript.
[2] Arts Council catalogue, p. 11.
[3] Nicolete Gray, 'David Jones', *Signature*, no. 8 (new series), 1949, p. 48. For a more extensive account of David Jones's lettering see Nicolete Gray, 'David Jones and the Art of Lettering', *Motif*, no. 7, 1961, pp. 69–80.

remarkable works largely incomparable with anything else being done at this time in the field of the visual arts. The other side of his achievement is to be found in the inscriptions, where he has reduced all to simplicity and made a unity of the meaning and the shape of words. These two factors are also at work in *The Anathemata* and the later short poems, where the meaning of the whole work is comparable to, say, the *Aphrodite*, while the constant use of seminal quotations in Latin or Welsh provides an incantatory counterpart to the inscriptions. It would, however, be unjust to praise these two aspects of David Jones's work to the detriment of that most prolific period of his life from 1925 to 1932. What he produced during this period is as polished and finished in its proper way as the later things. His engravings for *The Deluge* in particular must have a high place in a full assessment of his work. But perhaps the quality which is constant and which is found in those inimitable landscapes and window scenes is the feeling of holiness in the common object.

4
In Parenthesis

I

Until the late 1930s David Jones's reputation was as a watercolourist and engraver, but in 1937 he made his modest entry into the field of literature with a book that commanded the eloquent attention of a number of prominent critics, including James Agate and Herbert Read, who immediately recognized its importance not only as a 'war book' but also as a first-rate work of contemporary literature. *In Parenthesis* was almost the last book to emerge from the personal experience of the First World War. The War had been over for nearly twenty years when it was first published, though it had been finished some three or four years earlier. Despite this late start *In Parenthesis* is less a work of reminiscence than any narrative that had previously appeared. The autobiographical element, strong though it obviously is, has been subordinated to an overriding poetic intent, which has created of this material an independent work of art. The re-awakened concern with the literature of the First World War, which has been stimulated by its fiftieth anniversary and a long series of television and radio programmes, probably owes more to the current interest in history—especially that of the recent past, which helps to make the events of today more comprehensible—than to purely literary values. When there are no longer any people alive with personal memories of the War, we shall perhaps be able to judge its literary products with a greater degree of objectivity and know what is more than historically and sociologically valuable. David Jones's book has profited like many others from this renewed historical interest, and indeed two of the most recent critical discussions of it—by John H. Johnston[1] and Bernard Bergonzi[2]—have appeared in books dealing specifically with the literature of the War. But its value is not, I feel, dependent on this interest, but on intrinsic artistic merit, which is somewhat more difficult to estimate in the case of more narrowly autobiographical accounts.

I have referred to *In Parenthesis* as a 'war book', and this is clearly the most obvious category into which it may be put. But David Jones states in his preface: 'I did not intend this as a "War Book"—it happens to be concerned with war. I should prefer it to be about a good kind of peace—but as Mandeville says, "Of Paradys ne can I not speken propurly I was not there; it is fer beyonde and that for thinketh me. And also I was not worthi." We find ourselves privates in foot regiments. We search how we may see formal goodness in a life singularly inimical, hateful, to us' (pp. xii f.). There is a sense in which war books may become parochial, treating the vicissitudes of a soldier's life like the private intercourse of an in-group, with no glance or awareness of anything further. Such books are often of copious interest to soldiers themselves, though lacking in any permanent value to others. The soldier's life, while yet circumscribed and incomplete, attempts a spurious self-sufficiency. But there is also, as an antithesis to this view, as Frederic Manning said, 'an extraordinary veracity in war, which strips man of every conventional covering he has, and leaves him to face a fact as naked and as inexorable as himself.'[3] This latter view is that of *In Parenthesis*. It is because it exemplifies 'formal goodness in a life singularly inimical, hateful, to us' that its impact is so telling. Its subject-matter is not war as such, but life exemplified in the deeds and moods of war. The war may be seen—partly—as a parenthesis, but it is nonetheless capable of demonstrating the essence of life. For David Jones in so much of his imaginative writing—not only in *In Parenthesis*—the soldier is one of the basic human prototypes.

[1] John H. Johnston, *English Poetry of the First World War. A Study in the Evolution of Lyric and Narrative Form* (Princeton University Press, 1964).
[2] Bernard Bergonzi, *Heroes' Twilight. A Study of the Literature of the Great War* (Constable, 1965).
[3] Frederic Manning, *Her Privates We* (Pan Books, 1967), p. 58.

We can see this in the later poems such as *The Tribune's Visitation* and *The Fatigue*, but also in the depiction of the sleeping soldiers in the drawing of *Guenever* and of the multifarious figures surrounding the *Aphrodite in Aulis*. But the view is supremely expressed in this first book.

If we accept these limitations on the definition of *In Parenthesis* as a 'war book', we are still confronted with the problem of categorizing it. The matter of genre can certainly be overdone. In a broadcast talk on David Jones on 29 October 1954 T. S. Eliot touched on this very matter when he said: 'There are two questions which people are given to asking, often in a peremptory tone, about certain modern works of literature. The first is: "Is this poetry or prose?"—with the implication that it is neither. The second question is: "What is this book about?"—with the implication that it is not really about anything.' Works which cannot quickly be classified are liable to be submitted to this kind of question, the dubious relevance of which should then become apparent. An obsession with genre is characteristic of literary sensibilities nurtured on the classics and more or less preconceived notions on the nature of form. But the subject of war—and perhaps especially the new kind of war experienced between 1914 and 1918, which was quite different from anything before—constitutes an extreme demand on literary technique. We are accustomed, in classical and medieval times, to talk about the epic, sometimes the heroic epic, where battle is the focal point of poetry, but so often other factors enter into consideration here that we are forced to modify our concepts and recognize that even *Beowulf* is not simply or merely an heroic epic. With modern literature the distinctions are even more precarious, so that nomenclature becomes more self-evidently the matter of convenience that it really is. The novel is in any case a combination of the narrative with the drama and thus provides the frame-work for almost any kind of experimentation. If one notes the excursions into philosophy of Thomas Mann's *Magic Mountain* or the abrupt alternations of tone and form in *Ulysses* or the extravagantly mannered lyricism of Lawrence Durrell's *Alexandria Quartet* or the reduction to conversation of most of Ivy Compton-Burnett's novels, to mention only a few obvious examples, one already has some conception of the limitlessness of the novel as a genre and at the same time of its extensibility as a concept. William Burroughs has even undermined the notion of definite sequence in chopping his novels into sections which may be read in any order. In an experimental context of this kind *In Parenthesis* does not have to justify itself. In length and overall structure it may be said to be a novel, but in its use of language it is more akin to poetry.

What the book is 'about' is less open to discussion. As a narrative of war it presents a simple enough plot, centred on the personal experiences and reactions of Private John Ball as he moves off from the parade ground of his infantry camp to the port of embarkation for France and thus ever further into the front-line of the War. As the scene changes from day to night and from camp to trenches, the events and preparations lead slowly to the final battle, in which the platoon is destroyed and John Ball himself wounded. Such is the bald outline of what happens over a period of some seven months of the War from December 1915 to July 1916. Within this framework we are given as concentrated a picture of the feel of the War from the viewpoint of a private as can be found anywhere, a picture built up from a mass of fine details and precisely observed minutiae. Nowhere are the perceptions of the five senses more piercingly recorded than in *In Parenthesis*. This attention to the physical sensations of the soldier's life in a certain preference to purely emotional responses is highly characteristic of David Jones's method and links up with his emphasis on the concrete and the particular in his paintings and engravings. The meaning of things is discovered through physical manifestations and their interrelationships.

The reader of the history of the First World War is, I think, struck most of all by its curious purposelessness and amorphousness. Historians will no doubt discuss for ever the reasons for it. As A. J. P. Taylor writes:

> Men are reluctant to believe that great events have small causes. Therefore, once the Great War started, they were convinced that it must be the outcome of profound forces. It is hard to discover these when we examine the details. Nowhere was there conscious deter-

mination to provoke a war. Statesmen miscalculated. They used the instruments of bluff and threat which had proved effective on previous occasions. This time things went wrong. The deterrent on which they relied failed to deter; the statesmen became the prisoners of their own weapons. The great armies, accumulated to provide security and preserve the peace, carried the nations to war by their own weight.[1]

The accounts of the conduct of the War, given by historians and poets alike, only serve to underline the military and political incompetence with which it was pursued. In these circumstances one of the most marked features of the poems, novels and autobiographical accounts that were published was the attempt to make some kind of order out of what appeared to have none. Where could any sense or meaning be found in the dislocation of ordinary life and the dismemberment of families? To what could the shock and brutality of the War be related?

The most stirring reaction of the time—and indeed the one which even today is the most famous—was the call to idealistic patriotism sounded by Rupert Brooke in such poems as 'Peace' and 'The Soldier'. It is fashionable nowadays to debunk these sonnets as emotional rhetoric and to claim that they are shallow, pointing by way of contrast to the 'maturer' lyrics of, for example, Charles Sorley. But the very idea of patriotism is at present so threadbare and ridiculous that we are not in the best of positions to judge the impact of Brooke's appeal. Nonetheless, it did represent an astonishingly potent element in the experience of the beginning of the War, even if, as personal accounts of trench warfare percolated back home, the idealism began to fade among the soldier-poets themselves. In its place there grew up a stronger realism, based on actual experience and often bitterly ironic and full of social criticism. Siegfried Sassoon, for example, uses the lurid details of battle to deflate the high-flown platitudinous ideals of the civilian population, which had not wished to be in touch with the physical realities of the war situation in France. His poems and those of Wilfred Owen pre-eminently tried to deflect the apprehension of

[1] A. J. P. Taylor, *The First World War. An Illustrated History* (Penguin Books, 1966), p. 16.

the War from the unreal ideals of a world that could no longer be recaptured or re-established to the concrete facts of suffering and death. Many of these poems, with their taut descriptions and keen, terse phraseology, are assured a lasting place in the annals of English poetry. But most of them are lyrics or short poems and as such capture a moment or a mood which seems worthy of remembering, perhaps most frequently of anger, despair or savage meaninglessness. Occasionally, as in Edmund Blunden's 'Third Ypres' or Herbert Read's 'The End of a War', we get a lengthier, more reflective picture. But the poetry on the whole acts like the quick jab of the hypodermic needle, bringing a brief respite of relief to a lacerated body. Perhaps in some cases it is all that is possible.

There are, of course, also the reactions of the autobiographers and novelists. Here a much more comprehensive approach and wider vision is apparent, together with the looser texture and the alternations of tension and tedium or repetitiveness that necessarily accompany it. Because of their authors' distinction in other fields such books as Robert Graves's *Goodbye to all that*, Sassoon's *Memoirs of an Infantry Officer*, and *Sherston's Progress*, and Blunden's *Undertones of War* have found continuing appreciation. Among the large number of novels Manning's *Her Privates We* has been distinguished from others in being reprinted as recently as 1967 in a paperback edition. As autobiography is one of the most popular of literary forms, it is not surprising that Graves's, Sassoon's and Blunden's accounts of the War have survived so well. But war *novels* have to possess more than ordinary qualities to enable them to do the same. Bernard Bergonzi notes that 'Manning's close-textured prose maintains an effective balance between the salty vigour of the colloquial exchanges of the soldiers, and Bourne's probing, existential reflections' and that his 'philosophical concern provides an additional dimension and unifies the novel's disparate realistic observations.'[1] He further adds that the 'epic flavour' created by the blend of the particular and the universal is only found elsewhere in any like degree in *In Parenthesis*. Yet David Jones's book is not philosophical in anything like Manning's sense. It does not set

[1] *Op. cit.*, p. 193.

out to provide a ruminative analysis of the nature of war, though it does by other means give shape and definition to a particular experience. It is not without its significance that the kind of vision David Jones attempted was not achieved until so long after the War had ended. It was not until nine years after the War that he even began to write his book, and the detachment of these years enabled him to treat his material with less subjectivity. The lyrics of the War period itself sometimes suffer from a lack of emotional control, from an excess of passion. *In Parenthesis*, however, manages to fuse an extraordinarily vivid objectivity with a degree of emotional concentration that is rare anywhere. Nine years had not dulled the memory or the perceptions of the writer, but had allowed him a sovereign control over his subject-matter.

The objectivity of *In Parenthesis* has given rise to a good deal of talk about the epic qualities of the book. John H. Johnston in particular has taken the view that David Jones has sought to re-create an 'heroic vision' and has, in effect, produced a modern epic poem.[1] His thesis is based to a large extent on an interpretation of the allusions to the Old Welsh *Y Gododdin*, the *Mabinogion*, Malory's *Morte d'Arthur* and the *Chanson de Roland* as constituting an heroic standard according to which 'the narrative reality is... permeated with inherited racial traditions and legends which, as they accumulate by way of analogy or simple poetic enrichment, produce the effect of a vital and significant historical continuity.'[2] Johnston does not, however, attempt to define what he means by the term 'heroic' apart from literary references; he does not point to any precise moral code or outlook which alone would justify the use of the term. Indeed he admits 'that the action of *In Parenthesis* is not essentially heroic action [whatever that is]; the protagonist of the poem is hardly a protagonist at all, and he is certainly not made in the mold of the epic hero.'[3] Medievalists, who are wont to discuss the essential nature of the heroic more than students of modern literature, would have difficulty in determining whether the *Mabinogion*, in whole or in part, or Malory could legitimately

---

[1] *Op. cit.*, pp. 302ff.
[2] *Ibid*, p. 304.
[3] *Ibid.*, p. 303.

be considered as heroic or epic. The fact that a work is concerned with battle is not a sufficient criterion for judging whether it has heroic qualities. The literary references here do not establish a single, unified mode of vision, but serve rather as a context simply for *soldierly* activity. The concepts of the heroic and of epic require more definition than a historical sense. As Bernard Bergonzi points out, David Jones 'reproduces a sense of shared experience and transcends the limitations of the purely individual standpoint. But true epic... reaches out beyond the personal to appeal to a system of public and communal values which are ultimately collective, national, and even cosmic. And this Jones does not do; he may feel that Celtic myth is central and not peripheral to his understanding of British tradition, and he may have some success in persuading a discerning reader that this is so. Nevertheless, such knowledge will not already be there to provide a ready response in the consciousness of most of his readers.'[1] It is possible—indeed one is compelled—to agree with Johnston that the allusions to such works as the *Gododdin* and the *Chanson de Roland* are integral to the intentions of *In Parenthesis*, but I do not think one can use them to claim the qualities he wishes to see.

The literary references of *In Parenthesis* are an essential part of David Jones's assimilation of his experience of the War. John H. Johnston comments: 'The individual response does not serve merely as a focus for limited emotional reactions; through its relationship to the heroic past it is universalized and ennobled.'[2] It is by placing his account in this wider context that David Jones is able to make a more permanently satisfactory work than many other books that were written using the same basic material. The War is thus not experienced as something totally other, forming a kind of world in itself, with its own values and self-consistency. Its disruption of the normal order of life is made sense of by the reference to a historical background which is itself accepted as part of the normal order. In this way connexions are made which many men in trying to describe their emotions and experiences found difficult, if not impossible. To a limited extent Frederic Manning

[1] *Op. cit.*, p. 203.
[2] *Op. cit.*, pp. 304f.

had used a similar device in his Shakespearian epigraphs to each chapter of *Her Privates We*, but they are not quite so convincingly incorporated into the structure of the novel as David Jones's allusions. All the same they are a like attempt to give the War a more general validity.

The basic frame of reference to the elements of a soldier's life in *In Parenthesis* is provided by a number of works, of which the most constantly appearing are the *Gododdin* poems of Aneirin, the prose tales of the *Mabinogion*, Malory and *Henry V*, though Chaucer, Gerard Manley Hopkins, Caesar and the *Chanson de Roland* also have their part to play. Of all these one can only reckon Shakespeare, Malory (though most probably through some modernizing adaptor) and Hopkins as a reliable component of contemporary literary culture. Where, then, lies the significance of the medieval Welsh contribution, to take the most important first?

David Jones, in being half Welsh, is more conscious of Welsh tradition than many of his full-blooded compatriots. When the majority of Englishmen unthinkingly refer to Britain as England, they do so because—consciously or unconsciously—they regard Wales and Scotland (let alone the Isle of Man and the Channel Isles) as nothing more than appendages to England. Little Welsh or Scottish history is taught in English schools, except where it is part of the process of subjugation or political union. The English cannot even pronounce Welsh or Scottish place-names, so it is plain they will know nothing of their languages or literature. Yet it is not a perverse delight in what is obscure or irrelevant that leads David Jones to preface each of the seven parts of his book with quotations from the sixth century poem of the *Gododdin*, for this poem above all others symbolizes for him the unity of the Island of Britain that is at the centre of his historical awareness. It dates from a period when Welsh was spoken in southern Scotland and parts of northern England, and Aneirin, its author, was poet at the court of the tribe of the Gododdin (called by Ptolemy the Otadinoi), whose capital was at Edinburgh. In some hundred stanzas of irregular length, which preserve two redactions of different periods and are contained in the unique thirteenth century manuscript, the poem tells of an expedition of three hundred of the best men of the tribe against the English at Catraeth, i.e. Catterick.[1] The battle was fought for a week, and in the end only one man—the poet—returned to tell the tale at Eidyn (there are certain slight variations in numbers as between the details of the two redactions, but these do not radically affect the content). There is no continuous narrative strand to the poem, and thus it has a curious bittiness despite the vividness and punch of numerous passages. As the poem muses on the expedition, stanza after stanza mentions a particular hero by name and celebrates the nobility of his deeds, while at the same time the pathos of the poet's solitary survival remains to the fore.

Even the language of the *Gododdin* in the original is obscure, with the result that translation into English is highly problematic. Professor Kenneth Jackson's recent version provides the latest findings of scholarship on the subject, but the way in which his translation is set out, firmly embedded in a welter of notes (all useful, I may add), and hedged about with question marks and dots of omission, makes appreciation of the poetry very difficult. Skene's version reads very well from this point of view, but a comparison with Jackson shows how much of the former's text is probably inaccurate. It may be well then simply to quote a stanza as illustration from Anwyl's translation, since this is the one from which David Jones himself has worked:

> Men went to Catraeth: fame was theirs. Wine and mead from golden vessels was their beverage; for a year receiving honoured treatment there were three men and three score and three hundred with torques of gold. Of all that marched and stood over the overflowing liquor three alone escaped by their valour with the sword, the two war-hounds of Aeron and Cynon, now in the earth, and I from my stream of blood by virtue of my noble song. (p. 121).

(This stanza, referring to three survivors from the battle, comes from the later redaction of the poem, the A. text.)

---

[1] Translations into English have been published as follows: *The Four Ancient Books of Wales*, vol. 1, by W. F. Skene (Edinburgh, 1868); *The Gododin, and the Odes of the Months*, by William Probert (London, 1820); *Y Gododin. A Poem on the Battle of Cattraeth*, by John Williams ab Ithel (Llandovery, 1852); *The Gododin of Aneirin Gwawdrydd*, by Thomas Stephens, ed. Thomas Powel (London: Cymmrodorion Society, 1888); *The Book of Aneirin*, by Edward Anwyl (*Transactions of the Honourable Society of Cymmrodorion*, Session 1909–10); *The Gododdin. The Oldest Scottish Poem*, by Kenneth Hurlstone Jackson (Edinburgh University Press, 1969).

References to the fourteenth century collection of prose tales known as the *Mabinogion*, several of which date from a much earlier period, are also thickly strewn through the pages of *In Parenthesis*. It is as much through them as through Malory that Arthur, the *dux Britanniae* of the late Roman period, figures in the book. It is the tale of *Culhwch and Olwen* especially which David Jones delights in. But these allusions and those of Malory, while frequently strongly martial in tone, are not exclusively there for martial reasons. They represent, to be sure, the struggle of man against the forces of evil, both human and supernatural, but they also conjure up romantic associations of men and places, of desperate deeds and high aspirations, of failures, victories and treachery. They create a singularly appropriate atmosphere for the recounting of the deeds of a battalion of the Royal Welch Fusiliers, a regiment which, incidentally, with Robert Graves and Siegfried Sassoon among its number figures prominently in the literature of the War. The *Gododdin* and the *Mabinogion* emphasize the Welsh tradition, while Malory, Shakespeare and Hopkins take care of the English. It is not without its point that the Shakespearian allusions are to the histories and in particular to *Henry V* and Fluellen.

In this concern to create historical depth and a closeness of texture the Anglo-Saxon heritage comes off rather badly. *Beowulf* is mentioned not at all (possibly because its associations are continental and not insular), while only fleeting references are made to the *Battle of Maldon* and the *Battle of Brunanburh*. Anglo-Saxon poetry, for all its splendours, has yet to become a real part of the English tradition, taken for granted in the same way as Chaucer. This is as far back as the average Englishman goes, and the *Knight's Tale* with its evocation of the palace of Mars—again the echo of Rome—does duty for him. Perhaps the inclusion of phrases from the *Chanson de Roland* serves as a reminder that the England of tradition is cast in the mould of the Norman conquest. For if we do not know our Beowulf, we nonetheless all know of Oliver and Roland and the disaster of Roncevaux, and know immediately what is meant when David Jones talks of 'the intimate, continuing, domestic life of small contingents of men, within whose structure Roland could find, and, for a reasonable while, enjoy, his Oliver'

(p. ix). Such are the foundations of literary reference to the details and mood of a soldier's life. They are added to in a multiplicity of ways which demonstrate the author's desire to make more than an epitome of military values and feelings. The Latin quotations from the Roman missal and the constant Biblical allusions are the most cogent expression of this more comprehensive vision, but they are not the only ones.

The mosaic of literary reference extends from direct quotation in connexion with some particular event or observation to the structure of the whole work. For not only does each of the seven sections bear an epigraph from the *Gododdin*, but it also carries a title derived from one or more other literary sources to focus the particular theme of the section. Thus, the simplicity of the narrative outline of the book is complemented by the density of associations evoked at any given point, for these associations are the factors of order in the generally episodic structure. *In Parenthesis* is not a work of long sweeps of narrative or dramatic vigour, which carry the reader breathlessly on in unbroken continuity. It is carefully fitted together like a mosaic: each piece has its clear function in the whole picture, but it is nonetheless separate and distinct; there are no imperceptible gradations of colour, no blurrings of outline or fusions of one form with another.

The work as a whole may be divided into two roughly balancing halves, the first of which (Parts 1–4) describes the platoon's December departure from England, arrival in France, march to camp, general features of life in the trenches and the celebration of Christmas. The second (Parts 5–7) takes up the narrative again some six months later and covers the preparations for the great battle and the death and wounding in it of most of John Ball's friends and comrades. This second half thus parallels the movement of the first in its progression from the known to the unknown and from the familiar to the fearsome. The first part is more general in its descriptions and somewhat less closely textured in its allusions, while the second depends on an increasing particularity as the final battle is approached and the ghastliness of violence and death becomes universal. The book begins with more or less ordinary prose, which is the commoner vehicle of expression in the first four parts, though verse forms are also found especially in Part 3. But in the second half verse becomes more important until in the final section it dominates the whole of what is said. It seems likely that this development in texture and style corresponds to the growth of David Jones's own poetic awareness as he worked at the book, for the first sections are noticeably simpler and more straightforward than the latter ones. This is, however, as fortunate as it was inevitable, since it means that the book really does work up to a climax, which is expressed not only in terms of the action depicted, but also in the verbal technique.

If the epigraphs to each part of *In Parenthesis* send one back in each case to the *Gododdin* and thus punctuate the work with the spirit of Wales and the Middle Ages, the various headings provide a broader framework. The title to Part I—'The many men so beautiful'— gives us a point of departure that is both noble and positive, but the succeeding line in Coleridge's poem—'And they all dead did lie'— shows the bleak contrast that is to follow. *The Ancient Mariner*, as we have already seen, has been a continuing focus for David Jones's imagination, in his engravings, his poetry and his essays, and this is not the only place in *In Parenthesis* where it makes its mark. It is not without significance for its use here that David Jones is much concerned with the ideas of sacrifice and atonement in the *Ancient Mariner*, both in his illustrations and in his critical comments on the poem. At the very end of Part 7 he refers, for example, to John Ball's rifle hanging at his 'bowed neck like the Mariner's white oblation' (p. 184). So in making this quotation for the title of Part I he is alluding, obliquely enough, to that sacrificial aspect of the War which other poets made much of and which he himself also developed, but as a part rather than the whole of his own view.

The Shakespearian heading of Part 2—'Chambers go off, corporals stay'—from *Henry V*, a favourite source of reference for David Jones, gives a down to earth allusion to the two basic elements of battle—men and guns—and provides a fitting title for the settling-down of the men to their camp routines, once arrived in France. The atmosphere of day-to-day duties, lectures, parades, fatigues, marches, which is drawn here, is then, in the last paragraph, shattered by the scream of the first shell. As they continue in these surroundings, all of this grows to be a matter of course, but the first shell is described with a detail that only the first can produce through the change of consciousness that it brings.

As the heading to Part 1 brings associations with other artistic pursuits, so 'Starlight order' links up with a book of War reminiscences that David Jones illustrated about 1931, for its title—*March, Kind Comrade*—is a quotation from the line of Hopkins' 'The Bugler's First Communion' preceding the one that David Jones's title comes from. The two words of the heading have an obvious literal application to the night march, which occupies Part 3, but the whole context gives us a more explicit religious reference from this particularly Catholic poem of Hopkins:

> Frowning and forefending angel-warder
> Squander the hell-rook ranks sally to molest him;
>   March, kind comrade, abreast him;
> Dress his days to a dextrous and starlight order.

Part 4, which concludes the first half of the book, but nonetheless forms the central section of *In Parenthesis*, characterizes the action and descriptions by the title 'King Pellam's Launde'. Here the theme of the Waste Land, deriving from Malory and the anthropological and ritual analysis of the theme by Jessie L. Weston,[1] comes into its own. King Pellam, in Malory, is the king whose lands were laid waste as a result of the 'dolerous stroke' inflicted on him by Balin's spear. In him again, as in the figure of the Ancient Mariner, the idea of sacrifice is put foward. This whole complex of Malorian themes, expressed in the poetic content of Part 4 as well as in the title, recurs in the final section of the book, reinforcing the parallel structure of the whole work.

The heading to Part 5—'Squat Garlands for White Knights'—exhibits a synthesis of allusions to another poem of Hopkins and to *Through the Looking Glass*, arising from the fact that new shrapnel helmets were issued to all ranks early in 1916. Hopkins's poem, 'Tom's Garland' with its first line 'Tom—garlanded with squat and surly steel', caused a good deal of brain-racking to his friends Robert Bridges and R. W. Dixon, and so Hopkins had to write a

[1] For a discussion of this theme see below, pp. 181f.

letter explaining his adaptation of the Pauline image of human society as a body with many members to Tom, the navvy.[1] David Jones picks up the immediate visual analogy between Tom and the soldier's new appearance, but the context of the ordered, ideal commonweal of men resonates with it. The visual impact, however, is what connects this most serious poem with Lewis Carroll, for Alice 'thought she had never seen such a strange-looking soldier in all her life. He was dressed in tin armour, which seemed to fit him very badly, and he had a queer-shaped little deal box fastened across his shoulder, upside-down, and with the lid hanging open. Alice looked at it with great curiosity' (ch. 8). This humorous touch reminds one of the comedy of John Ball's appearance on the parade ground in the very first episode of the book—perhaps again a subtle indication of the parallelism of the two halves of the work.

The sixth section, 'Pavilions and Captains of Hundreds', provides another synthesis of allusions, this time to Malory and the historical books of the Old Testament. Both, however, are general references to the omnipresent pavilions pitched on the scenes of battle in Malory and to the captains of thousands and hundreds so frequently mentioned in the descriptions of Old Testament battles. In the kind of interlude before the final onslaught that Part 6 represents, this combination of allusions turns our attention to the setting of the scene, to the background that is sometimes taken for granted. For a moment, in the brief respite and strange calm that preludes the storm, there is time for a more general view.

It is perhaps, in the first instance, a little off-putting to realize that the title to the most moving, the most powerful, section of the book is a quotation from Lewis Carroll's *The Hunting of the Snark*. But anyone who has read even a little of the narrative literature of the War (the lyric is quite different in tone) will have seen that soldiers are rarely deserted by a sense of humour for long, no matter how desperate their situation. The outsider is apt to think that only a tragic, serious attitude befits the situations of mental hospitals, prisons and battle-fields, but a sense of humour is often

[1] *Poems and Prose of Gerard Manley Hopkins*, ed. W. H. Gardner (Penguin Books, 1954) pp. 234ff.

the only thing that enables them to be successfully coped with. 'The five unmistakable marks' by which the Snark may be recognized are its taste, 'which is meagre and hollow, but crisp', its 'habit of getting up late', its 'slowness in taking a jest', its 'fondness for bathing-machines', and its ambition. The profoundly scholarly question of the metaphysical import of these characteristics may safely be left to the erudition of one more learned than myself, perhaps a German. There seems, however, to be some small hint of irony in considering the Snark's habits as comparable with those of the Germans.

The technique of literary allusion by which David Jones so successfully remythologizes his material, stripping it of the hackneyed associations and tritely formulated ideals of tenth-rate poets and replacing them with more realistic notes, is closely akin to the work of Eliot, Joyce and Pound. *The Waste Land* in particular seems to provide a close parallel. Critics, when provided with such apparently circumstantial evidence, are apt to dwell on the matter of influences with peculiar loving care, and John Johnston, although he quotes from a personal letter David Jones wrote to him disavowing conscious imitation, gives a fairly lengthy account of the parallels between Eliot's poem and *In Parenthesis*. In conclusion he notes that despite their obvious differences, 'simply as specimens of poetry written between two great wars, their general relationships in the matter of technique can hardly be denied.'[1] David Jones's own reaction to this analysis is that poets are liable to write in similar ways about similar subjects more as a result of a common cultural background, because things are in the air, rather than through direct influence and imitation. It is interesting to note that the German poet Gottfried Benn said much the same in his introduction to an anthology of Expressionist lyrics. 'I think,' he wrote, 'that the influence of earlier literature on those young people who are disposed to create is not as great as is often assumed (probably to the discomfiture of literary historians). I would say rather that in the course of a cultural period inner states of mind are repeated, similar forces of expression, which had been extinguished for a while, re-appear—thus in Expressionism there was indeed a

[1] *Op. cit.*, p. 327.

repetition of the Storm and Stress period, but without a conscious relationship to Klopstock and Hölderlin.'[1] Critics frequently like to consider themselves more acute than the poets they write about, but when such highly articulate poets as Benn and David Jones express themselves in this way, scholars would do well to be cautious.

But if we pursue the question of influences a little further, now that it has been raised, what one would expect—and does find—is some positive relationship with the world of the visual arts. Probably the first thing that strikes most readers of *In Parenthesis* is the acutely visual imagination of the author. Such a detail as 'The Orderly Sergeant of "B" is licking the stub end of his lead pencil; it divides a little his fairish moist moustache' (p. 1) causes us to visualize the man immediately. A later description of waterlogged holes in the darkness dwells at greater length on the visual impact:

> Slime-glisten on the churnings up, fractured earth pilings, heaped on, heaped up waste; overturned far throwings; tottering perpendiculars lean and sway; more leper-trees pitted, rownse-pykèd out of nature, cut off in their sap-rising.
>
> Saturate, littered, rusted coilings, metallic rustlings, thin ribbon-metal chafing—rasp low for some tension freed; by rat, or wind, disturbed. Smooth-rippled discs gleamed, where gaping craters, their brimming waters, made mirror for the sky procession—bear up before the moon incongruous souvenirs. Margarine tins sail derelict, where little eddies quivered, wind caught, their sharp-jagged twisted lids wrenched back.   (p. 39)

This careful emphasis on what the eye sees, the precise detail of the physical objects and the kind of light in which they are seen, marks the descriptive technique of the entire book. It is the technique of one trained in the art of observation, the kind of writing that a painter such as David Jones would almost naturally do. The constant attempts to define the quality of light have in the sphere of words a similar mood to his concern with light and movement in such pictures as *Montes et omnes colles* or *Pigotts in Storm* or *Chapel in the Park*. But words are a different medium from paint, and in

---

[1] *Lyrik des expressionistischen Jahrzehnts* (Munich: dtv, 1963). Einleitung von Gottfried Benn, p. 7.

words, conscious though he always is of associations, he is more precise, more definite, than in his watercolours. The romanticism and diffuseness of much of his painting gives way to a clarity of outline in his writing. Perhaps there is a greater similarity here with his engravings. But in both painting and engraving David Jones is concerned with the representation of *things*. His perceptions of them may vary from pre-occupation with shape and rhythm to colour and mood, but it is in each case the essence of the *thing* at which he is aiming.

It is in this descriptive technique most of all that David Jones puts what he had learnt from painting and engraving to good use, but one cannot fail to remark that he uses paintings and artists as points of reference as well as works of literature. Among the artists mentioned in *In Parenthesis* are Paolo Uccello, Breughel, Hobbema, Fragonard and Signorelli. Uccello's *Rout of San Romano* in the National Gallery obviously captured his imagination.

> From where he stood heavily, irksomely at ease, he could see, half-left between 7 and 8 of the front rank, the profile of Mr. Jenkins and the elegant cut of his war-time rig and his flax head held front; like San Romano's foreground squire, unhelmeted; but we don't have lances now nor banners nor trumpets. It pains the lips to think of bugles—and did they blow Defaulters on the Uccello horns. (p. 2)

A little later, in the episode where the men are permitted to march easy and smoke, Mr Jenkins, one of the officers who is delineated more carefully than the others in the course of the book, is referred to with a touch of humour: 'The Squire from the Rout of San Romano smokes Melachrino No. 9' (p. 5). This is the most exact reference to a picture that there is in *In Parenthesis*, and how delightfully apt it is. Apt also is the allusion to Breughel in the passage where the soldiers are groping their way through the dark towards the front. 'The stumbling dark of the blind, that Breughel knew about' (p. 31) reminds us especially of his *Parable of the Blind Men*. In the lull of Part 4 the landscape is compared with the gentle pictures of Hobbema and considered a suitable setting for the visits of the men from Whitehall: 'They grace the trench like wallflowers, for an hour; as spirits lightly come from many mansions, and the avenues, where they sit below the pseudo-Fragonards cross-legged, slacked, or lie at night under a Baroque cupidon, guiding the campaign' (p. 93). The conjunction of Fragonard and the Baroque in connexion with the official visitors can hardly fail to point an ironic contrast between their imagined, frivolous ease and the rigours of the trenches. Baroque art is used again as a kind of symbol of lack of contact with reality when the forays of the aeroplanes are compared with 'Baroque attending angels' that 'surprise you with their air-worthiness' (p. 124). Something of the same feeling is present when the men, anxiously waiting for zero in Part 7, are characterized as 'those small cherubs, who trail awkwardly the weapons of the God in Fine Art works' (p. 156). These various allusions, which can be amplified by a further one to Signorelli's *Innocent* in the descriptions of the runner rousing himself from sleep (p. 128), are probably more immediate in their effect than the majority of the literary references. Maybe it is the humour, of different kind, so generally evident in their use that we find appealing.

II

The multiplicity of points of reference and allusion that are to be found in *In Parenthesis* reflect and reinforce the nature of the experience which it tries to unfold. Based on a peculiar set of circumstances, the book attempts a comprehensiveness of sensation and personal outlook by means of detailed description and the extensive use of literary, artistic and historical analogues. It pivots on the figure of Private John Ball, but it is not particularly his personal story. The choice of his name—that of the wandering priest executed in 1381 for his part in the Peasants' Revolt—is some indication of this, for with this name a historical link is forged, a cleric is identified with the lot of the common people, and his agitatory message of equality is put in the levelling context of war and death. Indeed although it is through the reactions of John Ball that we receive our picture of the War, we learn very little about the personal details of his life and background. As John Johnston says of the characters of the book, they 'are individuals, but they are distinguished from one another not so much by traits as by degrees of sensibility and insensibility. They live less by what they are and do than by what they see and feel.'[1] The various men (and women) who figure in the book are thus not present as characters in any usual understanding of the term, but as shifting focusses of a much larger reality.

Private 25201 Ball makes his first appearance in the work late on parade. He is not a man of heroic stamp, but simply an ordinary chap with ordinary problems. He finds the transition from civilian life to the Disciplines of the Wars disconcerting:

> Private Ball's pack, ill adjusted and without form, hangs more heavily on his shoulder blades, a sense of ill-usage pervades him. He withdraws within himself to soothe himself—the inequity of those in high places is forgotten...
> He put his right hand behind him to ease his pack, his cold knuckles find something metallic and colder.
> No mess-tin cover.
> Shining sanded mess-tin giving back the cold early light. *Improperly dressed, the Battalion being paraded for overseas.* His imaginings as to the precise relationship of this general indictment from the book to his own naked mess-tin were with suddenness and most imperatively impinged upon, as when an animal hunted, stopping in some ill-chosen covert to consider the wickedness of man, is started into fresh effort by the cry and breath of dogs dangerously and newly near. For the chief huntsman is winding his horn, the officer commanding is calling his Battalion by name—whose own the sheep are. (p. 2)

Such a description, combined with the author's admission that he was 'not only amateur, but grotesquely incompetent, a knocker-over of piles, a parade's despair' (p. xv), lends substance to the view that John Ball is nearer to David Jones's own personal situation than any other character in the book. But after his initial *contretemps* John Ball falls more or less into the corporate experience of the battalion, being occasionally singled out of the anonymity of officers' shouts and privates' complaints as they march off to the port of embarkation: 'No one said march easy Private Ball, you're bleedin' quick at some things ain't yer' (p. 4). On arrival in France he has adjusted sufficiently so as to have 'regained a certain

[1] *Op. cit.*, p. 288.

quietness and an indifference to what might be, as his loaded body moved forward unchoosingly as part of a mechanism another mile or so' (p. 19). It is through him that we feel the newness of the situation, discover that exploded bombs smell like pineapple and realize the absurdity of carrying the latch-key to Stondon Park. Then suddenly comes the first shell:

> He stood alone on the stones, his mess-tin spilled at his feet. Out of the vortex, rifling the air it came—bright, brass-shod, Pandoran; with all-filling screaming the howling crescendo's up-piling snapt. The universal world, breath held, one half second, a bludgeoned stillness. Then the pent violence released a consummation of all burstings out; all sudden up-rendings and rivings-through—all taking out of vents—all barrier-breaking—all unmaking. Pernitric begetting—the dissolving and splitting of solid things. In which unearthing aftermath, John Ball picked up his mess-tin and hurried within; ashen, huddled, waited in the dismal straw. Behind 'E' Battery, fifty yards down the road, a great many mangolds, uprooted, pulped, congealed with chemical earth, spattered and made slippery the rigid boards leading to the emplacement. The sap of vegetables slobbered the spotless breech-block of No. 3 gun.
>
> (p. 24)

The impact of this description is shattering. Its total awareness, the accuracy of visual and auditory detail, the rapid succession of words hammering at the same area of consciousness, and then John Ball's emotional reaction and the silent destruction of nature—all this has not been bettered anywhere.

We do not learn very much about John Ball's background and individual characteristics. He has a moustache that 'invests him with little charm' (p. 27), his luminous wrist-watch is a sufficiently important detail for it to be mentioned (pp. 59, 147)—he can tell others what time it is (p. 90). His aunt Woodman in Norwood, who is good enough to send him 'a satisfactory parcel' (p. 117), is the only one of his relatives to figure in his life and she is referred to three times in brief phrases. One imagines she sent the seed cake that Ball and his companions tuck into. In the midst of all this unpretentiousness it is a bit startling to find, when he picks up his India paper book, that it is Dunbar's 'Lament for the Makaris' he reads in his anthology. No doubt this, together with Dai's boast, is not meant as a personal characteristic, but his awareness of the inevitability of death for everybody is meant in the same representative way as Dai's claim to have been everywhere.[1] In any case, Ball's frequent sessions on guard, especially at night, allow his reflective spirit ample opportunity for pondering on the deep things of life. But when he is relieved, his mind and body are no different from anyone else's:

> ... He felt cheese to be a mistake so early in the morning....
> At the head of the communication trench, by the white board with the map reference, the corporal of a Vickers team bent over his brazier of charcoal. He offers an enamelled cup, steaming. Private Ball drank intemperately as a home animal laps its food, not thanking the kind agent of this proffered thing, but in an eager manner of receiving.
> After a while he said: Thank you sergeant—sorry, corporal—very much—sorry—thanks, corporal.
> He did not reach the Lewis-gunners nor his friend, for while he yet shared the corporal's tea he heard them calling down the trench.
> All of No. 1 section—R.E. fatigue.
> He thanked these round their brazier and turned back heavy-hearted to leave that fire so soon, for it is difficult to tell of the great joy he had of that ruddy-bright, that flameless fire of coals within its pierced basket, white-glowed, and very powerfully hot, where the soldiers sat and warmed themselves and waited to see what the new day might bring for them and him, for he was one of them, shivering and wretched at the cock-crow. (pp. 74f.)

Later on we get a lengthier account of the day-to-day comradeship of Ball, his friend the Lewis-gunner and Olivier:

> They talked of ordinary things. Of each one's friends at home; those friends unknown to either of the other two. Of the possible duration of the war. Of how they would meet and in what good places afterwards. Of the dissimilar merits of Welshmen and Cockneys. Of the diverse virtues of Regular and Temporary Officers. Of if you'd ever read the books of Mr. Wells. Or the poetry of Rupert Brooke. Of how you really couldn't very well carry more than one book at a time in your pack. Of the losses of

[1] Cf. Johnston, *op. cit.*, pp. 306f.

the Battalion since they'd come to France. Of the hateful discomfort of having no greatcoats with fighting-order, of how bad this was. Of how everybody ought rightly to have Burberry's, like officers. Of how German knee boots were more proper to trench war than puttees. Of how privileged Olivier was because he could manage to secrete a few personal belongings along with the signaller's Impedimenta. Of how he was known to be a favourite with the Regimental and how he'd feel the draught if he were back with his platoon. Of whether they three would be together for the Duration, and how you hoped so very much indeed. Of captains of thousands and of hundreds, of corporals, of many things. Of the Lloyd George administration, of the Greek, of Venizelos, who Olivier said was important, of whom John Ball had never previously heard. Of the neutrality of Spain. Of whether the French nation was nice or nasty. Of whether anyone would ever get leave and what it would be like if you did. Of how stripes, stars, chevrons, specialisations, jobs away from the battalion, and all distinguishing marks were better resisted for as long as possible. Of how it were best to take no particular notice, to let the stuff go over you, how it were wise to lie doggo and to wait the end. (pp. 139f.)

Such a conversation could have taken place among almost any intimate group of soldiers. It gives one a very homely picture of their lives and underlines how utterly average, straightforward and typical John Ball is meant to be.

Among the officers of the battalion David Jones expresses a certain reticent affection for Lieutenant Jenkins, the squire from San Romano. He is only twenty years old, and his youth makes him easier with the men than Sergeant Snell and he allows them to smoke while marching. 'Platoon drill was tiresome, but Mr. Jenkins was kind. He used to sit by the little stream where they got their washing-water, and look into it for long at a time without moving, whilst they smoked under the turnip-stack, with someone watching to see if anyone—the Adjutant, or that shit Major Lillywhite, was anywhere about' (p. 15). He is looked upon like the shepherd of a flock as he leads the soldiers in their night march, and even where his leadership is a little uncertain there is humour and loyalty in such criticism as makes itself felt: 'There's no kind light to lead: you go like a motherless child—goddam guide's done the dirty, and is our Piers Dorian Isambard Jenkins—adequately informed—and how should his inexperience not be a broken reed for us—and fetch up in Jerry's bosom' (p. 34). When we have seen him going about his business unobtrusively, appearing at regular intervals, though with nothing special about him noted, we are glad to hear that he 'got his full lieutenancy on his twenty-first birthday, and a parcel from Fortnum and Mason; he grieved for his friend, Talbot Rhys, and felt an indifference to the spring offensive—and why was non-conforming Captain Gwyn so stuffy about the trebled whisky chits' (p. 107). The War sometimes weighs with painful heaviness on this young gentleman, of whose sensitive reactions and upper-class background we are given brief glances, as for example at the Divisional baths: 'Mr. Jenkins would strike at midge-flies with his cane, and forget a bit about Talbot Rhys and laugh at the screaming Froggy brats by the fresh-painted white uprights of the canal bridge' (p. 110). The details are not very numerous, but they give us such a sympathetic picture of the man that we are deeply moved when the final battle brings his death:

> Mr. Jenkins half inclined his head to them—he walked just barely in advance of his platoon and immediately to the left of Private Ball.
>   He makes the conventional sign
> and there is the deeply inward effort of spent men who would
> make response for him,
> and take it at the double.
> He sinks on one knee
> and now on the other,
> his upper body tilts in rigid inclination
> this way and back;
> weighted lanyard runs out to full tether,
>   swings like a pendulum
>   and the clock run down.
> Lurched over, jerked iron saucer over tilted brow,
> clampt unkindly over lip and chin
> nor no ventaille to this darkening,
>   and masked face lifts to grope the air
> and so disconsolate;
> enfeebled fingering at a paltry strap—
> buckle holds,

holds him blind against the morning.
   Then stretch still where weeds pattern the chalk predella—where it rises to his wire—and Sergeant T. Quilter takes over.
(pp. 165f.)

The difference between Mr. Jenkins and Private Ball is finely drawn. A clear bond of sympathy is always apparent, in contrast to the feeling expressed about Major Lillywhite or the dull obtuseness of Corporal Quilter.

With Lance-Corporal Aneirin Merddyn Lewis another sensibility again is sketched in with deft strokes, for although Mr. Jenkins has a Welsh name, he has nothing of the spirit of Wales about him. The reaction of Lance-Corporal Lewis to John Ball's name being taken when he arrives late for parade is a succinct expression of the values he stands for: 'Temporary unpaid Lance-Corporal Aneirin Merddyn Lewis had somewhere in his Welsh depths a remembrance of the nature of man, of how a lance-corporal's stripe is but held vicariously and from on high, is of one texture with an eternal economy. He brings in a manner, baptism, and metaphysical order to the bankruptcy of the occasion' (pp. 1f.). We learn even less about Lewis's personal background than about Jenkins, for David Jones is less interested in the external details of a man's life than in the quality of his spirit. But in the trenches we are admitted into the secret corners of his being:

   Lance-Corporal Lewis looked about him and on all this liquid action.
   It may be remembered Seithenin and the desolated cantrefs, the sixteen fortified places, the great cry of the sea, above the sigh of Gwyddno when his entrenchments stove in. Anyway he kept the joke to himself for there was none to share it in that company, for although Watcyn knew everything about the Neath fifteen, and could sing Sospan Fach to make the traverse ring, he might have been an Englishman when it came to matters near Aneirin's heart. For Watcyn was innocent of his descent from Aeneas, was unaware of Geoffrey Arthur and his cooked histories, or Twm Shon Catti for the matter of that—which pained his lance-corporal friend, for whom Troy still burned, and sleeping kings return, and wild men might yet stir from Mawddwy secrecies. And he who will not come again from his reconnaissance—they've searched his

breeches well, they've given him an ivy crown—ein llyw olaf—
whose wounds they do bleed by day and by night in December wood.
    Lance-Corporal Lewis fed on these things.   (p. 89)

Lewis is here a focus for the history and culture of Wales. He laughs to himself at an incident from Welsh tradition that parallels his own business in the trenches of France; he remembers the legendary descent of the Welsh from Troy; he recalls the death of Llywelyn in 1282, the last of a long, continuous line of Welsh princes. There is a note of sadness in the fact that all this means nothing to his fellow-countryman from Neath, in this respect the typical South Walian. But Lance-Corporal Lewis represents something of this other kind of Welshman too, for he 'sings where he walks, yet in a low voice, because of the Disciplines of the Wars. He sings of the hills about Jerusalem, and of David of the White Stone' (p. 42). When he is 'spilled', however, in the battle, it is the fact that he 'worshipped his ancestors like a Chink' (p. 155) that is recalled, together with further allusions to other aspects of Welsh legendary tradition.

    The other men in the battalion are not so clearly delineated. Sergeant Snell remains a more or less impersonal officer, while Corporal Quilter is a man of severely down-to-earth character whose only concern seems to be discipline, digging and inspection. His promotion to Sergeant permits him a little testy sarcasm at the expense of Private Saunders, but otherwise we are told nothing apart from his pursuit of routine duties. Private Bobby Saunders demonstrates an archetypal form of skiving and its appropriate reward (p. 91), while his comrade Private Watcyn loses his promotion for absence from a parade (p. 109). The one who emerges most conspicuously from this motley crew is the unnamed man from Rotherhithe, who delights in a mouth-organ (p. 95) and is the subject of a cheery interlude in an *estaminet*:

> The man from Rotherhithe sipped very gravely his abominable beer; sometimes he held his slowly emptying glass to the light; when he replaced it on the marble, he did so without the faintest audibility. He looked straight-eyed and levelly; through bunched heads, through the Sacred Heart, done in wools, through the wall, through the Traffic Control notice, on the board outside, opposite;

> through all barriers, making as though they are not, all things foreign and unloved, through all things other and separate; through all other things to where the mahogany cornices of *The Paradise*—to the sawdust thinly spread...the turned spirals that support the frosted panes they call through, half-open, from the other bar, is a good job o' work.... Nat West put that in when they enlarged the house; he got the wood cheap when they broke up *The Golden Vanity*...at the Royal Albert, in the cholera year....Surrey Commercial stevedores call drinks for the Reykjavik mate...she's lying across the water and goes out tonight...she's bound for the Skagerrak with plant from Ravenhills. (pp. 112f.)

Such details are not in themselves matters of great import, but they are the stuff of life.

Lance-Corporal Lewis and Dai with the ill-fitting greatcoat are conscious or representative of living in a world where myth is a reality and not a poetic fiction. The particular myth against which their lives are seen is, as Bernard Bergonzi points out, 'an *ad hoc* frame of reference'; it is 'unique and non-generalizable, valid only for Jones's particular purposes in writing *In Parenthesis*.'[1] Nevertheless, it possesses great emotional power because all its elements are related to the continuity of historical, literary and legendary tradition in the Island of Britain. They are much more obviously and organically related than, for example, the diverse facts and fictions of Pound's *Cantos*.

But there is another range of experience against which, or rather, in which, the events recounted are also seen—that of religious ritual. Primarily, of course, it is the ritual of the Catholic tradition, but not exclusively so, for it is an anthropological fact that ritual plays an important part in the functioning of every kind of society and no more so than in its religious institutions. When John Ball catches sight of the moon on the night march, we are reminded of the association of the moon with the Virgin Mary and of the hill-shrines where the Annunciation was anticipated: 'In the cleft of the rock they served her in anticipation—and over the hill-country that per-bright Shiner stood for Her rod-budding (he kept his eyes towards the swift modulations of the sky, heaven

---

[1] *Op. cit.*, pp. 202f.

itinerant hurrying with his thought hasting)—but that was a bugger of a time ago' (p. 39). But in addition to such almost casual allusions there is a constant alignment of the physical events of the soldiers' existence with the ritual observances of Christendom, and this is more extensive than has generally been recognized. Reinforcing all this is, of course, the framework of liturgical reference and indeed the liturgical quality of much of the language.

The idea of sacrifice in a context of Christian discipleship provided one means whereby a number of War poets were able to interpret their own personal experience in a way that made some sense of it. Wilfred Owen is probably the poet of whom one first thinks in this connexion, for several of his poems are very strongly Christian in their imagery and in their mood of sacrifice. In a lyric this mood is often the sustaining force of the whole poem, giving it both substance and impact. In a longer work, such as *In Parenthesis*, the religious mood can not—at least nowadays, whatever was possible in the medieval epic—take the foremost place. It is fidelity to the day-to-day events and not any unifying mood or theme that counts first of all. Like the allusions to Wales and Malory, the religious references of *In Parenthesis* give a wider relevance to the action and details of life in the war situation; they are an essential part of the general human experience that the whole book depicts. Some of the allusions—to well known Biblical figures, to phrases from the liturgy and the objects of ritual—will be obvious to most readers, but what is perhaps most remarkable is the way in which the seemingly casual word or reference keeps alive throughout the whole of the work an atmosphere of latent transubstantiation. At almost any point the trivial act or tawdry object may be transmuted into a thing of numinous significance.

The account of the parade and the departure in Part 1 gives us a good indication of David Jones's technique with its deft use of the single telling word or phrase to evoke an important mood. The parade is characterized by a 'silence peculiar to parade grounds and to refectories', 'the silence of a high order' (p. 1), in which Captain Gwyn is able to continue 'the ritual words by virtue of which a regiment is moved in column of route', while Corporal Quilter's part is to intone (p. 3). When the men have left the camp,

David Jones notes that 'the liturgy of a regiment departing has been sung' (p. 4). In this ritual the officers take on the aura of the Good Shepherd: 'the officer commanding is calling his Battalion by name—whose own the sheep are' (p. 2). And later as the blistered soldiers march on to their port of embarkation, we hear how 'it is his part to succour the lambs of the flock' (p. 6). These are analogies that come easily to this situation, but there is a more particular liturgical setting for this initial enterprise—the events of Easter. In the practice of the early Church it was common for catechumens to be baptized on Easter Eve, and certainly the ritual of the parade ground and the departure is that of an initiation. Indeed, as Lance-Corporal Aneirin Merddyn Lewis ponders on the event, his pre-occupation with the vicarious nature of military authority and with the deeper aspects of the situation 'brings in a manner, baptism, and metaphysical order to the bankruptcy of the occasion' (p. 2). The Biblical words that ring in Lance-Corporal Lewis's mind occur in fact in the context of the Good Friday sacrifice, for they are Jesus' words to Pilate—'Thou couldest have no power at all against me, except it were given thee from above' (John xix, 11). The march itself is not compared with any element of the Crucifixion story, but with the massacre of the Holy Innocents (p. 6), but when they embark for France the imagery of death and resurrection, baptism and a new birth, is again used, for in the voyage across the Channel they are 'shrouded in a dense windy darkness' (p. 8). Here, perhaps, we have a coalescence of the crossing of the Styx with the Entombment of Christ, and the final paragraph of Part 1 brings the analogy with the discoveries of the first Easter morning: 'and on the third day, which was a Sunday, sunny and cold, and French women in deep black were hurrying across flat land—they descended from their grimy, littered, limb restricting, slatted vehicles, and stretched and shivered at a siding. You feel exposed and apprehensive in this new world' (p. 9). What is so skilful about these analogies is their unobtrusiveness. David Jones is content to give a hint here and there, sometimes more, sometimes less obviously, and to allow his readers to make their own connexions. The analogies are not, I think, worked out in a systematic whole, each piece cohering absolutely, but every allusion has its proper place precisely where it is made. So the references to the Good Shepherd, the Holy Innocents, baptism and the Resurrection do not necessarily fit together each to each, but they are details of a broader frame of reference which is used to illuminate the primary events of the book at particular moments. There is no attempt to model the action of the entire work on an extensive religious analogy, though there may be episodes, such as this in Part 1, where one theme recurs in various modifications.

In Part 3 we hear again of 'the ritual of their parading' (p. 27) and how 'the liturgy of their going-up assumed a primitive creativeness, an apostolic actuality, a correspondence with the object, a flexibility' (p. 28). The religious framework of both this section and Part 7 is made apparent by the quotations from the Good Friday offices which precede the details of the action in each case. In Part 3 the words are given in English, but the increased solemnity of Part 7 and the ultimate sacrifice of death is marked by the use of Latin. Biblical and liturgical references punctuate most of *In Parenthesis*. Sometimes it is a well-known figure who is referred to, such as Lazarus (p. 43) or Jonathan and Absalom (p. 163); sometimes the words themselves take up or echo phrases from the Old and New Testaments. One of the most successfully sustained analogies occurs in the passage describing the activities of Christmas morning. It begins (p. 65) with a number of allusions which establish the religious—as opposed to the purely Christian—significance of the time and place, for it is described as 'the time of Saturnalia' and the proximity of the wood (Mametz Wood) is associated with the reverence that Tacitus tells us the ancient Germani paid to the woods and groves that were their holy places (p. 66).[1] This anthropological—and thus implicitly universal—setting is filled in by a further reference to Odin, whose hanging of himself on the windy tree is probably modelled on the Christian Crucifixion, and by the allusion to St Boniface, the 'Apostle of the Germans', who is said to have chopped down a sacred tree in the territory of the heathen Saxons and who was later martyred by the heathen Frisians. In the reference to the Anglo-Saxon monk Boniface we are brought back in a curious way to the actual situation in which the soldiers find

[1] Cf. *Germania*, ch. 9.

themselves 'on Christmas Day in the Morning' (p. 68). The clearly Christian scale of reference now appears with the comparison of the hessian coverings round the soldiers' necks with 'tied amices' and the characterization of their duty as 'serving their harsh novitiate' (p. 70). We are thus prepared for the explicit analogy between the Lance-Corporal's distribution of rations and the Holy Communion. As the men cluster about him, bringing as it were their offertory, the Lance-Corporal takes on the quality of a priest as 'he makes division, he ordains' (p. 72). When he doles out the issue, there are a whole series of reminiscences of the moment of communion:

> Dispense salvation,
> strictly apportion it,
> let us taste and see,
> let us be renewed,
> for christ's sake let us be warm.
> O have a care—don't spill the precious
> O don't jog his hand—ministering;
> do take care.
> O please—give the poor bugger elbow room.   (p. 73)

And yet, despite the obvious holiness of the moment, there is no attempt to impose a spurious devotion on it. The oaths and ordinary soldierly language are not muted or modified, but on the contrary they are lifted up into the ritual context. The ritual is not debased by them, but they are raised by it:

> Each one in turn, and humbly, receives his meagre benefit. This Lance-jack sustains them from his iron spoon; and this is thank-worthy.
> Some of them croak involuntary as the spirit's potency gets the throat at unawares.
> Each one turns silently, carrying with careful fingers his own daily bread....   (pp. 73f.)

The description of the battle in Part 7 is similarly full of religious allusions, but here they are not so much to observances and rituals as to the theme of death and sacrifice in its manifold aspects, but culminating of course in the Passion of Christ. This begins with the reference to the site of battle as 'the place of a skull' (p. 154) and the soldiers' waiting for their final orders as the Agony in the Garden. As the battle grows worse, those who still have their business to do 'do it quickly', as Jesus told Judas when he was about to betray him (John xiii, 27) (p. 177). But as death overtakes all, there is a difference from the Passion Story, for there are no 'weeping Maries bringing anointments' (p. 174). The theme of the Passion is predominant in this last section of the book, but we are reminded in addition of the tactics of Joshua at the siege of Jericho (Joshua vi, 1ff.) as the soldiers wait for their orders (p. 159), we hear of the deaths of Jonathan and Absalom in the list of exemplary heroes (p. 163). The testing of Shadrach, Meshach and Abednego, the Three Holy Children, in the fiery furnace (Daniel iii) makes a further appropriate reference in the context (p. 164), while later on we find an allusion to the parable of the Good Samaritan:

> But O Dear God and suffering Jesus
> why dont they bring water from a well
> rooty and bully for a man on live
> and mollifying oil poured in
> and hands to bind with gentleness.   (p. 173)

The wounded men are looked on as martyrs in their sacrifice, being carried away from the field:

> Carrying-parties,
> runners who hasten singly,
> burdened bearers walk with careful feet
> to jolt him as little as possible,
> bearers of burdens to and from
> stumble oftener, notice the lessening light,
> and feel their way with more sensitive feet—
> you mustn't spill the precious fragments, for perhaps these raw bones live.
>   They can cover him again with skin—in their candid coats, in their clinical shrines and parade the miraculi.   (p. 175)

The horror and torment of death and wounding sears through the concluding section of the book; nowhere is its bloodiness and suffering disguised. In all this the specifically Christian allusions are perhaps a means whereby the finality of earthly life may be muted. For man is made 'a little lower than the angels' (Ps. viii, 5) (p. 154), and the soldiers' saucer hats are like 'helmets of salvation' (Ephesians vi, 17) (p. 157). At the point of death the soldier turns to the Mother of Christ and voices the liturgical response 'let our cry come unto thee' (pp. 176f.). And in the last few lines of the book the 'comfortable waters' (p. 186) evoke the well-known phrases of consolation of the 23rd Psalm. The emphasis of the book nonetheless remains on the facts of physical suffering and death. The recurrent invocations of Biblical themes, liturgical phrases and ritual actions do not in any way minimize this or devalue it. Their function is rather to underline the fact that the religious moment breaks into the whole of a man's experience, penetrating it at every point.

The religious motifs of *In Parenthesis* emerge quite naturally from the primary description of the soldier's life. In the combination of the universal idea of ritual with particular allusions to Christian and Biblical themes they are perhaps a more immediately valid factor of unity in the book than the Welsh and Arthurian complexes. Their claim of universality is more easily apparent. In any case, they must be seen as an equally important means whereby the discontinuity of experience felt by the soldiers in the War is, at least partially,[1] overcome. In this fragmentation of life, which is reflected in the book by its 'episodic structure, even the brief ejaculation 'Christ have mercy' (p. 115) may have its function in relating the fragment of experience to a continuity outside it.

III

Earle R. Swank, in his discussion of the book as an experimental novel, sees—apart from this use of literary, religious and historical reference as a kind of 'objective correlative'—the main experimental features as lying in the author's use of language. Here we have 'the obvious derangements of syntax and conventional usage'

---

[1] Earle R. Swank, 'David Michael Jones: *In Parenthesis*' in Arthur T. Broes and others, *Lectures on Modern Novelists* (Pittsburgh: Carnegie Institute of Technology, 1963), pp. 70ff.

and an attempt by David Jones to force the reader 'to provide a sonic character to the prose so that the additional signals of meaning ordinarily so richly present in speech can be restored as a tool of the literary artist'.[1] The language of *In Parenthesis* requires a detailed investigation such as Swank calls for. Such an analysis cannot be embarked on here, though some comment is clearly necessary, for David Jones has a tone and style of his own in his use of words. It matters little in this context whether we are content, with Swank, to refer to *In Parenthesis* as prose and a novel or whether we consider the rhythms and the typography to bring the work nearer to poetry. There is still an unconventional use of language. One of the devices that quickly strikes the attention of the reader is the frequent change of tense in the narrative sections of the book. To call this a device is to emphasize the conscious skill of the author in using it, but as one reads *In Parenthesis* the changes of tense do not obtrude themselves. On the contrary, they appear so natural in their context that the reader is perhaps only subconsciously aware of their effects. The use of the historic present in combination with the simple past tense is by no means as usual in English writing as it is, for example, in French or German, where frequent alternations of tense in ordinary narratives are liable to put the novice English reader off his balance. David Jones has, I feel, successfully adapted this device for his own purpose. It fits so smoothly into the shifting focusses of awareness, the changing moods, that mark the composition of *In Parenthesis*. If we look at the opening passage of Part 1, we have a very good illustration of the effects produced by the changes of tense.

The passage begins with a dramatic exchange between the sergeant and a number of other soldiers, punctuated by an elliptical sentence without a verb, which nonetheless is not devoid of action. The immediacy of this exchange is followed up by another sentence with no main verb: it is the state of affairs which is important. There is then a transition to a description in the present tense, linked with further verbless sentences. When Private Ball's late arrival is noted, we have a further dialogue, and then the use of the past tense with Lance-Corporal Lewis's 'remembrance of the

[1] *Ibid.*, pp. 74, 75.

nature of man'—for only one sentence—introduces another dimension, a kind of historical distance and objectivity, which is repeated from a different viewpoint when we are told that 'Corporal Quilter on the other hand knew nothing of these things'. What follows straight away after this in the description of John Ball's predicament is a remarkably dextrous use of tenses showing important psychological changes of focus. Ball 'withdraws within himself to soothe himself' (present tense), and from this position of withdrawal views Mr Jenkins objectively (past tense), but is forced by the reminder of the squire of San Romano into a personal reaction (present tense) about the difference in medieval and modern battle equipment. He then reverts to his own situation (past tense), discovers that he has no mess-tin cover and is eased back into a new realization of his plight by an epic simile (present tense) of an animal being hunted. The simile links up with San Romano, and the 'chief huntsman' becomes the 'officer commanding' who is 'calling his Battalion by name'. The present situation is once more all-important, though the alternation of tenses continues, indicating the rapid shifts of viewpoint from which the episode is seen at one and the same time.

Such a use of tense changes is characteristic of *In Parenthesis* and could be equally well illustrated in any number of passages throughout the book. But it is also instructive to note how many sentences, in this passage as in others, are lacking in finite verbs. There is drama in the scraps of conversation and bawled-out commands, there is narrative in the simple progression of the uncomplicated plot, but there is also—and this one would expect from a painter—a good deal of careful descriptive observation. Here, of course, there is much loving attention to detail. Often the syntax is no different from that ordinarily used, but occasionally the verbs are suspended, and we get a series of participial constructions, which correspond rather curiously to the way in which a good film in the midst of a more or less conventional narrative sequence suddenly makes us conscious of a quite new, distinctive and concentrated visual sense. This kind of impact is made, for example, in the night march in Part 3 of *In Parenthesis*, where the normal use of verbs gives way to participles:

> Sometimes his bobbing shape showed clearly; stiff marionette jerking on the uneven path; at rare intervals he saw the whole platoon, with Mr. Jenkins leading.
> Wired dolls sideway inclining, up and down nodding, fantastic troll-steppers in and out the uncertain cool radiance, amazed crook-back miming, where sudden chemical flare, low-flashed between the crazy flats, flood-lit their sack bodies, hung with rigid properties—
> the drop falls,
> you can only hear their stumbling off, across the dark proscenium.
> (p. 37)

There is no lack of movement in such a description; the lack of finite verbs does not bring about a static atmosphere. What we have is a syntactic reflexion of the superimposition of a new vision on the narrative progress.

The visual sense that is made so acute in *In Parenthesis* owes much to the astonishingly wide range of adjectives and adverbs deployed with such accuracy and effect throughout the work. In particular David Jones has a keen eye for changes of light and darkness—they are key-points in his watercolours too:

> The rain stopped.
> She drives swift and immaculate out over, free of these obscuring waters; frets their fringes splendid.
> A silver hurrying to silver this waste
> silver for bolt-shoulders
> silver for butt-heel-irons
> silver beams search the interstices, play for breech-blocks underneath the counterfeiting bower-sway; make-believe a silver scar with drenched tree-wound; silver-trace a festooned slack; faery-bright a filigree with gooseberries and picket-irons—grace this mauled earth—
> transfigure our infirmity—
> shine on us. (pp. 34f.)

But the adjectives are not only visual, but also conjure up a mood to give us a deeper, fuller appreciation of the moment:

> At intervals lights elegantly curved above his lines, but the sheet-rain made little of their radiance. He heard, his ears incredulous, the nostalgic puffing of a locomotive, far off, across forbidden

fields; and once upon the wind, from over his left shoulder, the nearer clank of trucks, ration-laden by Mogg's Hole. (p. 50)

The adjective seems to be almost the most important part of speech in *In Parenthesis*, for it is not the events that the book recounts that make it such a profoundly satisfying work, but the way in which the events are seen and experienced. In this it is the adjective, together with the simile, the metaphor and the allusion, which creates the exactness and the subtlety of mood.

Although these remarks on David Jones's language have so far concentrated chiefly on the pictures and images they evoke, there is, as Earle Swank has indicated, an important sonic quality in it. As David Jones says in his introduction:

> I frequently rely on a pause at the end of a line to aid the sense and form. A new line, which the typography would not otherwise demand, is used to indicate some change, inflexion, or emphasis. I have tried to indicate the sound of certain sentences by giving a bare hint of who is speaking, of the influences operating to make the particular sound I want in a particular instance, by perhaps altering a single vowel in one word. I have only used the notes of exclamation, interrogation, etc., when the omission of such signs would completely obscure the sense. (pp. xi f.)

In this way the individual inflexions of the variety of men in John Ball's platoon are made present and audible to us. Whole passages in the book cry to be read aloud and not merely with the eyes:

> G. S. O. 1—thet's his ticket—the Little Corporal to a turn—they're bringing up his baton—wiv the rations.
> Wiv knobs on it,
> green tabs an' all.
> Rose-marie for re-mem-ber-ance.
> Green for Intelligence.
> Where's yer brass-hat.
> Flash yer blue-prints.
> Hand him his binocular. (p. 78)

This is the rough and ready lingo of the private, spontaneous, direct and salty. It is far enough removed from the minute descriptions and dense allusiveness of other sections of the book, but it is equally convincing and perhaps truer to the original experience of the War.

But even in those sections where conversational exchanges are completely absent, the language resounds with delight in the words and their pure sound:

> Half-minds, far away, divergent, own-thought thinking, tucked away unknown thoughts; feet following file friends, each his own thought-maze alone treading; intricate, twist about, own thoughts, all unknown thoughts, to the next so close following on. (p. 37)

The repetition here of words and sounds and the alliteration provide the exact linguistic counterpart to the mechanical following of each other of the soldiers in their trench march. In other places the repetition of words and phrases has a liturgical quality about it, echoing the versicles and responses of community worship. But the delight in language goes on further to the use of recondite expressions, to words of Latin origin which lend dignity to the theme and contrast strongly with the broad colloquialisms. This conjunction of uses reaches its splendid apogee in the rhythmic resonances of Dai's boast:

> I am '62 Socrates, my feet are colder than you think
> on this
> Potidaean duck-board.
>   I the adder in the little bush
> whose hibernation-end
> undid,
> unmade victorious toil:
> In ostium fluminis.
> At the four actions in regione Linnuis
>   by the black waters.
> At Bassas in the shallows.
> At Cat Coit Celidon.
> At Guinnion redoubt, where he carried the Image.
> In urbe Legionis.
> By the vallum Antonini, at the place of boundaries, at the toiling estuary and strong flow called Tribruit.
> By Agned mountain.
> On Badon hill, where he bore the Tree.
>   . . .

> Let maimed kings lie—let be
> O let the guardian head
> keep back—bind savage sails, lock the shield-wall, nourish the sowing.
> The War Duke
> The Director of Toil—
>   he burst the balm-cloth, unbricked the barrow
> (cruel feet march because of this
>   ungainly men sprawl over us).
> O Land!—O Brân lie under.
> The chrism'd eye that watches the French-men
> that wards under
> that keeps us
> that brings the furrow-fruit,
> keep the land, keep us
> keep the islands adjacent.   (p. 80, 82)

Despite the allusiveness of this passage, which often makes it difficult to understand, the force of the words, the use of anaphora and parallelism, and especially the reverberations of sound and rhythm completely capture the reader and make the literal understanding of the literary references a secondary matter. This very strong sonic quality of the whole book made it a natural target for adaptation for broadcasting, and in a condensed version by Douglas Cleverdon, together with specially composed haunting music by Elizabeth Poston, it has been broadcast four times on the BBC Third Programme.

In many ways *In Parenthesis* is not an easy book: it is one that almost invites the attention of scholars and critics. And yet this has not happened to the extent that it deserves, probably because it is a book which eludes ordinary definitions and appreciations. It is the kind of work which forces the critic, when he has made his attempt at judgement, to admit how tentative and inadequate his remarks are in face of the book itself. *In Parenthesis* has many levels at which it can be read so that the reader will discover new things and new relationships in it each time that he dips into its pages. It is a book that can give the ordinary reader as well as the literary critic much direct, simple enjoyment. It is a work that communicates even before it is understood.

5
The Anathemata

I

When David Jones's second book, *The Anathemata*, was first published in 1952, several reviewers, especially those who were themselves poets, were generous in their praise of the author's achievement. Kathleen Raine, writing in the *New Statesman and Nation* (22 November 1952), felt that book-reviewers' standards were 'made ridiculous by the appearance of a work of art of permanent value' and confessed herself 'embarrassed for want of honest words in which to convey this judgment of David Jones's *Anathemata*.' Another reviewer in *The Listener* (1 January 1953) asserted that '*The Anathemata* can scarcely fail to be counted a great book, as *In Parenthesis* is counted,' and the as always anonymous critic of the *Times Literary Supplement*, though on the whole cautiously sympathetic, described it as 'this fascinating work'. But perhaps Edwin Muir, writing in the *Observer* (2 November 1952), struck the key that has remained dominant when he talked about its 'obscure delight' and the fact that 'it does sometimes achieve communication on a level where few poets attempt to communicate.' The distinction of *The Anathemata* was recognized in its gaining the Russell Loines Memorial Award for Poetry in 1954.

The balance of critical praise was, however, stormily redressed in the last issue of *Scrutiny* (Vol. XIX, No. 4, October 1953) with a notice of considerable bitterness by J. C. F. Littlewood, who clearly thought that David Jones needed putting in his place for his 'posturings', 'affectations' and 'preciosities'. As much as anything Littlewood seemed discountenanced by the enthusiasm and some of the claims put forward by admirers of David Jones's poem. The fact that part of it was broadcast on the BBC Third Programme he saw as possible only in terms of a literary fashion, defined by the cult of impersonality and under the unhealthy influence of Eliot's religious views and the thraldom of *Finnegans Wake*. He tried to stamp *The Anathemata* as 'a new (Roman Catholic) *Waste Land* by a new (London-Welsh) T. S. Eliot.' But however negatively Littlewood judged it, he nevertheless thought it important enough to be worth nearly four pages of mordant comment.

Since the comments of the reviewers there has been very little in the way of detailed criticism of *The Anathemata*, although the handful of general articles on David Jones have added their small measure of appreciation. Nor has the poem been much noted in histories of literature or works of general critical interest. A remark in the introduction to a recent selection of *Longer Contemporary Poems* (Penguin Books, 1966) comes therefore somewhat out of the blue in claiming *The Anathemata* as one of the five 'major poetic efforts of our era' (the other four are Eliot's *Waste Land*, Pound's *Cantos*, Hugh MacDiarmid's *In Memoriam James Joyce*, and William Carlos Williams's *Paterson*). This is probably a premature judgement, though it may reveal itself to be true. As yet the poem has scarcely been assimilated into the consciousness of those knowledgeable on twentieth century poetry.

II

The Anathemata is more obviously a poem than *In Parenthesis*, though parts of it are printed as continuous prose. But apart from this it similarly defies attempts at easy classification in terms of genre. It shares the qualities of chronicle, epic, drama, incantation and lyric and is at the same time none of these and more than all put together. It is thus very difficult to answer the enquirer who wants to know what sort of a work it is and what it is 'about'. The poet himself defected in his own description of it as 'fragments of an attempted writing', and yet this does contain a necessary truth, precious though the description might seem. He is right to call it an attempt—an attempt at a vision of Britain, not just as these islands appear now in the mid twentieth century, but as they appear through the deposits of many cultures over aeons of time. And the fragments are inevitable, since the knowledge of one man must be fragmentary, though he may possess a perception of essentials and the things that will stand for others and be the light shining in the darkness. Each poet seeks to recreate the world in his own image—that part of the world that he sees—but the overwhelming number, especially at present, confine themselves to the fraction, the aspect, the minute detail of life, on which they put the imprint of their vision. What distinguishes such works as the *Cantos* or *Finnegans Wake* or *Ulysses* and *The Anathemata* is the fact that they are attempts to depict a *universum*; they represent a totality including the whole of history. This historical perspective, if the word is not too external in its connotations, is the animating force of *The Anathemata*, but it needs to be analysed before it can be properly understood. Wittgenstein said of philosophy that 'the problems are solved, not by giving new information, but by arranging what we have always known',[1] and David Jones's 'attempted writing' can also be seen in these terms. He uses the data of history, the ever-accumulating fund of knowledge, and arranges them in such a way as to make them point to the dignity of labour in the diverse service of man and God. This last sentence puts brusquely and crudely one vital aspect of the poet's work, not only in *The Anathemata*, but also expressed in various essays, especially 'Art and Sacrament' and 'The Utile'.[2] Nevertheless, it is important to be aware of this from the beginning, since the vision with which we are confronted is both strikingly positive and through and through Christian, two exceedingly unfashionable qualities for the mid twentieth century. Perhaps only one firmly and deeply rooted in the Catholic tradition and with a keen awareness of what human creation demands could mould 'what we have always known' into a work of such subtle dimensions as David Jones has achieved.

The moving forces in his literary material are many and varied.

---

[1] Ludwig Wittgenstein, *Philosophical Investigations* (Blackwell, 1953), para. 109, p. 47e.
[2] *E & A*, pp. 143ff.

The fact that he is a devout Roman Catholic explains the constant reference to the Bible, the missal and medieval Latin hymnody in the form of direct quotation, allusion or paraphrase, and this source provides the basic framework for his ideas and their exposition. Equally important is his mixed Welsh and Cockney parentage, which gives him access to the deepest strata of emotions about Britain, the oldest Celtic Britain, and about London, the feelings that probably only a born Londoner can really have. No one else has ever better expressed that community of spirit and culture that there ought to be between English and Welsh, but which the English have by and large brutally and arrogantly ignored. The great link in this respect is the Arthurian legend, represented especially by the classical works of Malory, together with the tales of the *Mabinogion*, though with much more that the average Englishman will never have heard of. And then the material reaches back further still to the heydays of Greece and Rome, to Troy and all that went before it in the world's pre-history. In fact, in his long preface to the book the poet quotes as shedding light on his own work a remark from the introduction to Nennius's *Historia Brittonum*: 'I have made a heap of all that I could find.' As regards the subject-matter, this is probably the most accurate summary of what we find in *The Anathemata*, but St Irenaeus provides the best antiphon—if I may use that ecclesiastical metaphor—on the technique of organization of the subject-matter: '*Nihil vacuum neque sine signo apud Deum*'. This dictum of a second century saint marks above everything else the continuity of the tradition in which David Jones stands. In the Christian scheme the signs are, of course, related to God and Christ, but Baudelaire's sonnet 'Correspondances' in substituting nature shows the continuing attractiveness of the idea apart from its specifically Christian use. It needs no special insight to point out that the sign, under the more usual name of 'image', is the most widely known and used device of poetic technique, but there are few writers who have explored and almost systematized its use with such telling effects as the author, who would probably prefer to be called the maker, of *The Anathemata*. The very word chosen as the title, glossed with such loving care and at such length in the preface (pp. 28f.), is indicative of the many strands of thought running through the fabric of the poet's vision, as he himself says:

> So I mean by my title as much as it can be made to mean, or can evoke or suggest, however obliquely: the blessed things that have taken on what is cursed and the profane things that somehow are redeemed: the delights and also the 'ornaments', both in the primary sense of gear and paraphernalia and in the sense of what simply adorns; the donated and votive things, the things dedicated after whatever fashion, the things in some sense made separate, being 'laid up from other things'; things, or some aspect of them, that partake of the extra-utile and of the gratuitous; things that are the signs of something other, together with those signs that not only have the nature of a sign, but are themselves, under some mode, what they signify. Things set up, lifted up, or in whatever manner made over to the gods.

This description distils the method and theory underlying the composition of *The Anathemata* and points to the sense in which the 'heap of all that I could find' is meant to be understood. The following passage, taken from the section entitled 'The Lady of the Pool', may perhaps give a brief introductory indication of the way in which the signs, culled from the most diverse sources, are combined and transmuted:

>   On the ste'lyard on the Hill
> weighed against our man-geld
>   between March and April
> when bough begins to yield
>   and West-wood springs new.
> Such was his counting-house
>   whose queen was in her silent parlour
> on that same hill of dolour
>   about the virid month of Averil
> that the poet will call cruel.
>   Such was her bread and honey
> when with his darling Body (of her body)
>   he won Tartary.   (p. 157)

The subject is the crucifixion of Christ, one of the central themes of the whole poem, but the way in which the theme is treated is by allusion to a whole host of related ideas. There is no explicit naming of either Christ or Mary, and this is, I think, because David Jones is concerned with the universal aspects of the Christian doctrine of the Atonement (or at least one of the long-standing interpretations of the meaning of the death of Christ). For him, it is not a question of talking about the Crucifixion because its truth is certain on the authority of the Church and the scriptures, but because he sees it as worked into the very fabric and being of the universe. In this way we get the unexpected alignment of God the Father and the Virgin Mary with the king and queen of *Sing a Song of Sixpence*. The alignment perhaps jars a little, as nursery rhymes and dogmatic theology are not usually linked in most people's minds, but deeper study of these children's rhymes frequently reveals unsuspected general truths. Much of this passage derives from the Good Friday processional hymn of Venantius Fortunatus, the *Vexilla regis*, and the use of the word 'Tartary' instead of 'hell' is particularly interesting in linking the Christian idea with the concepts of Roman and Greek mythology. Then, of course, there is the connexion made between the medieval poem of *Alison* and *The Waste Land* in the references to April, behind which lies the idea of vegetation and fertility rites as a further manifestation of the archetype of death and rebirth in man's religious awareness. So in these few lines of David Jones we have a fair specimen of his way of joining together disparate motifs into a larger whole in which they are still clearly identifiable.

The twentieth century has seen an extensive use of the art of collage in visual modes of expression, where the juxtaposition of objects has often had either a pure pattern or a representation of the contemporary experience of chaos as its dominant effect. *The Anathemata* is, in its way, a literary collage, but with the important difference that it is not meant as pure pattern or as representative of chaos, but rather as representative of order. The signs cohere; the heap is in fact a pile, as the Victorians would have put it, an edifice.

The Anathemata is not, however, an ordinary kind of edifice. Its structure is not as clearly apparent as the more or less linear narrative of *In Parenthesis*. But neither is it made by the simple additive technique which enabled Whitman to think of his *Leaves of Grass* in terms of the structure of some vast cathedral with aisles and side-chapels built on to a central nave and chancel. *The Anathemata* finds its principles of construction more akin to the tradition of medieval Welsh poetry, about which Gwyn Williams writes illuminatingly and with reference to David Jones in the foreword to his anthology of Welsh verse, *The Burning Tree*:[1]

> The absence of a centred design, of an architectural quality, is not a weakness in old Welsh poetry, but results quite reasonably from a specific view of composition. English and most Western European creative activity has been conditioned by the inheritance from Greece and Rome of the notion of a central point of interest in a poem, a picture or a play, a nodal region to which everything leads and upon which everything depends. The dispersed nature of the thematic splintering of Welsh poetry is not due to a failure to follow this classical convention. Aneirin, Gwalchmai, Cynddelw and Hywel ab Owain were not trying to write poems that would read like Greek temples or even Gothic cathedrals but, rather, like stone circles or the contour-following rings of the forts from which they fought, with hidden ways slipping from one ring to another. More obviously their writing was like the inter-woven inventions preserved in early Celtic manuscripts and on stone crosses, where what happens in a corner is as important as what happens at the centre, because there is often no centre.

These remarks shed a helpful light on what a reader of *The Anathemata* might at first consider to be a formless, inchoate mass of deep thoughts and recondite allusions. There is no clearly conceived centre to the work, or rather, to adapt St Augustine's definition of the nature of God, the poem is a circle whose centre is everywhere and whose circumference is nowhere. For the important substance of the poem is to be found at every point in it. The direction and intention of the words are apparent from the start. The transmutations, the transference of significance from one thing to another, the transparency of things—all these are hymned in the very first words:

> We already and first of all discern him making this thing other. His groping syntax, if we attend, already shapes:
> ADSCRIPTAM, RATAM, RATIONABILEM...and by pre-application

[1] Gwyn Williams, *The Burning Tree* (Faber, 1956), p. 15.

> and for *them*, under modes and patterns together theirs, the holy
> and venerable hands lift up an efficacious sign. (p. 49)

The act that is here being obliquely described is the consecration of the bread and the wine used in the celebration of the mass, which stands as the supreme expression of man's universal pre-occupation with ritual and the sacramental. David Jones is primarily concerned about the fact that man as a species is a maker of signs and thus a 'sacramental animal'. Even palaeolithic man, he reminds us, 'juxtaposed marks on surfaces not with merely utile, but with significant intent; that is to say a "re-presenting", a "showing again under other forms", an "effective recalling" of something was intended.'[1] Ritual actions and the shaping of things into art-forms are an essential part of the way in which man orders the world that surrounds him and finds meaning in it and his own life. The theme of this first section of the poem is given by its title, 'Rite and Foretime', and the allusions to the mass have to be understood in this context. The contrasts between different times and places for such a celebration follow immediately on this initial statement of the consecration, though yet the act intended has the same validity:

> These, at the sagging end and chapter's close, standing humbly
> before the tables spread, in the apsidal houses, who intend life:
> > between the sterile ornaments
> > under the pasteboard baldachins
> > as, in the young-time, in the sap-years:
> > between the living floriations
> > under the leaping arches. (p. 49)

This technique of contrast and comparison in the ritual practices of man through the ages runs through the entire section and, indeed, through most of the poem, though the focus shifts from the varied procedures of ritual and sacrifice to many other aspects of man's sign-making activity. At every point in the poem the reader will encounter some important contribution to the total theme, but he will find it difficult to say at any specific point that he has reached the centre or the climax.

There is an extreme fluidity in the poem's structure of ideas.

---

[1] 'Art and Sacrament', *E & A*, p. 155.

It is more like the sea with rivers running into it and islands rising out of the depths than any building no matter how complicated; it is like the 'riverrun' of *Finnegans Wake* in its circularity. And yet there are principles of construction about the work, as the division into eight named sections most clearly shows. Before dealing in greater detail with particular parts and aspects of the poem it will probably be of use to attempt here a brief analysis of the eight sections.

The first four sections deal with the cultural deposits of Britain in linked historical-geographical terms. In this way the first half of *The Anathemata* consists of an ordering of the material, beginning in the mists of pre-history and working progressively and exploratively to a point where, with the discovery of Britannia by the Romans, the separate identity of Britain begins and all historical levels are seen at once. Broadly speaking, the development of civilization—as far as we in Britain are concerned—coincides with geographical changes of focus. The beginnings are seen in general European terms, the bounds being sufficiently loose to include those lands of the near East, especially Palestine, Egypt and Mesopotamia, whose religion and culture lie at the origins of much of Europe; and the time is 'fore-time'. From this the poem moves forward to the hey-day of Mediterranean civilization and the incorporation of Britain into it. Time and place become more specific, and the links of culture are caught up in an extended sea image which goes through the whole gamut of names for it—Greek, Latin, Welsh and German (as representing the Teutonic stock of the English)—from the Mediterranean to the English Channel:

> Now nor'-east by north
>   now east by north, easting.
> Sou' sou'-west the weather quarter
>   by what slant of wind
> they brought her into the Narrow Sea
>   Prydain's *camlas*!
> that they'll call Mare Austrum
>   *Our* thalassa!
> The lead telling fifty in the chops.
> Then was when the top-tree boy

>   from *his* thalassa over their *mare*...
>   cried to his towny
>   before the mast-tree
>   cries louder
>   (for across the weather)
>   to the man at the steer-tree:
>   Pretáni-shore! Cassitérides!
>   we've rounded their Golden *Cornu*.   (pp. 101f.)

The first two sections contain the most important of the introductory material and are followed by two much shorter ones, which continue the process of becoming more specific. 'Angleland' brings the invasions of the continental Teutons and defines the geography by their name. 'Redriff' pinpoints the place to the south bank of the Thames, to Rotherhithe. (Those of us who are not Londoners are liable to find some of the allusions less transparent from now on, but David Jones is assiduous in his annotations, and a map is also often of great assistance.)

The last four sections of the poem reshape the basic material no longer in directed, historical-geographical terms, but through larger circles of images. There is no break in the poem, for what had been marked by precise geography in 'Redriff' is taken up by the extensive section on 'The Lady of the Pool', where the manifold appearances of *das Ewig-Weibliche* are concentrated in the Pool of London and its surroundings. This section is succeeded by one of a much more obviously composite order, as its title 'Keel, Ram, Stauros' indicates. In this complex section the world of nature and the world of the utile are seen diversified in the living tree and the wood that forms a primary material of man's creative endeavour. In the three metamorphoses the tree is dedicated to the divinities of the sea, to the god of war, and to Christ in turn. Appropriately, it is the 'keel' which dominates the section and provides the organic link with the preceding 'Lady of the Pool', for the Church is known as 'the ship of Christ' and the name for the central part of most churches in the West, the nave, derives from the same image in a more concrete form. The seventh section, 'Mabinog's Liturgy', moves to the theme of birth in a broader Celtic setting and combines the continuing incantatory mood of the poem with the repertoire of a *mabinog*, a poet embarking on his career, telling the *mabinogi* or the tale of the birth and infancy of Christ, but with many references that range farther afield:

> In the first month
> in the week of metamorphosis
> the fifth day past
> at about the sixth hour after
> > the dusk of it
> toward the ebb-time
> > in the median silences
> > > for a second time
> again in the middle night-course
> > he girds himself.
> Within doors, attended
> > with lamps lighted.
> No hill-*pastores* lauding
> > for Burning Babe
> > for Shepherd-Bearer.
> > > Nor now far-*duces* star-night
> nor swaddlings now:
> his *praetexta* is long since cast.
> > Is it the tinctured *picta*
> he puts on?
> Yes, and the flowered *palmata*
> > by anticipation:
> this *is* 'his own raiment'.
> Not *Lalla, lalla, lallla*
> > not rockings now
> nor clovered breath for the health of him as under the straw'd crucks that baldachin'd in star-lit town where he was born, the maid's fair cave his dwelling. (pp. 193 f.)

The imagery of the Passion in this quotation is taken up again in the final section, linking in the double formula of 'Sherthursdaye and Venus Day' both religious and profane elements and showing the Arthurian context of Galahad's successful quest of the Holy Grail together with the inherited background of the Greco-Roman world-view.

The eight section titles focus brightly on the important moving forces of *The Anathemata*. They isolate aspects of the poet's enterprise, but at the same time no single aspect can be seen entirely separately. The sections are constantly interrelated, and motifs recur, sometimes amplified, sometimes allusively, often in a completely different setting, with the result that the whole work has a kind of circularity. This is seen most clearly in the imagery and signs of Christianity, especially in the extensive use of liturgical allusions and the very definitely liturgical flavour, linguistically and structurally, that the poem in general possesses. The first and last sections display this circularity with the emphasis in the beginning on ritual observances as a general attribute of man and concluding with the ramification of associations with Maundy Thursday and Good Friday. A progression is visible in the way that the ideas have been unfolded, but the underlying principles to which the poet is pointing remain essentially the same. As the medieval carol puts it, *Alpha es et O*, or, as the quoted folk-tale formula runs: 'It was a dark and stormy night, we sat by the calcined wall; it was said to the tale-teller, tell us a tale, and the tale ran thus: It was a dark and stormy night...' This circularity of composition reflects a profound sense of the unity and order of life in David Jones's view of the world, and it is no accident that so many of his quotations and allusions should be medieval in their origin, for it was during the Middle Ages in particular that this ordering was most strongly experienced. The circularity symbolizes also the inclusiveness of the ideas and images deployed. Because of the rootedness of the imagery in the inheritance of the past there is a timeless quality about the whole work, and this is because the things referred to are seen both for their own sake, for their own intrinsic value, and *sub specie aeternitatis*. There is no blind historicism about *The Anathemata*: the past lives, it is part and parcel of the present. The deposits, as the author likes to call them, transcend their purely historical, objective sense and appeal to levels of meaning both higher and deeper than themselves.

III

The Anathemata is recognizably a work by the same person who wrote *In Parenthesis*. This is perhaps most apparent in the texture and allusive technique of the two works, especially when one compares those sections of *In Parenthesis* in which the typography points to a more deliberately 'poetic' intention with more or less any section of *The Anathemata*. A comparison of this kind also helps one to realize more clearly the limitations of thinking of *In Parenthesis* as a 'war book'. In a sense (however restricted) the narrative of the soldiers' experience is really a peg (though a pretty substantial one) on which a very particular way of looking at and interpreting human action is hung. In both works David Jones is concerned with

> The adaptations, the fusions
> the transmogrifications
>   but always
> the inward continuities
>   of the site
>   of place.   (*A*, p. 90)

In *In Parenthesis* this mode of vision and interpretation focusses on the very concrete experience of the soldier in the trenches, on the objective details of his day-to-day life. By contrast *The Anathemata* is more abstract and general. Its subject-matter cannot be as easily defined and circumscribed as that of *In Parenthesis*, where the reader is immediately aware of the primary object of the poet's attention, even if he does not straight away recognize the source of the allusions which give it depth and meaning. In *The Anathemata* one may not see so quickly or so clearly exactly what is being talked about, as the poet seems to define his subject as he goes along. The difference between the two books reminds one very much of cinematic technique with the earlier book showing a constant precise definition of outline and detail, while the later work exhibits numerous changes of focus, more degrees of clarity and blurring, more daring juxtapositions.

In perceiving the inner similarities and differences in the two works, one is also, whether one likes it or not, pushed into making a comparative evaluation of them. Some critics have made accessibility their criterion of judgement and thus preferred *In Parenthesis*. Certainly the narrative structure carries the reader on with its simple progression and emotional content, however much or little he comprehends of the way in which this is related to other aspects of life and history. It is the narrative structure which makes *In Parenthesis* more amenable to conventional criteria of judgement than *The Anathemata*. It is easier to evaluate it by comparison with other works on similar themes, and this comparison inevitably makes the book into a 'war book'. It is possible that if *In Parenthesis* were not generally considered a 'war book' it would not enjoy such a high reputation. But conversely, the application of the same criterion of judgement to *The Anathemata* necessarily contributes to a false evaluation of the work because it does not have a narrative outline, because it does not have a clear focus of attention. *The Anathemata* is a far more ambitious work than *In Parenthesis*, though of course this does not necessarily mean that it is a more successful one. In the final analysis the comparative evaluation of the two books can only be settled by the admission of the reader's own personal preference and priorities and not by purely literary criteria, because literary criteria are not the only things involved in judgement. It is not possible to say whether simplicity of structure is artistically more satisfactory than interweaving of themes or that a linear progression is preferable to circularity of construction. Perhaps the whole thing depends on whether you think that war is a more appropriate metaphor for the meaning of life than the perception of the numinous in art and religion. In a way it is rather like the discussion about whether the *Iliad* is a greater work than the *Odyssey* or vice versa: the discussion most often tells more about the personal psychology of the critic than of the poems themselves. But however this may be, it is true to say that *The Anathemata* presents a more complex stage of the allusive poetic technique already so important in *In Parenthesis*, together with an increased proportion of the work printed typographically as poetry. There is thus a discernible development in poetic form, but this in itself cannot be evaluated positively or negatively. It is only in terms of the total impact of the work that any judgement can be made. But if every work of art is made in the way that is proper to it, there can be no absolute judgement as to whether it is better or worse than some other work of art, unless the intention in the making of them were identical. It is not possible to say

THE ANATHEMATA

that a Sung vase is objectively more beautiful than a Ming vase.

It is evident that *In Parenthesis* is a much more popular work than *The Anathemata*. The later book in this respect suffers from a number of drawbacks: its theme (or one of its themes) is religious awareness at a time when regard for religious values is at a very low ebb; it places a premium on consciousness of the whole of man's history in an age that lives for the present and the future; it views the data of experience by the light of analogies and symbols that the mid twentieth century appears to have lost the capacity for using in its emphasis on the literally true; it is a hymn to order and meaning in a period which experiences more keenly the forces of chaos and randomness. There is probably no one more conscious of these drawbacks than David Jones himself, and in his Preface to *The Anathemata* he mentions the problems they raise:

> The artist deals wholly in signs. His signs must be valid, that is valid for him and, normally, for the culture that has made him. But there is a time factor affecting these signs. If a requisite now-ness is not present, the sign, valid in itself, is apt to suffer a kind of invalidation. This presents most complicated problems to the artist working outside a reasonably static culture-phase. These and kindred problems have presented themselves to me with a particular clarity and an increasing acuteness. It may be that the kind of thing I have been trying to make is no longer makeable in the kind of way in which I have tried to make it. (p. 15)

Despite all this, there are straws in the wind which might reasonably indicate that the twentieth century attitudes outlined above are neither permanent nor absolute and that David Jones, rather than being behind his time, is somewhat ahead of it. Perhaps he has tried to do something which is not yet possible rather than 'no longer makeable'. Let me try to make clearer the kind of thing I mean.

First of all, the question of religion. The current widespread rejection of religion is in part a rejection of the dogmatic assumptions of a large section of the Christian Church that are felt to be unjustified for a number of reasons: because they reflect an earlier stage of imperfect human knowledge, because they are unnecessary or irrelevant, because the Church also has failed to interpret its symbols, and for various other reasons too. But to a considerable degree the alienation of many from the Church is an alienation from the organization and not, necessarily, from religious experience. This is not the place to propound a sociological explanation for the queer position of the Church in our society. All that I am trying to say is that the prevalent form of rejection of religion is the rejection of certain accidental or superficial features and not a denial that religious experience as such exists. Many people, perhaps most people, when pressed will argue against the doctrines or dogmas of some branch or other of the Church, but will nonetheless accept the experience of the numinous as valid. They will deny a particular view of the nature of God, but accept that there are strange forces in the universe that scientific knowledge is unable to give an explanation of and call these forces supernatural. The revulsion is thus against authoritarian pronouncements on matters of belief, for at the same time as men are experiencing a widespread reaction against traditional forms of Christianity there is a growing interest in the sphere of comparative religion and in such techniques as yoga and Zen. Such interest is on the one hand anthropological and on the other mystical. Now these are precisely the aspects of religion that are to the fore in *The Anathemata*. Of course, the poem focusses most distinctly on the accumulation of Christian, and more specifically Catholic, data in the way of rites and liturgy, but they are the nearest to hand. The reader is not required to 'believe' them any more than he is required to 'believe' any poetic material. When the poem begins, one is at first inclined to think that this is a Christian, and thus exclusive, poem, but with the turn of the first page the Christian priest (who has never been called such explicitly, but is referred to only by the pronoun) receives his first name as a 'cult-man':

> The cult-man stands alone in Pellam's land: more precariously than he knows he guards the *signa*: the pontifex among his house-treasures, (the twin-*urbes* his house is) he can fetch things new and old: the tokens, the matrices, the institutes, the ancilia, the fertile ashes...the palladic fore-shadowings: the things come down from heaven together with the kept memorials, the things lifted up and the venerated trinkets. (p. 50)

With this passage it becomes clear that David Jones is interested in the phenomenon of religious awareness as such. As a Catholic he naturally gives pride of place to the signs and symbols and to the mythology of Christianity, but he seems hardly less interested in the myths of Greece and Rome and the rituals of prehistoric man. The conviction with which the poem carries its readers thus depends on the extent to which the poet makes living and real the multitudinous links and identifications which he himself experiences between the beliefs and practices of very various religions. It is through anthropology rather than theology that we most easily enter the poetic intention of *The Anathemata*.

What, then, of the matter of history? We are seeing at the present time a number of reactions against the study of history or at least of the less than immediate past, and this reaction has spread in many cases to the sphere of literature also. In the newest universities the antipathy towards studying anything that goes back beyond the period of the Renaissance and the Reformation is peculiarly marked. The classics have been eliminated quite deliberately from the courses offered by some places, not because of financial stringency but because they are considered irrelevant. The development of the natural and applied sciences obviously demands that an increasing part of the school curriculum should be devoted to them, which means that Latin, for example, is gradually being crowded out. In English studies the position of Anglo-Saxon is continually being debated. This attenuation of interest in the older periods of literature and history corresponds to or is the external expression of a failing sense of historical continuity. This is perhaps the real situation of the mid twentieth century: its appreciation of things—and certainly of history and the arts—is atomistic. We may be able to glimpse a kind of beauty or achievement in an old building or a statue, for example, but on the whole we prefer it to be isolated in a museum rather than create traffic jams for people on the move. We do not really like to live with the past, because it hampers us in our current aims. This tendency is most marked in the United States, where a few areas of historical and architectural interest are museumized and thus made sterile, and anything else is knocked down. But it is difficult for the things of the past to live when they cannot be seen in their proper context and in relation to other living things.

In the midst of all this understandable concern for utility and contingent devaluation of the past, it is surprising to realize just what a popular appeal archaeology is now making. Perhaps especially through television programmes, but also through appeals to the popular imagination in colour supplements and magazines, there is a wide interest in the discoveries of archaeology from such far-flung sites as Çatal Hüyük in Turkey, Abu Simbel, Masada, L'Anse aux Meadows in northern Newfoundland (where proof of Viking settlement has been found), and South Cadbury, to name only a few of the places that have excited public attention. The number of paperbacks on particular excavations and on the basic principles of archaeological research is continually increasing. Archaeology brings with it, amidst all the painstaking detail and tedious, careful digging and sifting, the possibility of some romantic discovery, maybe even something that will change the evaluation of a culture. It is the lure and thrill of the unfamiliar that has created popular support for this un-utilitarian pursuit. But there are also the refinements of scientific technique which bring respect as well as the advantage of a name with a suffix that links it to many of the natural sciences. But however the scholar may evaluate this interest in archaeology, it is certainly one of the most vital spots in present-day historical awareness. The twentieth century is in the extraordinary position that at no time has it been easier for men to gain information about what other men have achieved, both throughout the whole world and down all the ages of history, and at the same time that there are so few individuals who have even a relatively superficial awareness of the totality. The man who knows something about everything has been replaced by the one who knows all about not quite nothing, but a very little bit indeed.

In this hopeless-looking situation David Jones has made an attempt to express some of the 'inward continuities'. He has taken some of the fragments of man's past and tried to fit them together. He has begun far back in the realms of prehistory and ranged over the entire world for his material. Out of his own enthusiasms he has collected and, I think, successfully arranged a multiplicity of vivid and brilliant glimpses of man's lasting objects of concern. It is particularly apt that two of the contributions to a recent collection of essays on David Jones's total achievement should be by scholars whose main work lies in the field of prehistoric archaeology. One of them, Nancy Sandars, writing about the present state of our culture emphasizes the fragmentation it is undergoing:[1]

> Everything is flying apart like our universe itself according to one interpretation, because 'the centre cannot hold'. In general, the well-made objects, the right actions, are presented to us as scattered, too soon dissipated, too small, tiny gestures quickly lost. Against this David Jones shows us a world that is a whole, concentrated and converging, a logical palimpsest where ages and persons juggle their differences and are found to be one age and one person. Dai and Taliessin, the Lady of the Pool, tutelar of *our* place and her Sea Captain, the hunter of the hog and the Trwyth. To understand what we are (and are not) by the light of what we have been is, it seems, the purpose and the achievement. 'We were then *homo faber, homo sapiens* before Lascaux and we shall be *homo faber, homo sapiens* after the last atomic bomb has fallen.' The history and prehistory of man is conterminous with the history and prehistory of man-the-artist.

Nancy Sandars then goes on to reiterate how much knowledge of the lost art and literature of the past of countries far removed from our own is now available to us, though as yet unassimilated. 'But it is just this sort of assimilation of the past into the present,' she writes, 'this putting it to work, acknowledging not so much our interest in it as its interest in us, which is so novel and almost shocking in *The Anathemata*.'[2] In a similar vein Stuart Piggott expresses something of his personal response to the poem in recounting his feelings on first seeing the famous Upper Palaeolithic sculpture known as the Venus of Willendorf:[3]

> And as I held this numinous figure, the first words that flashed into my mind were not technical archaeological reflections on Gravettian *art mobilier* of 20,000 years ago, but a quotation—
> Who were his *gens*-men or had he no *Hausname* yet

[1] N. K. Sandars, 'The Inward Continuities', *Agenda*, SI, p. 93.
[2] *loc. cit.*, p. 95.
[3] Stuart Piggott, 'David Jones and the Past of Man', *Agenda*, SI, p. 76.

no *nomen* for his *fecit*-mark
      the Master of the Venus?
   whose man-hands god-handled the Willendorf stone
      before they unbound the last glaciation.
The Anathemata had bitten deeply into the consciousness of at least one archaeologist.

But even those who are not archaeologists must surely have experienced a similar response of wonder and curiosity as to what the makers of these strange objects were like that lived so long ago and in such remote places, and in these words from *The Anathemata* they find their own thoughts echoed and given a deeper resonance.

The weight of historical interest in *The Anathemata* lies to a very large extent in the periods before the Renaissance—in prehistorical times, in the ancient world of classical Greece, Rome and Palestine, in the Middle Ages, where the contribution of the Celtic and the Christian Church tends to outweigh all else. It is one of the poem's limitations that the post-medieval world is not really satisfactorily integrated into the whole work. The Lady of the Pool certainly belongs to some indefinite period of this later time, and Ebenezer Bradshaw, David Jones's grandfather, mediates to us a little of the atmosphere of the turn of the century in 'Redriff', but the links between the deposits of the remote past and those of the present and recent times are rather tenuous. There is not quite enough from the last five centuries in the way of reference to convince those who have not inwardly experienced it of the unbroken spiritual continuity. There are tokens of this continuity in several allusions to the First World War, the linking of Chamberlain's slogan of 'Peace in our Time' with the *pax Romana* of Augustus (p. 186), the oblique references to Nelson (p. 114), the Vienna of Johann Strauss (p. 59), and the wreck of the *Schiller* off the Scillies in 1875 with the loss of 300 lives (p. 100). Nonetheless, such references (which could be added to a little) are too scanty to perform effectively the function of continuity over the most recent phase of man's history. Against all this, one could of course claim that the last five hundred years are so obviously part of our conscious inheritance that there is no need for particular things to be insisted upon beyond those which have been mentioned. If one looks at *The Anathemata* in the context of David Jones's other writings, it is clear that he values a great deal of the achievements of this later period, but that his greater concern is to rescue what others have not been as quick to recognize the value of.

In turning from the matter of historical awareness to the problems raised by literary symbolism it is apparent that this is yet another facet of the same question. The alienation of modern society from the past has forced probably most poets into the construction of new patterns of symbolic reference, simply because the traditionally acceptable allusion to, say, classical mythology has become opaque. The images and metaphors no longer produce the associations and reactions that were possible in previous centuries. In this predicament the majority of modern poets have sought their validity not in a universally valid tradition of literary reference, but rather in the acuteness of purely personal experience. They have tried to create new relationships on the basis of individual psychology and universal phenomena. They shun the use of proper names. It is a retreat into an inner, private world without any readily identifiable social involvement. The reader's recognition of the meaning of a poem depends on his identification at an empirical and emotional level with the persona, the 'I', of the poem. It is an extreme position to take, but given the disintegration of social values that characterizes the mid twentieth century, it is the most obvious course to pursue.

David Jones takes a position at the opposite pole of experience, at least so far as *The Anathemata* and his later poems are concerned. It is a position as open to criticism as the one just outlined, since in its very attempt to build the foundations of social (and this means also literary and historical) cohesion in poetry it is liable to become as obscure as the poetry which exists on the basis of an intense private vision. But if one's theme is civilization, what other thing can one do? A full comprehension of civilization is in any case a matter of continuous effort, and the initial obscurity of *The Anathemata* derives from the fact that the reader is being continually presented with new concrete information as well as with the elements of emotional and psychic states that he is, perhaps, more familiar with because he can, at least partly, recognize them in himself. David Jones is fully aware that he is stretching the capacity of his readers' knowledge. He realizes that he cannot take it for granted that his readers will know what he is talking about from the simple angle of information, so he has copiously annotated his works. In this, of course, he is not alone among modern poets. The example was set by T. S. Eliot in his notes to *The Waste Land*, though they convey far less information of immediate value than David Jones's and were confessedly appended in order to make the poem itself of sufficient length to be published separately. Other poets who have followed in Eliot's footsteps are Marianne Moore and Edith Sitwell, though Pound, whose later work would profit most from such a procedure, has presented his readers with nothing at all and thus made his work a matter of extreme difficulty to understand. David Jones's annotations serve the practical purpose of opening up 'unshared backgrounds'.[1] They are not an affectation. Indeed, it would be more of an affectation not to provide any guide of this kind, as the poet himself recognized. The critic who talks about a poem or a work of art justifying itself in its own terms and in its own internal structure, without any outside information, is forgetting that what makes anyone able to appreciate a poem is the fact that he brings some knowledge of his own to it. If that knowledge is not there—and in poetry that is not contemporary with the reader it can hardly be there without some historical discipline—his understanding of the poem will be limited, but the fault surely lies in the reader and not in the poem, unless the poem is so deliberately private as to elude any possibility that the reader could be in possession of the information required to understand it. This latter state of affairs seems not infrequently to be the case with Pound's *Cantos*.[2]

In a way, David Jones's notes are an educational technique. He is trying to make it possible for his contemporaries to get something of vitality that he himself feels in the symbols, images and references that the modern world has largely discarded. In this way, by demonstrating his own relationship with the symbols of the past,

[1] Preface to *The Anathemata*, p. 14.
[2] Cf. Noel Stock, *Reading the Cantos. A Study of Meaning in Ezra Pound* (Routledge, 1967).

he is attempting to break down the isolation of the twentieth century and to re-establish the continuities of human experience. As he says in his Preface (p. 10), 'If one is making a painting of daffodils what is *not* instantly involved? Will it make any difference whether or no we have heard of Persephone or Flora or Blodeuedd?' His own answer is an emphatic 'yes', and although the change from brush to pen brings its own problems the answer to the question remains the same. The Lady of the Pool cries, in the opening lines of that section, '*Who'll try my sweet prime lavendula*' (p. 125), but she experiences something of the difference and metamorphoses quickly enough:

> An' in this transfiguring after-clarity he seemed
>   to call me his
> ...Fl—ora...*Flora Dea* he says...whether
>   to me or into
> the darks of the old ragstone courses?
>   ...how are you for conundrums, captain?   (p. 131)

But we need to fit into this the information of the note to *Flora Dea* too, for 'it has been said that the name of the goddess Flora was used as a mystical or secret name for Rome'. The passion for names and for sounds, for their literal and for their hidden meanings, lies at the heart of David Jones's poetry. He would approve of the four questions that W. H. Auden would put to all critics to test their discernment:[1]

> 'Do you like, and by like I really mean like, not approve of on principle:
> 1. Long lists of proper names such as the Old Testament genealogies or the Catalogue of ships in *The Iliad*?
> 2. Riddles and all other ways of not calling a spade a spade?
> 3. Complicated verse forms of great technical difficulty, such as Englyns, Drott-Kvaetts, Sestinas, even if their content is trivial?
> 4. Conscious theatrical exaggeration, pieces of baroque flattery like Dryden's welcome to the Duchess of Ormond?'

If a critic could truthfully answer 'yes' to all four, then I should trust his judgement implicitly on all literary matters.

---

[1] W. H. Auden, *Making, Knowing and Judging* (Clarendon Press, 1956), pp. 19f.

All these aspects of poetry that Auden is demanding that the critic should like are present to a greater or lesser degree in *The Anathemata* and are an essential part of its fascination.

IV

If much of David Jones's basic material consists of the deposits of the past, his technique is by contrast very much of the present. Of course it is false to think that one can divide up his work in this arbitrary way, since the historical 'content' cannot or does not exist apart from the 'form' in which it is perceived. The 'material' is determined by the 'technique' in which it is presented. The aim of *The Anathemata* could not have been achieved in any other way and certainly not at any other time. David Jones is a quarrier of matter from the past, he is a conservationist in this respect, but as regards poetic technique he belongs to the experimental vanguard. This alone should make the critic pause in his judgements.

The prosody of *The Anathemata*, like that of most rhymeless modern verse, is hard to analyse. In rhymed verse one can recognize the reason for ending a line at a particular point, but in much modern poetry the end of a line often appears to be entirely arbitrary or to have more to do with the printed shape of the poem on the page. In any case, the traditional distinguishing marks of verse and prose are no longer considered relevant to critical discussion. What matters more is the pitch of the words, the level of consciousness at which they are to be appreciated. In his lecture on *Poetry and Drama* T. S. Eliot said:[1]

> We should aim at a form of verse in which everything can be said that has to be said... but if our verse is to have so wide a range that it can say anything that has to be said, it follows that it will not be poetry all the time. It will only be poetry when the dramatic situation has reached such a point of intensity that poetry becomes the natural dramatic utterance, because then it is the only language in which the emotions can be expressed at all.

This kind of assessment applies to the various forms of language that make up the literary technique of *The Anathemata*, though David

[1] Quoted in M. C. Bradbrook, *T. S. Eliot*, Writers and their Work, No. 8 (Longmans, Green & Co., 1958), p. 53.

Jones marks his transitions typographically, whereas Eliot prints even his most banal and prosaic dramatic utterances as verse. In his Preface David Jones gives a brief guide to his intentions:

> I intend what I have written to be said. While marks of punctuation, breaks of line, lengths of line, grouping of words or sentences and variations of spacing are visual contrivances they have here an aural and oral intention. You can't get the intended meaning unless you hear the sound and you can't get the sound unless you observe the score; and pause-marks on a score are of particular importance. Lastly, it is meant to be said with deliberation—slowly as opposed to quickly—but 'with deliberation' is the best rubric for each page, each sentence, each word. (p. 35)

Nonetheless, it would be well-nigh impossible to transcribe accurately—that is, as the printed page has it—even David Jones's own recorded reading of sections of his own poetry on the basis of the aural impression. Despite everything, the relation between the printed version and the spoken version is nothing like as close or as predictable as is the case with rhyming verse or other forms with a regular rhythmic structure. But when all this is said, there are still sound and stress patterns which differentiate the flow of words from the non-repetitive patterns of ordinary prose.

The key to the prosody of *The Anathemata* is to be found in the development of antiphonal structure and parallelism on the basis of versicles and responses in the Catholic liturgy and the antiphonal singing of the Psalms, which are themselves constructed on the principle of parallelism. The essential feature of these two forms is that the whole utterance is divided and the parts balance each other, sometimes by similarity, sometimes by contrast. When one is reading large sections of the poem to oneself, one feels almost a necessity for two voices to give expression to this division and balance. The following passage from 'Middle-sea and Lear-sea' may perhaps illustrate this:

> Twelve hundred years
>   close on
> since of the Seven grouped Shiners
>   one doused her light.

> Since Troy fired
>
>   since they dragged him
>   widdershins
> without the wall.
> When they regarded him:
> his beauties made squalid, his combed gilt
>   a matted mop
> his bruised feet thonged
>   under his own wall.
> Why did they regard him
> the decorous leader, *neque decor...*
> *volneraque illa gerens...* many of them
> under his dear walls?   (p. 84)

This is not the more or less one-to-one parallelism that is characteristic of the Psalms, but a more complicated kind of arrangement. The passage falls into two parts, based respectively on the parallel statements beginning with 'since' and on the variations 'When they regarded him' and 'Why did they regard him'. The 'since' sequence is not a matter of absolutely equal balancing, for the long first clause is balanced by two shorter clauses, to the second of which is added a further modification in two parts, connected this time by alliteration—'widdershins/without the wall'. Moreover, the 'since' clauses form a kind of chiasmus within the section from 'Twelve hundred years' to 'without the wall'. The second part of the passage pivots on the use of the word 'regard' at the beginning and of 'wall' at the end. The 'when' sequence clearly centres on the fate of Hector; the 'why' sequence introduces into this the image of the Suffering Servant from *Isaiah*, with which Christian theology has associated the Passion of Christ. The contrasts of the first section are reflected in the structure of half-lines, whereas in the second section the contrasts are subsumed in the continuous, though very loosely connected, whole lines. The opposing conceptions of 'the decorous leader' and the Suffering Servant are yoked into one line because of the single root of the words applied to them. It would be possible to imagine other typographical arrangements of the words that form this whole passage that might be satisfactory, but there would not be in them the clear indications of the underlying structure and careful balancing of small units that we have observed and which are as clear a guide as could be given of the way in which the poem is meant to be read aloud. This kind of construction represents the most frequently found pattern in the composition of *The Anathemata*. It is not based on a strict system of measured equivalents, whether of clauses or of word-stresses, but the two interlock. Some of the balancing clauses or words will be found to consist of a closely similar stress-pattern, whereas others gain their equivalent value from the sentence-structure.

Such passages as the one just analysed show the underlying hieratic tone of large sections of *The Anathemata*. The deliberation in reading that David Jones asks for is obviously liturgical in its associations. The words are carefully chosen and must be given their due weight. But this is not the whole story: there are other types of structure which vary the mood and intensity of the book. Curiously enough, it is in the section called 'Mabinog's Liturgy' that we find some of the longest passages where the overriding factor in composition is the creation of a continuous flow of speech and not the liturgical balancing we have just considered. Take this passage, in which the poet describes the beauty of Gwenhwyfar, the wife of Arthur:

> Within this arc, as near, as far off, as singular, as the whitest of the Seven Wanderers, of exorbitant smoothness, yet puckered a little, because of the extreme altitude of her station, for she was the spouse of the Director of Toil, and, because of the toil within,
>   her temples gleamed
> among the carried lights hard-contoured as Luna's rim, when in our latitudes in winter time, she at her third phase, casts her shadow so short that the out-patrol moves with confidence, so near the zenith she journeys.
>   If as Selenê in highness so in influence, then as Helenê too: by her lunations the neapings and floodings, because of her the stress and drag.
>   ...for she was the king our uncle's wedlocked wife and he our father and we his sister's son.   (pp. 197 f.)

This passage is printed as prose apart from the isolation of the phrase 'her temples gleamed', the beginning of the second sentence with the conditional clause placed at the end of the line, and the rather oddly tacked-on quotation from Malory at the end of the passage. Yet the distinction between the two types of structure is probably not as pronounced as the typography suggests. The words run smoothly, but there is an undercurrent of parallelism and contrast which closely resembles the balancing of phrases that is characteristic of the other main kind of structure. We can readily see this, for example, in the comparison 'as near, as far off, as singular, as the whitest of the Seven Wanderers' and in the equation of Selenê and Helenê and the double formulas of 'by her lunations the neapings and floodings, because of her the stress and drag'. Within this short passage there are other features such as alliterative patterns and the repetition of single words which show how carefully constructed even the 'prose' of *The Anathemata* is. But not everything can be explained in terms of the passage quoted, understood by itself. The unit of composition is much larger than this, and the isolation of the phrase 'her temples gleamed' receives part of its value from its semantic connexion with the initial words of the sequence relating Helen with the Virgin Mary and Gwenhwyfar, that is, 'Brow of Helen!' (p. 194). Similarly, 'for she was the spouse of the Director of Toil' links up with a previous clause '(for she was the wife of the Bear of the Island)' (pp. 195f.). In addition to these unmistakable structural elements, there is the whole complex of repeated images, especially of lights and the moon, which unify the complete sequence. The final sentence, which appears rather disconnected from what precedes it on account of there being no linking image, is justified by its association of the fateful marriage of Guinevere and Mordred with the abduction of Helen, whose name begins the sequence.

The two passages that I have briefly analysed above are typical of the two chief modes of composition in the poem. They are not opposed to each other, but represent merely the kind of variation that is possible on the basis of comparison and contrast, which is the mark of the poem's structural patterns. This variation derives from different realizations of the generally unified kind of syntactical patterns in David Jones's writing. His syntax is overwhelmingly substantival, verbs play a quite subordinate role most of the time and are often completely lacking, so that the sentence structure is largely built up by the addition of substantival and adjectival phrases. In the passage just quoted, the 131 words contain only six finite verbs—*was, gleamed, casts, moves, journeys* and *was* again. Moreover, even these verbs are not very important carriers of meaning in the context. There are certainly words derived from verbs, but these appear in the non-finite forms of participles and verbal nouns—*exorbitant, puckered, carried, hard-contoured, neapings* and *floodings*. In this way the very syntax of the poem mirrors the theory of juxtaposition, comparison and identity that reinforces the work's main theme. Against all this, the division into 'verse' and 'prose' is merely one of relative emphasis.

When it comes to vocabulary David Jones is liable to tax his readers to the uttermost. This is, of course, part and parcel of his substantival style, for there are more things and abstractions in the universe than actions and processes, each having its proper name and each name being capable of modification by an illimitable range of adjectives. David Jones is an inveterate user of the less familiar strata of English words derived from Latin and Greek, but even this does not always give him sufficient scope for the precise nuance that he wishes to capture. In this position he resorts to other languages for a particular word, especially to Welsh, Latin and Greek, but also to French and German. This use of language cannot, however, be discussed apart from the actual subject-matter of the poem, for the choosing of a word is not a question so much of style or level of discourse, but rather of the precise object that has to be named and the associations that have to be evoked in that particular context. The language is thus not obscure (which implies a profundity of theme plumbable only by initiates or a failure on the part of the writer to make himself understood), but technical. Thus, one of the difficulties in properly appreciating 'Rite and Fore-time' is the use of technical terms from geology and prehistoric archaeology, but as numerous aspects of these two disciplines form part of the essential subject-matter of the section it would be unreasonable to object to the language. The following passage is a typical enough example of the vocabulary in this section:

> As, down among the palaeo-zoe
>   he brights his ichthyic sign
> so brights he the middle-zone
>   where the uterine forms
> are some beginnings of his creature.
> Brighter yet over the mammal'd Pliocene
>   for these continuings
> certainly must praise him...   (p. 74)

In these lines David Jones expresses his understanding of the universally manifested marks of the divine in terms of geological time. Where man is concerned, the spirit of the divine is more clearly felt, but the point here is to show this spirit at work even before man recognizably existed. Even so, the choice of the precise form of the word to represent the palaeozoic, mesozoic and tertiary periods has a deliberate significance relating it to other ideas and concepts. Thus, with *palaeo-zoe* we have an unassimilated Greek word to indicate the oldest animal life in a collective nominal form. This is followed by an English adaptation, *middle-zone*, which changes the reference from living things to a spatial conception, and it is linked with the former word by the phonetic similarity of the second element in each compound. Then, the *Pliocene* division of the third geological period, defined by its characteristic of showing mammal life, is introduced with its technical name. The use of the word *ichthyic* connects the Greek-derived technical vocabulary with the symbolic meaning of the fish in early Christianity, and this needs to be a Greek form because the Christian significance originates from an interpretation of the letters of the Greek word as initials for words meaning 'Jesus Christ, God's Son, Saviour'.

But apart from these technical terms we find some other words that are highly characteristic of David Jones's language. He is very fond of using the word *bright* as a verb meaning 'to make bright', and this is a clear reflex of his preoccupation with nominal and adjectival concepts. The other idiosyncrasy stems from the same root, and this is the use of newly-created past-participle forms, evidenced here in 'the mammal'd Pliocene'. The most noticeable of these forms are derived from nouns, e.g. 'tabernacled flame'

(p. 85), 'each brined throat' (p. 103), 'schisted Ocrinum' (p. 106), but in addition to these past-participles there are a considerable number of verbs derived from adjectives on the pattern of *bright*, used both as finite verbs and as past participles, e.g., 'the darked bay's wide bowl' (p. 108), 'to white/the horse-king's *insulae*' (p. 97), 'the blueing waters' (p. 95), 'the warp of mist/that diaphanes the creeping ebb' (p. 100). These are just a few instances of the way in which David Jones pushes all the resources of language into getting the exact word that he wants for the context.

On the other hand, while these minute particulars are precisely named and described, there is an obliquity about the central themes around which they revolve. There is a constant tension between the concrete and the general. At the beginning of the poem it is by inference that we realize that the action being described is the celebration of the mass, for the word *priest* is never used. Until we hear of the 'cult-man' standing in Pellam's land (p. 50), it is only a masculine pronoun that stands at the centre of the poet's words. Then we are told of the 'pontifex' and later of 'this man', but on the whole the pronominal usage sticks. Because of this we can be led into accepting the identification of 'the master of the Venus[,]/whose man-hands god-handled the Willendorf stone' (p. 59) with the man 'so late in time' who 'shows every day in his hand the salted cake given for this *gens* to savour all the *gentes*' (p. 50). We have not been forced to name this man in a way that would exclude us from relating him to some other. The fact that he is referred to by a pronoun makes identifications of all kinds more fluid and natural. Sometimes, however, the reader may be at a loss to know who is being referred to by the pronoun and flounder rather in the mass of particulars, not knowing quite how to make sense of them. 'The Lady of the Pool' is especially difficult in this regard, since the 'he' and the 'she' that form the centre of consciousness seem to be in a continuous process of changing their face. Different periods of history mingle almost imperceptibly into each other so that all times become 'now' and all places become 'here'. The encounter between 'him' and 'her' is between the discoverer of Britain and Britannia. Again, the use of the personal pronouns prevents any permanent, exclusive identifications, and if the reader is not always sure of the central reference, this perhaps is only a reflexion of the difficulty of definition and naming that we experience anyway. In other sections of the poem the 'he' and 'she' are meant to be understood primarily as Christ and the Blessed Virgin, but the use of these names explicitly would have completely vitiated the correspondences and identities that are being built up. It would have made a poetic statement into a theological one. It is interesting to note that the word *Christ* is used only three times in the course of the whole poem. It is never used when any aspect of, for example, the Nativity, the Passion or the Crucifixion is being described, but only as an expletive, in a parenthesis, or in a compound phrase (such as 'a cure o' Christ', p. 129). The Virgin Mary is, however, referred to once or twice in a more meaningful context as the 'Maiden' and by the Welsh form of her name 'Mair'.

V

In his Preface to *The Anathemata* David Jones comments on the structure of his work as follows:

> What I have written has no plan, or at least is not planned. If it has a shape it is chiefly that it returns to its beginning. It has themes and a theme even if it wanders far. If it has a unity it is that what goes before conditions what comes after and *vice versa*. Rather as in a longish conversation between two friends, where one thing leads to another; but should a third party hear fragments of it, he might not know how the talk had passed from the cultivation of cabbages to Melchizedek, king of Salem. Though indeed he might guess.
>
> Which means, I fear, that you won't make much sense of one bit unless you read the lot. (p. 33)

There is, I think, more of a shape, if not a plan, to the poem than David Jones gives himself credit for. Harman Grisewood goes so far as to speak of a 'narrative' that is 'subordinate to the inner meaning and contemporary relevance of the events' and then goes on to say: 'The sequence of the events—Eucharist, Voyage, Conquest, Nativity, Eucharist, Calvary—is presented not as a chronicle of happenings but as manifestations of what is proper to Western man and indeed in certain characteristics to man himself.'[1] This

[1] Harman Grisewood, *David Jones, Writer and Artist* (BBC Publications, 1966), p. 15.

postulated sequence of events is rather too schematic in its divisions and nomenclature, though it does correspond to the main currents of the poem. But the more one reads, the more one finds that the elements of eucharist, voyage, conquest, nativity and Calvary are to be found at almost every part of the book, if not explicitly, then by association. Harman Grisewood in talking about eucharist and Calvary, for example, is stressing the undergirding Christian concept of the work, while David Jones's own section-titles emphasize the universally human character. He talks of 'rite' rather than eucharist, of 'Mabinog's Liturgy' rather than nativity, of 'Sherthursdaye and Venus Day' rather than eucharist and Calvary. Similarly, even one of the sections Harman Grisewood thinks of as belonging to the theme of conquest incorporates the idea of the Cross and thus of Calvary in the word *stauros*. So closely interwoven are the themes of the poem that a close reading of a section is probably more helpful than an attempt to define the larger units of the poem too specifically.

The last section of the poem, 'Sherthursdaye and Venus Day', marks, as David Jones has said, a return to the beginning, but with the difference that it presupposes all that has been said between. The words of the title pick up the 'Sherthursdaye bright' of the first section (p. 51) and the 'Gwener-Frigdaeg' of 'Mabinog's Liturgy' and the 'Venus-Day' of 'Middle-sea and Lear-sea' (p. 96), as well as linking the ritual meal of Maundy Thursday with the sacrifice of Good Friday. But indeed the whole section is carefully integrated with what has gone before, and almost all of David Jones's key images and even words re-appear here in this final synthesis. The beginning of the poem and to an ever greater extent the middle sections are full of questions (see especially the opening passages of 'Angle-land', 'Redriff' and 'The Lady of the Pool'), but this last part is more confident in its tone. It has its questions, to be sure, and in fact ends with two, but they are rhetorical, whereas most of the others are suggestive. This question form seems to be a fundamental aspect of David Jones's method, giving hints of what might have happened and what links can be made, but also involving his readers in some measure in his own thoughts. The technique is comparable to the delicate suggestiveness of his watercolours. I think especially of the paintings such as *Manawydan's Glass Door* and *The Chapel Perilous*, whose titles from legend add another dimension to our reactions.

The first sequence (pp. 224–7) centres on the figure of the Saviour, whether the sacrificial victim of Christianity, or the god Odin, or the fairy-tale hero Peredur. It is clear that the central figure of the whole section is Christ, but it is only the other heroes through whom aspects of him are seen who are mentioned by name. In a way this is rather like the Jewish avoidance of the name of God as being too holy for men to use, and it ties in with the fascination of names generally for David Jones that the ultimate reality should be nameless. The titles applied to him here—

> Bough-bearer, harrower
> torrent-drinker, *restitutor*.
> . . .
> Marquis of demarking waters
>   Warden of the Four Lands

—recall a previous catalogue (pp. 207f.) of broader scope, but there the harrower is Arthur. The swift focussing on the events of Maundy Thursday—

> Her Thursday's child
> come far to drink his Thor's Day cup:
> At night, within
>   at his lit board.
> Without in the night-grove
>   far side the torrent-bed

—links up verbally with the same juxtaposition in a sequence from 'The Lady of the Pool' (p. 157), where a number of other associations are evoked that have already been touched on (see above, pp. 5f.). The allusion to Thor's Day paves the way for the comparison with Odin, who also, as the Eddic poem, the *Hávamál* (stanza 138), relates, sacrificed himself to himself. (This allusion is also to be found in *In Parenthesis*, p. 67). After this the sequence turns to Peredur, who was the saviour hero of the Maimed King and the Waste Land in the Welsh story that corresponds to the legend of the Grail in its better-known versions by Chrétien de Troyes, Wolfram von Eschenbach and Sir Thomas Malory. But Peredur is a man and not a god, and his history is a quest on the pattern of the medieval knight-errant seeking an adventure. In his being called a 'margaron-gainer' we are reminded of the Biblical parable of the pearl of great price (Matthew xiv, 45f.), but more particularly of the other times that the word is used. For Helen of Troy is alluded to as a margaron (p. 56), and one of the ships in 'The Lady of the Pool' is given that name (p. 135). Moreover, in the last few lines of the poem the Church, 'his well-built *megaron*', seems to be identified as Christ's 'undying Margaron' (p. 243). In this way, a host of powerful images are linked through the use of the one word with its happy phonetic similarity to *megaron*, 'temple'. The English word 'pearl' alone could not have brought together this diversity of references. The lines on Peredur then lead back to more explicit connexions with the ritual theme of 'Rite and Fore-time' by way of the Roman auguries, which declare the time appropriate for action. For as Peredur's asking of the question causes the rivers once more to run and the land to become fertile, so the ritual of the eucharist 'can do more than any grain' (p. 227). Both are a means to salvation.

After another short sequence, which pursues some of the images already introduced and connects the practices of the Roman soldiery with the First World War, the section returns to the institution of the sacrament of the Lord's Supper, which is 'germ of all:/of the dear arts as well as bread' (p. 230). This action is viewed as a new beginning, confirming but superseding the actions of the past: 'Levites! the new rite holds/is here/before your older rites begin' (p. 230). Rome is invoked, and also Triptolemus, Demeter, Liber, Ceres and the Egyptian god Horus, in the synthesis of ritual meaning that is being attempted here.

The next sequence turns more on the question of place than on unity of intention, and David Jones here uses the story of Abraham, 'the wanderer-duke' (p. 232), and his sacrifice of Isaac to continue his theme. Abraham's journey led from Beersheba via 'Liknites' cave of bread' (Bethlehem) to the 'land of vision', where Jerusalem was to stand, and he was to go

> On to one of the mountains there
>   on an indicated hill

> not on any hill
>> but on Ariel Hill
> that is as three green hills of Tegeingl
> in one:
>>> the hill of the out-cry
>>> the hill of dereliction
>>> the *moel* of the *mamau*
> that is all help-heights
> the mound of the in-cries.   (p. 233)

Again, the verbal reminiscences recall the hill sequence of 'Rite and Fore-time' (pp. 53ff.), and the particularity of the hill is insisted upon—'not on any hill/but on Ariel Hill'—though it seems that all hills partake of its significance. Once more the use of an unusual, learned word serves to link a number of passages. *Oreogenesis* takes us back to the hill sequence already mentioned, but also to the 'pre-Cambrian oreos-heavers' (p. 67) and the 'New Light' that beams 'through all oreogeny' (pp. 73f.) in the geological passages of the first section. It is a different kind of association from the notions of sacrifice, but subtly and unobtrusively evoked in this ritual context to enlarge its significance. From hills we go to the one who cries on 'the hill of the out-cry' and so into a further, amplified catalogue of titles and descriptions of Christ, where quickly the hill images yield to water images, which provide some kind of parallel to the omnipresence of the sea in the sections from 'Middle-sea and Lear-sea' through to 'The Lady of the Pool'. The climax of this sequence comes in the poignant identification of the psalmist's 'hart [that] desireth the water-brooks' (Psalm xlii, *Book of Common Prayer*) with Christ on the cross, crying 'I thirst':

> As the bleat of the spent stag
>> toward the river-course
> he, the *fons*-head
>> pleading, *ad fontes*
> his desiderate cry:
>> SITIO   (p. 237)

The section then increasingly centres on the Passion theme. At this point David Jones uses a modification of one of his favourite devices for specifying the time. In his annotation he reminds us of the traditional hour of 3 p.m., at which Christ died on the cross, but in his text he defines this by reference first to the Roman changing of the guard, and second to the nautical watches. In this way he underlines the importance of the Roman heritage in our culture and the omnipresence of the sea. This type of indirect definition of time, here reduced to a matter of the time of day, is particularly evident in the opening lines of 'Mabinog's Liturgy' and more or less throughout 'Middle-sea and Lear-sea', where, however, a great deal more of the historical background is evoked. The reference to Roman practice is followed up by a very skilful vignette of Pontius Pilate at his siesta at the hour of the Crucifixion:

> It is the empty time
>   after tiffin
> and before his first stiff peg.
> The fact-man, Europa's vicar
> the Samnite of the Pontian *gens*
> within the conditioned room
>   sleeps on
> secure under the tiffany.
>   They sting like death
> at afternoon. (p. 239)

In the last four pages of *The Anathemata* the images of sacrifice grow more and more dense and complex as so many of the significant ideas of earlier sequences are associated with them. Not only are we reminded of the Gilyak hunters, who in a sense worship the bear they hunt for food (cf. also p. 62), but of the birds which 'each, after his kind, must somehow gain his kindly food' (p. 240). The meaning of the Passion is not confined to mankind, but is at the centre of the universe's very being: there is a place for the sleeping dog, Argos, as he sleeps out his life (cf. also pp. 79, 192), and for the beast in the stable, present at the Nativity. And at the same time it is the spot where Abraham was prepared to make his sacrifice of Isaac and for this received the lasting blessing of Yahweh, and it is the spot where Galahad successfully achieved the quest of the Holy Grail. All these things maintain their individuality, linked though they are in the reality that they point to:

> He does what is done in many places
> what he does other
>   he does after the mode
> of what has always been done.
> What did he do other
>   recumbent at the garnished supper?
> What did he do yet other
>   riding the Axile Tree? (p. 243)

Perhaps one might say in conclusion that *The Anathemata* is an attempted demonstration of the truth of the words attributed to Christ in the Oxyrhynchus Papyri: 'Lift up the stone and there shalt thou find me: cleave the wood, and I am there.'

6

The work in progress

Since the publication of *The Anathemata* in 1952 David Jones has been occupied with the writing of a further work, parts of which he has allowed to see the light of day in various magazines and other publications, mostly with the indication that they are merely fragments of a larger 'work in progress'. As yet they have not been collected in one book (though all except two were printed together in the issue of *Agenda* devoted to David Jones's work), nor have they reached the point of completion. Comments on them are thus necessarily tentative, especially as they are subject to textual revision and to modification as their function within the scope of the finished work becomes apparent.

The fragments were published in the following order:

(1) *A, a, a, Domine Deus* (1955; minimally revised and with the addition of a few more lines 1967)
(2) *The Wall* (1955; 1967)
(3) *The Tribune's Visitation* (1958; published separately and with notes 1969)
(4) *The Tutelar of the Place* (1961; 1967)
(5) *The Dream of Private Clitus* (1964; 1967)
(6) *The Hunt* (1965; 1967)
(7) *The Fatigue* (1965)
(8) *The Sleeping Lord* (1967)

Of these various pieces *A, a, a, Domine Deus* is much the shortest, covering barely a page, and has no obvious close connexion with the others. *The Wall*, *The Tribune's Visitation*, *The Dream of Private Clitus*, and *The Fatigue* are related in being centred on the experience of Roman soldiers in Palestine at the time of the Incarnation, while *The Tutelar of the Place*, *The Hunt*, and *The Sleeping Lord* are more concerned with the Island of Britain and its domestic and universal *numina*. Tony Stoneburner, who is the only person to have discussed the relationship of fragments (2) to (7), rightly views *The Hunt* as 'tangential' to this group, but suggests an ingenious connexion.[1] However, the publication of *The Sleeping Lord* tends to underscore the ingenuity of this suggestion and would lead me to view the fragments as having two fairly distinct focusses, with *The Tutelar of the Place* providing a link between them. David Jones has stated that this fragment does belong with the other Roman ones, but he has not made any such explicit statement about *The Hunt* or *The Sleeping Lord*. Nor has he said anything about the sequence in which the various fragments are designed to be read. The reader is thus very much thrown back on his own resources for his understanding of what he reads.

In some ways the fragments of the work in progress read like a synthesis of *In Parenthesis* and *The Anathemata* in that David Jones has returned to the figure of the soldier as manifesting a central experience of the human race, while at the same time being concerned with the differences and correspondences of human perceptions throughout the world and its history. But whereas the experience of the soldier in *In Parenthesis* was primarily autobiographical and personal, however much it was deepened and objectified by allusions and connexions that were strongly felt, the soldiers of the work in progress have retreated into the objectivity of history and have become in addition the vehicle for a critique of our own time. The emphasis of *In Parenthesis* is on reporting the nature of experience, that of the fragments on evaluating it; and this latter is possible because David Jones sees much of the Roman empire and its practice as forming a remarkable parallel to our own twentieth century world. In this way, perhaps more clearly than anywhere else apart from one or two of his essays, he takes issue with contemporary life, its sense of deracination, and its will to

[1] Tony Stoneburner, 'The Work in Progress', *Agenda*, SI, p. 142.

destruction. The viewpoints that he presents, however, range more widely than those of *In Parenthesis*, where the continuities are vouched for by many, and ignorance ('Corporal Quilter on the other hand knew nothing of these things', p. 2), rather than disagreement, represents the opposite pole. *The Tribune's Visitation* more than any other poem David Jones has written is an argument, a discussion of the issues raised by a universal government, rather than an affirmation of the need for roots. This poem and *The Fatigue* (to a lesser degree) give us the position of those in authority as the counterbalance to the delineation of the privates, whose thoughts and feelings form the focus of *The Wall* and *The Dream of Private Clitus*. Putting these four together and relating them to *The Tutelar of the Place* and the two Celtic pieces, we have the beginnings of a work of wider scope than either *In Parenthesis* or *The Anathemata*.

Although David Jones's poetry is not subjective or concerned with the minutiae of personal lives like much modern verse, it derives nonetheless from traceable personal experience. This experience, in the case of the Roman fragments, is one of place rather than of event. The primary event in David Jones's life remains throughout his poetry the experience of the trenches, and both the Roman poems and *The Hunt* draw heavily on this. The places that exercise his imagination are more various, and it is his visit to the Holy Land in 1934 during a period of convalescence that seems to have given the main focus for the Roman fragments. But the day-to-day routine and the language used to describe it are those of a British soldier in the First World War. Duckboards, bivvies, chitties, and the like mingle with the technical terms of Latin military vocabulary and make the two relevant to each other. An attempt at historical verisimilitude would in any case have been out of joint with David Jones's purpose, for although he aims at accuracy in his details, it is the interrelationship of details that interests him, an interrelationship which is not bound to one time or one place. When the tribune asks, 'Should all the aunts on Palatine knit you Canusian comforts, or shall we skin the bear of Lebanon and mount the guard in muffs?' we are reminded of the continuities in a soldier's life, of the physical discomforts and deprivations that he suffers, regardless of whether he is a Roman on guard-duty in Jerusalem or a Londoner in the trenches of northern France. The historical detail that tells us the comforts might be Canusian rather than merely woollen is typical of David Jones's delight in the particular, for Canusium was a Greek town in Apulia and was famous for its wool.

The setting of the four Roman pieces is Syria Palaestina and the time is that of the Passion of Christ. The soldiers are most clearly identified in *The Dream of Private Clitus*, where Clitus, the central figure, is from Rome itself, while the companion to whom he relates his dream is called Oenomaus and comes from Elis, and the companion in his dream is a Celt, Lugobelinos, whose name changes down the ages to Llywelyn. Roman, Greek and Celt as soldiers, together with the frequent allusions to the Limes Germanicus both here and in *The Tribune's Visitation* and the situation in Palestine, effectively determine the geographical limits of Roman power and show the inclusiveness of their empire. Rome or the *imperium Romanum* is in fact the world. Time and time again through these poems the world is insisted upon. The walls that the soldiers march are 'the walls that contain [or maintain] the world'; Jerusalem it is implied is 'the world city' (*The Wall*). In *The Tribune's Visitation* the tribune declares:

>   It's the world-bounds
>   we're detailed to beat
>   to discipline the world-floor
>   to a common level
>   till everything presuming difference
>   and all the sweet remembered demarcations
>   wither
>   to the touch of us
>   and know the fact of empire.

And in *The Dream of Private Clitus* the soldier whose dreams know few bounds says:

>   That'ld be a difficult thing to dream, Oenomaus:
>   Dea Roma, Flora Dea
>   meretrix or world-nutricula
>   without Brasso.

Here, then, the chief centurion, the sergeant bawling his orders, is elevated and included in the world order represented by Rome, now goddess, now harlot, now affectionate nanny.

As this last quotation indicates, the world is not seen from one aspect only, leveller though Rome may most often seem to be. It may be seen through the eyes of a soldier, but since the typical Roman was both farmer and soldier, his eyes can truly see for all. What is the nature of this world? Each of the fragments gives a different answer to this question, ranging from the confession of ignorance in *The Wall* to the blind fulfilment of an inscrutable command in *The Fatigue*. But it is clear that whatever Rome does and whether she does it for good or ill, she is far from understanding in all its profundity the meaning of her action. Not for nothing did medieval Christianity imagine Longinus, the Roman centurion who pierced the side of Christ, as being blind; and yet, within the divine purpose, the same can be said of Rome as Rome says of its soldiers:

> From where an high administration deals in world-routine,
> down through the departmental meander
>   winding the necessities and accidents
>   the ball rolls slowly
>   but it rolls
> and on it your name and number.   (*The Fatigue*, p. 12)

The Roman fragments all presuppose Palestine as their physical location and the time of the Passion as their date, though this is far from being apparent from the actual words of the poems themselves. It is certainly only dimly discernible in *The Wall*, which begins with the admission of the ordinary soldiers that they are in the dark about what is happening:

> We don't know the ins and outs
>   how should we? how could we?
> It's not for the likes of you and me to cogitate high policy or
> to guess the inscrutable economy of the pontifex
>   from the circuit of the agger
>   from the traverse of the wall.

This mood of uncertainty goes right through the poem, repeating in a slightly modified form this very beginning, and emphasized in its insistent use of question rather than statement. The wall itself is undifferentiated; there is nothing to tell us that it is in Palestine. On the contrary, all the plain geographical references are to the city of Rome itself, except for the Omphalos—Jerusalem was commonly thought of as the navel of the world, at least during the Middle Ages. Five of the seven hills of Rome are mentioned by name; the wolf that suckled Romulus and Remus, the founding fathers, is alluded to, and their mother Ilia is invoked with the spirit of Rome herself. Their father, Mars, is referred to under his own name, and as Ares, and also as the Strider. Amidst the welter of cults and deities there can only be an oblique allusion to the new religion that will subsume the rest—'the maimed king in his tinctured vesture, the dying *tegernos* of the wasted *landa* well webbed in our marbled parlour, bitched and bewildered and far from his dappled patria far side the misted Fretum'. *The Wall* is almost a cry of despair in its long sequence of rhetorical questions about the nature of the signs of destiny. What was the purpose of these things? Why did the Romans cultivate order in the way they did?

                did they parcel out
per scamna et strigas
            the *civitas* of God
that we should sprawl
            from Septimontium
a megalopolis that wills death?

The questions continue unanswered, perhaps unanswerable, and the night covers all. It is both literal and metaphorical, physical and metaphysical—'so cold it is, so numb the intelligence, so chancy the intuition'. It is a conclusion that holds out little hope; the old ideals seem to have changed and hardly for the better. Irene, the personification of peace, has been substituted for Mars, but the change would seem to be one of name only, for Irene cradles in her arm the god of wealth, Plutus, who figures but slightly in the living pantheon that David Jones celebrates and of whom he caustically remarks: 'and they say that sacred brat has a future'. Meanwhile the soldiers remain.

The Wall is a kind of choral monologue voicing the thoughts of the ordinary soldier; *The Tribune's Visitation* starts off with a quick exchange of question and answer that swiftly turns into an address to the troops by the inspecting tribune. It is a more complex piece than *The Wall*, and the issues already raised in the earlier poem are sketched in more clearly. The wall we now know to be 'this parched Judaean wall' and the city to be Jerusalem. We even learn by inference the name of the corporal with the 'good Samnite face'—'Private what? Pontius what?/A rare name too, for trouble.' This detail fixes the chronology of the piece as several years before the events of *The Fatigue*. *The Tribune's Visitation* is a poem of great pathos, in which the tribune exemplifies in his own recollections of home the schizoid character of Roman endeavour. All the evocations of loved objects and places are forced to give way to the great negative of uniformity, which spells out death. The tribune is a man whose head is disconnected from his heart. He speaks the words of authority, he justifies the 'world-plan' that is the instrument of 'world-death'. Or rather he attempts to do so, for in speaking to the soldiers his heart continually battles with his head:

> I would speak as Caesar's friend to Caesar's friends. I would say my heart, for I am in a like condemnation.
>
> I too could weep
>   for these Saturnian spells
> and for the remembered things.
>   If you are Latins
> so am I.

And when he has poured out his thoughts and is about to pull himself together to face his task once more, he realizes how near he has come to a betrayal of the authority he serves and gathers the men together in a parting rite to symbolize their unity. In this final passage the analogy between the tribune and Christ that had been becoming increasingly apparent now becomes explicit in the tribune's breaking of the 'barrack bread' and drinking of the 'issue cup'. The military context of this Communion (which David Jones had already used with great delicacy in *In Parenthesis*, Part 4) gains a good deal of its force from the fact that the very word 'sacrament' derives from the *sacramentum* or oath of allegiance that the Roman soldier swore to his superior. The whole of this passage is filled with Biblical and especially New Testament phrases, which have a curiously ironic flavour since the tribune, in the very performance of his unifying act, thinks to have laid the ghost of other rites and memories:

> So, if the same oath serve,
> why, let the same illusions fall away.
>
> Let the gnosis of necessity infuse our hearts, for we have purged out the leaven of illusion.   [1 Corinthians, v, 7]

How very much there is of St Paul, the only apostle who was himself a Roman, in the echoes of the tribune's words!

>   for all are members
> of the Strider's body.   [Romans, xii, 4 f.]
>   and if not of one hope
> then of one necessity.
> For we all are attested to one calling
> not any more several, but one.   [Ephesians, iv, 4]
> . . .
> If then we are dead to nature
>   yet we live
>   to Caesar   [Romans, vi, 11]
>   from Caesar's womb we issue
> by a second birth.

All of this represents the positive side of the tribune's being. He has here become the instrument of a greater power even than Rome, a power of which he has dim premonitions, but to which he tries to say no. It is this negative aspect, however, which stands at the centre of the poem and takes up the dual image of death and empire that we have already noted in *The Wall*. The tribune sees himself assisting in the funeral obsequies of a dying order, compelled against his better judgement to be a rationalist and a defender of unified control.

> We are men of now and must strip as the facts of now would have it. Step from the caul of fantasy even if it be the fantasy of sweet Italy.

The tribune speaks of Rome, of the tributary streams that are 'lost in the indifferent sea', of the Roman Sea that is 'tideless and constant, bringing the norm, without variation, to the several shores', of the hills that are 'levelled to the world-plain'. He speaks of things that are Roman, but he speaks with a twentieth century voice:

> What then?
> > Are we the ministers of death?
> > of life-in-death?
> do we but supervise the world-death
> > being dead ourselves
> long since?
>
> Do we but organise the extension of death whose organisms withered with the old economies behind the living fences of the small localities?

The Tribune's Visitation is, I think, the most outspoken of David Jones's criticisms of a world from which he finds himself increasingly alienated, but it is not a poem of mere anger or disgust: it is a poem of involvement in the state of a civilization. The tribune has a definite place in his society, he has a job to do, however much he feels himself torn between the claims of 'the things of known-site' and his duty towards the Autocrator and 'world-hegemony'. The poet does not view dispassionately or from the outside.

The Dream of Private Clitus is a much more loosely constructed fragment than any of the other three Roman pieces, and the greater part of it is written in prose paragraphs rather than lines of poetry. In content it forms something of a counterpart to *The Tribune's Visitation*, being essentially an evocation of the Earth Mother as she is depicted on a relief from the Altar of Peace, which stood in the Campus Martius facing the Via Flaminia in Rome and is now in the Uffizi Gallery in Florence. Thus, despite the dismissive remarks of the tribune, the Mother Goddess exerts her fascination in the potent realms of the subconscious to the extent that Lugo calls in his sleep 'Modron' and 'Porth Annwfyn', which Clitus interprets as 'Matrona' and 'Gate of Elysium'. We are told that Clitus dreams his dream in Roman Jerusalem, but this is not the place that excites his imagination. On the contrary, it is the Limes Germanicus (as it is also in the opening lines of *The Tribune's Visitation*) and particularly the Teutoburg Wood, where Varus and three entire divisions had been slaughtered by Arminius in A.D. 9, that he recalls in his dream, where the tall trees and their 'striving branches' point forward to the splendours of Gothic cathedrals. The importance of time and place is further emphasized by the individualizing of the soldiers whose experience is here made visual and concrete. The tribune was representative and nameless; the privates, whose lives are nearer to the earth and who tremble before its *numina*, have become persons—Clitus, Oenomaus, Lugobelinos. Finally, the dream is broken by the voice of Brasso, the archetypal sergeant, the Primus Pilus Prior. Not that Brasso bears no relation to the substance of the dream. As in all the best dreams, he participates in its reality through sharing some of its qualities. Some of the gilt of the divine rubs off on him when we hear that, like Minerva born fully armed from the head of Jupiter, 'Some say he was born shouting the odds, in full parade kit, with a pacing-stick under his cherubic little arm, in the year that Marius reorganized the maniples and put the whole works on a proper, professional, cohort footing.' Others, however, would date this back to the very foundation of Rome, to the mother of whom it is said that she

> was ventricled of bronze
> had ubera of iron
> and that at each vigilia's term
> she gave him of her lupine nectar
> and by numbers.

Such a picture precisely invokes the magnificent Etruscan sculpture of the Capitoline Wolf (*c.* 500 B.C.) that is now in the Museum of Conservatori in Rome.

With *The Fatigue* the scene returns more resolutely to Palestine, and its details refer more precisely to the events of the Passion, for not only are we clearly in 'Salem City', but our attention is turned directly to 'Skull Hill', which keeps its central position to the end of the poem, where it becomes 'Lle'r Benglog' and, finally, simply 'The Tumulus'. As with David Jones's other shapings of the

Crucifixion story, the imagery used is of multiple origin, to the effect that everything leads to it. We are reminded of the striking vision of the Anglo-Saxon poem, *The Dream of the Rood*; of the fate that befell Hector at the fall of Troy that Vergil depicted with such concision; of the sacrifice that the Norse god, Odin, made to himself on the Windy Tree. All of these are images that David Jones has used in other places, sometimes more than once already, but they are interwoven with further details which make the fact of the Crucifixion concretely Roman. The four nails by which Christ (never mentioned by name) was nailed to the cross are 'of Danubian iron', the reed by which the soldiers smote him and also offered him the sponge of vinegar is a 'tall reed from up-stream reaches', and the sponge itself is 'from tidal Syrtis' in north Africa. Laverna, the Roman goddess of malefactors, is also invoked. But we get in addition such transmutations as the Five Wounds inflicted on the body of Christ being interpreted as the *phalerae* or medallions that signified battle-honours for Roman soldiers. Similarly, in a passage where rats and flies symbolize the horror and repulsiveness of what has now become 'world-*cloaca*' in the world plan, the sacrificial beast is decorated with a 'murex-dyed lemniscus', the ribbon which was attached to a wreath of victory.

Between them *The Tribune's Visitation* and *The Fatigue* follow the story of the Passion from the Upper Room of the Last Supper to Calvary. In them the Roman soldiers act as they are commanded and as duty prescribes, but they are the unwitting instruments of a 'world plan' that is not of their making. *The Fatigue* is much the most concretely imagined of the four fragments, for the querulous uncertainty of *The Wall*, the negated mythologies of *The Tribune's Visitation*, and the dream vision of Private Clitus have given way to a proposed action, which is described in circumstantial detail and realistic mood as well as universalizing analogies.

The relation of the three Celtic fragments to the Roman ones is as yet not clearly defined. If it were not for the fact that David Jones has explicitly given *The Tutelar of the Place* a position among the Roman pieces, one would be inclined to consider them separately. Certainly the frame of reference of both *The Hunt* and *The Sleeping Lord* is very different from that of the Roman ones in its specific

Welshness, though *The Tutelar of the Place* occupies a hinge position between the two groups. In effect, it is the answer to the concept of uniform empire propounded in *The Tribune's Visitation* and sets forth the love of the particular in terms of place:

> She that loves place, time, demarcation, hearth, kin, enclosure, site, differentiated cult, though she is but one mother of us all: one earth brings us all forth, one womb receives us all, yet to each she is other, named of some name other...

Private Clitus dreams of the Earth Mother, and *The Tutelar of the Place* is her celebration. The phraseology of the poem is liturgical, its form basically a litany. But together with the ritual invocations goes the lore and language of the nursery-rhyme, reflecting the depths of folk-knowledge that reaches beneath the ordinary levels of consciousness. Man has become a child in the presence of the Great Mother:

> When she attentively changes her doll-shift, lets pretend with solemnity as rocking the womb-gift.
> When he chivvies house-pet with his toy *hasta*, makes believe the cat o' the wold falls to the pitiless bronze.
>   Man-travail and woman-war here we see enacted are.

Man and woman are Jack and Jill; they are comforted by familiar words:

> here's a rush to light you to bed
> here's a fleece to cover your head;

and amid the rites of the folk dance they remember 'where sits the queen *im Rosenhage* eating the honey-cake, where the king sits, counting-out his man-geld'. They are 'little children' about to say their prayers, asking for protection against the terrors of 'the requirements of the Ram with respect to the world-plan'. The litany that then follows is constructed on a complex pattern of anaphorical periods beginning with 'When they' and containing striking parallel clusters of titles of the Mother Goddess. The whole of this passage is a kind of latter-day reworking of David's famous psalm of cursing (Psalm cix), particularly in such prayers against the impersonality of bureaucracy and *Gleichschaltung*. Such a section as that dealing with precise measurement and assessment, with its plea:

>   notch their tallies false
> disorder what they have collated

fits almost exactly the context of David's psalm, though mainly the prayer in such circumstances is not vindictive, but simply for protection. In keeping with the nursery rhyme allusions and imagery, the great power that stands behind the *mercatores*, *negotiatores*, *missi*, and other agents of imperium is symbolized in the figure of the Ram, who is thus seen in the final line of the poem as the deadly counterpart of the Lamb, whose name brings hope. The sheer repetition of the name of the Ram and his abominations creates a feeling of ominous terror which is all the more effective for being undefined in its ultimate origin:

> When they come with writs of oyer and terminer
>   to hear the false and
>   determine the evil
> according to the advices of the Ram's magnates who serve the Ram's wife, who write in the Ram's book of Death.
> In the bland megalopolitan light
>   where no shadow is by day or by night
> be our shadow.

The Ram may conquer in the short run, 'world-winter' and 'world-storm' may descend over the earth, but the Great Mother provides a refuge and her nature promises a new birth.

Perhaps *The Tutelar of the Place* can be regarded as some kind of parallel to the desolation of the disciples at the time of the Crucifixion, and thus *The Hunt*, as Tony Stoneburner has suggested, would correspond to Christ's Harrowing of Hell. More obviously, *The Hunt* is a reworking of the story of Arthur's pursuit of the Boar Trwyth across the south of Wales, which is told in the tale of *Culhwch and Olwen* in the *Mabinogion*. But we have seen elsewhere how Arthur is viewed as a Christ figure, and numerous details in *The Hunt* fill out this added dimension to Arthur's story. His 'twisted diadem' corresponds to Christ's crown of thorns; his bones are 'numbered' (cf. Psalm xxii, 17), his feet 'scarred'.

Arthur undertook the hunt 'for the healing of the woods', as the Suffering Servant brought healing with his stripes (cf. Isaiah liii, 5). In the last few lines of the fragment David Jones makes his analogy apparent through his statement

>   because this was the Day
> of the Passion of the Men of Britain
>   when they hunted the Hog
> life for life.

But it is a theme which is not limited simply to Arthur and Christ: it is an endeavour in which mankind ('the Men of Britain', 'when they hunted') as a whole is involved. It is difficult, however, to see a connexion between *The Hunt* and the Roman fragments in terms other than these derived from the Passion analogies. The Roman setting has been completely replaced by the Celtic, and this is perhaps the case because David Jones sees an answer to the problems posed by Rome and world dominion only in the unique vision of the Celts, concerned as they are for the unity of the 'deposits' of the Islands of Britain. They can see the Saviour figure, because they actually had the experience of Arthur as their leader against the invading Anglo-Saxons. One can perhaps see a link with *The Tutelar of the Place* again in the fact that the earlier poem allegorizes Rome in the figure of the Ram, while *The Hunt* has as its quarry the Hog whose path of destruction and ruin is more to be inferred than spelt out in detail. Both poems are concerned with the battle against bestiality.

The latest of the fragments so far published is that entitled, provisionally, *The Sleeping Lord*, and it is also the longest. Thoroughly Celtic like *The Hunt*, it follows up the theme of Arthur as the Saviour figure, using the powerful and widespread folklore motif of the king who is rumoured after his death to be sleeping and waiting for a resurrection at which he will release his people from their bondage. This motif, about which Norman Cohn has written in a rare combination of erudition and enthusiasm,[1] was especially popular in the Middle Ages in Europe, and in Britain it was, of course, primarily attached to the person of King Arthur. In *The Sleeping Lord* David Jones does not restrict the motif to

[1] *The Pursuit of the Millenium* (Mercury Books, 1962; Paladin, 1970).

Arthur, though his use of the Arthurian titles 'the Bear of the Island' and 'the Director of Toil' makes him certainly the central point. The fragment begins in a very similar mood to the geological passages in the 'Rite and Fore-Time' section of *The Anathemata*, and indeed the whole of the fragment is intimately related, probably more so than any of the others, to the earlier book. It is accordingly far more difficult to say what it is about than is the case with the Roman fragments, so widely does it range. It is a poem that keeps changing its focus, moving from the world of nature to the interior world of enclosed spaces, from the celebration of creation to the celebration of ritual, from history and prehistory to the present day. The Wales of David Jones's imagination is most often the Wales of the Middle Ages, but in *The Sleeping Lord*, as elsewhere in these fragments, he is more conscious or at least more explicit in what he says of the modern, industrialized world:

> Are his wounded ankles
> > lapped with the ferric waters
> that all through the night
> > hear the song
> from the night-dark seams
> > where the narrow-skulled *caethion*
> labour the changing shifts
> > for the cosmocrats of alien lips
> in all the fair lands
> > of the dark measures under
> . . . .
> > Is his royal anger ferriaged
> where black-rimed Rhymni
> > soils her Marcher-banks
> > Do the bells of St. Mellon's
> toll his dolour
> > are his sighs canalled
> where the mountain-ash
> > droops her bright head
> for the black pall of Merthyr?

A quite considerable portion of the poem is written in this question form and reminds one of the interrogatory vein of *The Wall*. But whereas *The Wall* concludes with a feeling of unknowingness and passive endurance, the prevailing tone of *The Sleeping Lord* is one of hope. The questions asked, though phrased in the form of open questions, subtly imply the relevance of the Saviour theme to all the precise beings and things that they evoke. The question is, in fact, positively answered:

> So whether his lord is in hall or on circuit of the land, he's most like to be about somewhere, you can count on that.

The ritual that then follows is a commemoration of the men of Britain from the time of the Roman occupation (here a link with the Roman fragments is provided) and onwards. The diversity and extent of the commemoration is brought to a focus in three capitalized phrases: the sacrificial blood of 'the Incarnate Logos', 'shed PRO VOBIS ET PRO MULTIS'; the priest acting 'FOR THESE ALL'; and 'the respond: *ET LUX PERPETUA LUCEAT EIS*'. What is important is the inclusiveness and universality of the intention of the rite and the promise of perpetual light in the end. Perhaps the whole of the fragment can be summed up in a few lines which come only a little further on, after a long allusion to the ravages of the Boar Trwyth. They are lines of an austerer character than David Jones is used to write, but they nonetheless have a curiously reverberative quality:

> Tawny-black sky-scurries
> > low over
>
> Ysgyryd hill
> and over the level-topped heights
> > of Mynydd Pen-y-fal
> > cold is wind
> > grey is rain, but
> > BRIGHT IS CANDELA
>
> where this lord is in slumber.

The work in progress follows very much in the footsteps of *The Anathemata*. Its themes and the way in which they are treated all derive from the same common vision. Yet I think it could be claimed that these various fragments are perhaps sharper and more critical in their relationship to the disjointed world of today.

David Jones has his favourite motifs, whether the smaller ones of allusion and reference or the larger archetypal themes, but he does not stand still. As he takes issue with the cultural disintegration of our time, he finds himself more than ever grasping to words and things Welsh for their simultaneous particularity and sense of continuity. This is especially the case in *The Sleeping Lord*. Even where industry has created its wastes in the valleys of Glamorgan and Monmouthshire, the memory of the Muses has not been erased from man's mind. But when they are asleep, the objects dear to them have to be salvaged and displayed in all their intricacy for those who come after.

7
Essays and occasional writings

A number of David Jones's essays on matters relating to the nature of art and the artist have been mentioned and quoted from earlier in this book. They were especially relevant for an understanding of his intentions and techniques, whether in the sphere of the visual arts or in the field of poetry. They are, however, only a few of many 'occasional papers' that David Jones has written on a wide variety of topics and most of which Harman Grisewood edited in the collection entitled *Epoch and Artist*, published in 1959. These writings, which comprise a few substantial essays, broadcast talks, reviews and letters, form intensely interesting background material for people who wish to learn more about his *materia poetica* and about his art generally, but they have a very considerable interest in themselves as the expression of a highly inquisitive, reflective and sympathetic mind. The editor divided them into four sections, which roughly speaking centre on Wales, the theory of art, the British cultural inheritance, and particular artists or writers. They were written over a period of about thirty years, but one can see in them and through all the diversity of subject-matter the same mind at work, the same central concerns. David Jones is not a philosophical writer, even when he is writing about the theory of art. He writes imaginatively rather than discursively, and he allows his associations and passions to carry his thinking rather than subject himself to logical progressions. Because of this his writing has a lively, growing quality and more impetus than the frequent dull-as-ditchwaterness of a more careful mind. He writes of his loves, and he writes of the particular. His imagination dwells on the concrete, the tangible, and the minute particulars of human experience, for it is through them that the great universals alone can reveal themselves.

The first group of essays deals with Wales. One might say more accurately that it deals with the idea of Wales, for David Jones's Wales is one that probably the great majority of Welshmen would find it difficult to recognize as the Wales in which they live. But then a great many Welshmen have been alienated from much of their heritage because of the cultural dominance of England, with the result that what is commonly acknowledged as the Welsh heritage turns out to be the folksy production dear to the pockets of the day-tripper tourist and the rousing hymn-singing of a male voice choir. Of course, this is part of the inheritance, but only part. In any case, Wales is a divided country, divided between the industrial South and the rural North with at least two of its focal points—Chester and Shrewsbury—actually in England. David Jones's own connexions in some measure bring these divisions together, since his family came from Holywell and the longest period that he himself spent in Wales was at Capel-y-ffin and thus not far from the dirty mining valleys. But it is not really the Wales of today that excites him, though the industrial scene makes its appearance in a few of his paintings and figures importantly in *The Sleeping Lord*: it is the Wales of before Llywelyn, of before the fatal battle of 1282, when the Welsh (rather than Wales) were custodians of the 'tradition of the conceptual unity of the Island' (p. 45). This is the central fact for David Jones. He is not interested in Wales as a separate country; he is interested in Wales as embodying the inheritance of Britain. This is why the period of the Principality is of minor significance for him, for with it Wales literally became provincial and no longer universal, even in its ideals and aspirations.

Perhaps for the majority of Britons the facts of this distant period of history are so many dry bones, but David Jones has, I feel, a way of breathing them into life. In reading his reflexions we quickly become aware of the reality, for example, of Vortigern the Thin, of Brân the Blessed, and Owain Glyn Dŵr, so much does he talk of them as if he had just been in conversation with them a few days before. He speaks of them in such a way that those of us who are not Welsh can realize that there is something of *our* past in them too, and indeed other writers like Gerard Manley Hopkins and George Borrow have provided us with a perhaps readier entry into this other world. One of David Jones's most suggestive essays in this respect is his talk on 'Wales and the Crown', broadcast by the BBC in connexion with the Coronation of Elizabeth II. This talk is highly characteristic of David Jones's way of tackling a subject; nobody else could have composed a talk about the Coronation like this. Who else would have thought to link Llywelyn, the last *princeps Walliae*, and Helena, the mother of the Emperor Constantine, with the woman about to be crowned queen? But both these figures were signs of the monarchy of Britain. Llywelyn was 'the last bodily representative, the visible sign or sacrament of a tradition of rulers that were already established when Augustine of Hippo began on *The Confessions* in A.D. 397, that is to say, exactly two centuries before the *other* Augustine came to Canterbury' (p. 41). And Helena, traditionally of British origin, is 'in Welsh legend or in material mixed with Welsh legend... almost Britannia herself. In that tangled story, she passes from pseudo-history into the realm of true myth. We discern her as the eternal matriarch. In the Welsh secular tale, *The Dream of Macsen Wledig*, she is a figure of numinous beauty, whose Welsh brothers conquer Rome. And in Christian hagiography she is associated more than any other woman —except one—with that instrument on the hill

    Where that young Prince of Glory died.' (p. 44).

What do we have then in these two personages of history but a witness to the long unity of the Island of Britain in Llywelyn, and an archetype of matriarchy related to the central mysteries of the Christian religion? When Llywelyn was killed in December 1282, he was wearing, so we are told, a relic of the Cross; its finding (historically a matter surrounded by considerable doubt, but nonetheless popularly credited for that) is accorded to the zeal of the empress Helena. In this way do we find the most complex interconnexions. In the scheme of the whole essay the link between Llywelyn and Helena provides merely the basis for numerous other associations. David Jones is as prodigal of proper names and precise accounts in his essays as he is in *The Anathemata* or Dai's boast in *In Parenthesis*. Moreover, one does not have to go far with them before the shades of Rome are conjured out of the mists of time or the signs of the Passion discerned in almost every place.

This talk about the Coronation exemplifies the most persistent factor in David Jones's work. It is ostensibly about the relationship between Wales and the Coronation, but David Jones finds it impossible to prevent other things from crowding in. His way of looking at things is so unified that he cannot talk about Wales without talking about the things of religion and of art, the *imperium Romanum* and the British Empire. The Coronation is of course an act of religious significance, but even when David Jones is writing about Welsh poetry, it is the same sort of consideration which leads him to say of Celtic art: 'It was just this total oneness of form and content that the unflinching integrity of Joyce was determined to achieve in literary form; it was not for nothing that he looked steadfastly at a page from Kells' (pp. 63f.). The religious momentum, the historical perspective, the swift and natural juxtaposing of art forms are always present, whatever the subject under discussion. The supremely important discovery is that everything ultimately belongs together.

The essay on 'Welsh poetry', actually a review of Gwyn Williams's anthology *The Burning Tree*, is particularly helpful in showing the reader just how rich and powerful this poetry is and in giving us a bit more of an insight into David Jones's peculiar delights. He singles out the lines of poems that have especially caught his imagination, producing them like texts for a meditation. Indeed, the one from Aneirin which in English runs 'The bards of the world appraise the men of valour' he has chosen to stand, together with other words, as an inscription at the front of *Epoch and Artist*. Again with reference to Aneirin he comments: '*Gwyr y aeth Catraeth*, "Men went to Catraeth"; how natural it is for us of this generation to substitute for Catraeth, *y ffosydd*, "the trenches"; and you don't have to think long to see how the Welsh for trench came to be *ffos*' (p. 57). With what deftness and concision the sixth century battle, the First World War and the Romans are joined together! One could say of David Jones's own writing what he says of the Welsh: 'This is a very compressed sort of poetry and deceptively simple statements are juxtaposed with a most moving effect' (p. 57). His own mode of working and thinking is so clearly at one with what he finds in this old Welsh poetry that it is inevitable that he should quote it and use Welsh words and phrases everywhere in his own work. Inevitably also we find him in this same piece commenting at a little length on what moves him in Gruffudd ab yr Ynad Coch's *marwnad* or elegy on 'The Death of Llywelyn ap Gruffudd'. Even in translation this is a remarkable poem, and it makes one realize something of the power and fascination that this crucial man must have exercised.

The title of David Jones's collected essays stresses his twin interests of history and art, but he is equally concerned with the idea of place. His essays on 'George Borrow and Wales' and 'The Viae' are the clearest illustrations of this devotion. Borrow's book belongs to the mainstream of English travel-books with its fondness of retailing episodic encounters with local worthies and characters, but Borrow managed to visit a good many places of historic and legendary moment as well as use the opportunity for improving and showing off his Welsh. David Jones reminds us that he went to Dafydd ap Gwilym's grave at Strata Florida and drank from the source of the Wye on Plynlimon (as the maps spell it). *Wild Wales* is, however, as much a book about Borrow as about Wales, and since David Jones is more interested in the country than the man, the latter part of his introduction to the book attempts to relate Borrow's experiences to those of Giraldus Cambrensis in his *Description of Wales* and to the *Mabinogion*, and also to make some assessment of the cultural position of Wales both in Borrow's day and since. He ends, therefore, with a lament on the passing of the old Wales that the 'megalopolitan technocracy' with which he has to live tends to do nothing but applaud and hasten. He does not quote from Donne, but all that he has to say is but a restatement of 'No man is an island... Ask not for whom the bell tolls: it tolls for thee'. The fact that there is only 'one boat-builder in Anglesey, one sawyer in Montgomery, no corn-mill in all Flint, one quilter in Glamorgan, etc.' (p. 81) is an impoverishment for everybody and not only those who live there.

This concern for things Welsh and the peculiar contribution of the Celts in general to our perception of the nature of man comes out in further talks and letters that David Jones has written since the publication of *Epoch and Artist*. In a number of letters to the *Times* he has lamented the neglect of Wales and Welsh needs in the deliberations of Parliament, the impoverishment of our island heritage through the loss of a language, and the fact that no students of the University of Wales should have volunteered to help at the excavations at Sycharth, where Owain Glyn Dŵr had one of his principal residences. But more interesting than all these is a talk that he gave entitled 'The Dying Gaul' (*Listener*, 7 May 1959), which attempts an imaginative and more or less thumb-nail sketch of the Celtic contribution to European culture. His point of departure is two illustrations to T. G. E. Powell's book *The Celts*— the first of the Roman marble copy of an original bronze erected at Pergamon by Attalos I and known as the Dying Gaul, the second of a man's head carved in soft stone from the National Museum at Prague. From near the beginnings of our knowledge of them the Celts seem to have been subject to pressure from stronger peoples, but they have been a long time dying, and in their tenacity they have preserved things that have been a source of fructification for others. Curious though the man's head at Prague may seem, it has been recognized to portray an essential likeness of one contemporary Welshman! The continuities exist over a period of more than two millennia, and even where the Celtic languages have yielded ground almost entirely, their spirit, their devotion to the particulars of place and tradition, have been potent in the work of such writers as Joyce, at one and the same time both quintessentially Irish and European.

It would be possible to go through the rest of *Epoch and Artist* commenting on each further essay, review or letter, but this would probably turn out to be a rather dull affair in comparison with simply reading the pieces themselves. For one thing, most of them do not have a plain, straightforward argument that can be summarized in a couple of sentences. Those that deal with matters of art and poetry have already been discussed elsewhere, and reference has been made to various other writings incidentally. All of them shed light on what David Jones has tried to do in his poetry, and in a sense they can thus all be thought of as autobiographical since they represent aspects of his own way of looking at the world. Though some of them were commissioned, they nonetheless all centre on themes that are fundamental to him. They have nothing in common with the clever essays that such a person as Graham Greene seems able to produce at the drop of a hat. Occasionally their phraseology becomes mannered or ponderously precise in a way that reminds us that David Jones does not write easily. But most of the time he convinces us of the importance of what he is trying to put across, and because he writes 'within the limits of his love' (Preface to *The Anathemata*, p. 24) he writes with enthusiasm and delight of what he has discovered. A person reading what he has to say on 'The Myth of Arthur' will find in these 45 odd pages a marvellous distillation of how the Arthurian myth still lives after nearly 1500 years. He may not be able to find the precise fact or reference that he is seeking, but he will savour its mystery and experience something of its varied fascination, for David Jones has a rare talent for evocation. The composite scholarly volume, *Arthurian Literature in the Middle Ages*, edited by Professor R. S. Loomis, will probably serve him with more up-to-date information and a vaster range of subject-matter, but it is scarcely likely that anyone could compress and express its contemporary poetic significance better than David Jones.

Most of David Jones's occasional writings were done for publication in Catholic periodicals or in volumes such as the commemorative book *For Hilaire Belloc* that would have a large Catholic readership. This naturally had its effect on what he wrote, since he could take for granted a common religious faith. Yet though the tenets of Catholicism and especially the phraseology of the Roman missal form the constant basis of David Jones's thoughts, his vision is curiously free and personal (a fact that Saunders Lewis remarked upon in a recent television interview on the BBC). His involvement is liturgical rather than theological or intellectual, and it is this which makes his writings significant to more than just Catholics. They are concerned with that part of the human spirit that works and reacts according to the heart and the emotions, which occurs at a deeper level than thought or reason. In this connexion it is interesting to note what he wrote in a letter to the *Tablet* on the subject of the disappearance of the *Vexilla Regis* from the Holy Week liturgy. The final paragraph of his letter begins: 'As it is largely on the *feel* of the cult-practice that most of us rely in assessing what the Church intends us to think, each change of any sort in a ritual is more formative of our thought than is perhaps realized; so it is important that we assess aright this particular change.'[1] The same voice speaks here as speaks in praise and defence of things Celtic. It speaks of the necessity for the spirit of man to feed on more than what is justified simply by economic, technical and rational considerations. Man may be characterized as a rational animal, but his deepest actions and reactions result from forces that are emotional and instinctual rather than philosophical.

[1] 'The Holy Week Liturgy', *Tablet*, 7 April 1956, p. 330.

8
The Arthurian World

Although David Jones's poems (apart from *The Hunt*) cannot be thought of as Arthurian in the sense of, say, Charles Williams's *Taliessin through Logres*, the Matter of Britain is nonetheless of critical importance in his work as a whole. Allusions to those Arthurian tales and personages that formed one of the most popular and brilliant themes of medieval European narrative gleam like jewels among the pages of *In Parenthesis* and *The Anathemata* and, to a lesser extent, the extracts so far published from the work in progress. Two of the essays included in *Epoch and Artist* are concerned with the Arthurian legend in a wider sense; and the two illustrations reproduced in *The Anathemata* and such paintings as *Guenever*, *The Four Queens*, and *Trystan ac Essyllt* are superb realizations of the Matter of Britain in purely visual form. Arthur first makes his appearance in Welsh poetry in a few cryptic references of early, but uncertain date, about which scholars write with great circumspection since the manuscripts tend to be late, but seem to preserve much archaic material. But certainly before the Normans arrived, Arthur had become the focal point of various tales or legends, and following the Conquest his magnetism as a literary figure only increased. Geoffrey of Monmouth and Chrétien de Troyes saw to it that he gained general European currency during the Middle Ages, but in Britain his fame has never dwindled. The Arthurian legend is curiously tenacious in the island of Britain. Indeed, if anything, the nineteenth and twentieth centuries are richer in imaginative works of Arthurian literature than any previous century.

THE ARTHURIAN WORLD

Many people today will have made their acquaintance with King Arthur and the knights of the Round Table through T. H. White's novels collected under the title *The Once and Future King* or through Walt Disney's film *The Sword and the Stone* or the musical *Camelot*, both based on White's book. That the film at least, and perhaps also the book, may be regarded as more suitable for children than for adults is not without its point, for towards the end of the Preface to *The Anathemata* David Jones declares that one of the Books for the Bairns dealing with King Arthur's knights was the book that he most liked hearing read as a child. That was some sixty years ago, but in the foreword he contributed to R. W. Barber's book *Arthur of Albion* (1961) he tells how a friend of his discovered her child in tears over 'a child's popular version of what is called in Malory, "The moste pyteous tale of the Morte Arthur Saunz Gwerdon".' This brings us, so far as David Jones's artistic use of the Matter of Britain is concerned, pretty well to the heart of the matter, as the English-speaking peoples, for better or for worse, derive the common basis of their knowledge of the Arthurian legend from the works of Sir Thomas Malory. Malory's version, finished in 1469 and first printed by Caxton in 1485, was composed at a strategic time in the history of the English language so that, five centuries later, it is still the standard version and readily readable. Moreover, his skill in manipulating his material was such that Professor Eugène Vinaver, Malory's latest editor, claims that 'he alone in any language could thus have poured into the modern mould the sentiment which the Middle Ages had created.'[1] This compilation of eight romances, popularly known by the title of the last as the *Morte d'Arthur*, is the chief source of Arthurian reference for David Jones, though the medieval Welsh romances and tales of the *Mabinogion* run Malory a close second. The combination of Welsh and English in this way is characteristic of David Jones's vivid awareness of the essential unity of the deposits and culture of the whole of Britain.

In his long essay entitled 'The Myth of Arthur', first written for the volume *For Hilaire Belloc* (1942) and revised for publication in *Epoch and Artist*, David Jones has given the most coherent statement of his feeling for the Arthurian legends. The accounts of scholars

[1] *Arthurian Literature in the Middle Ages*, ed. R. S. Loomis (Oxford, 1959), p. 552.

are often necessarily matter-of-fact, classifying and noting points of origin and obscure philology, playing down questions of evaluation or relevance, so that David Jones's essay is a very real complement to their work in sketching the contemporary importance of the material. As he says, 'What makes the Arthurian thing important to the Welsh is that there is no other tradition at all equally the common property of all the inhabitants of Britain (at all events of those south of the Antonine Wall), and the Welsh, however separatist by historical, racial and geographical accidents, are devoted to the unity of this island' (p. 216).

The second part of this essay contains a longish appraisal of Malory's art and technique, quoting a good number of passages, many of which are key motifs in *In Parenthesis*, *The Anathemata*, and the work in progress. The first of these presents Balin and Balan, while the others are mainly concerned with Lancelot—the episode of the Chapel Perilous, the love that the Fair Maid of Astolat bore him, and his role in the final catastrophe, the *Morte* proper. The significance of these *momenta* in the poetry will be discussed later; here we need merely note the qualities in Malory that are of general consequence to David Jones. He himself mentions the 'determination' and the 'unmistakable intention' he finds in Malory, 'this feeling of men doing things, good or bad, "to the uttermost"'. Malory's understanding of chivalry is fundamentally martial,[1] depending on deeds achieved to enhance the knight's prowess rather than on adventures undertaken in the service of a lady. It is more often concerned with the concrete details of battles and tournaments rather than with such ideals as might motivate the encounters. The loves of Lancelot and Tristram may occupy many of Malory's pages, but his stories are not primarily love-stories, as the treatment of the love-theme in the *Book of Sir Tristram* amply shows. This aspect of Malory, the martial chivalry, makes reference to him peculiarly apt in *In Parenthesis*, which is in fact the most distinctly Malorian of David Jones's works. But the allusions are not confined to the common theme of martial endeavour: there is also the world of the supernatural, which is especially to the fore in

[1] Cf. P. E. Tucker in *Essays on Malory*, ed. J. A. W. Bennett (Oxford University Press, 1963).

Malory's account of the Sankgreal and such episodes as that of Lancelot's visit to the Chapel Perilous. The symbolism of the Holy Grail in Malory is adumbrated in the qualities that Galahad manifests in achieving the quest; it is an ideal of Christian asceticism and purity and represents the supreme adventure to the Arthurian circle. The Christian aspect, which is also apparent in some earlier versions of the Grail legend, is, however, combined by David Jones with the ritual archetype held to underlie it by Jessie Weston in her influential book *From Ritual to Romance*. Malory was almost certainly unaware of any such archetypes in his work, being more concerned with the story, as most medieval secular writers were, but David Jones's work is especially devoted to the ordering of diverse phenomena, to the alignment of similars. Malory's world is composite and heterogeneous in accordance with its origins, though he tried to give it a kind of unity, as his reference to 'the hoole book of king Arthur' indicates. It thus forms a remarkable frame of reference for David Jones's attempts at ordering his world and experiences.

But in works which are not primarily Arthurian (I except *The Hunt*), what is the function of Arthurian motifs? The answer to this question varies, of course, according the the nature of the work and also according to its position in the work, and this despite the fact that several of the motifs recur, both within one and the same work and in different ones. In appending notes to his poems David Jones shows the necessity for elucidating the references for those to whom Malory and the *Mabinogion* are not as familiar as they are to himself, but this in itself is scarcely sufficient for the impact of the reference to be properly felt. The reader who does not intimately know and feel in his bones the *human* relevance of, for example, the tragic story of the two brothers Balin and Balan, who killed each other before they realized the other's identity, will fail to appreciate the reverberations of the last five lines of 'Angle-land' in *The Anathemata*:

(O Balin O Balan!
         how blood you both
the *Brudersee*
         toward the last phase
of our dear West.)

Here the colonization of Britain by the Angles, coming from what is now Germany, is seen with an eye to the present, to 'the fratricides / of the latter-day' and the two World Wars. The allusion to Balin and Balan particularizes and personalizes the general events of our own time by reference to a well-known English example of a motif that is widely current in world literature. The use of a number of German words in this particular section and the influence (felt in other places as well as here) of Spengler's *Decline of the West* makes the allusion all the more pregnant. The Arthurian reference is a challenge to further reading.

In the brief preface to *In Parenthesis* Malory is specifically invoked and the tone of the work set by the comment that the landscape of battle spoke 'with a grimly voice' (Malory, VI, 15). This is also the first Arthurian allusion in the body of the work itself, occurring in the initial pages of Part 3, where the account begins to assume a more poetic form. The detailed factual description of the mustering of the soldiers, their unnoticed departure for France and their settling into camp behind the battle lines, given in Parts 1 and 2, now yields to 'Starlight Order'. The soldiers set out on a long night march into the trenches. They pass through a barrier, beyond which lights are prohibited, their sense of horror and fear growing, like Lancelot at the Chapel Perilous:

> Past the little gate
> into the field of upturned defences,
> into the burial-yard—
> the grinning and the gnashing and the sore dreading—nor saw he any light in that place.

The fitness of this allusion need not be dwelt upon, but we should note that in the last moments of consciousness in the death scene at the end of Part 7 the same episode of the Chapel Perilous is invoked, where Lancelot insists on keeping the sword he took from the dead knight in order to heal a wounded knight, 'whether that I lyve other dye'.

Towards the end of the night sequence, in the watch, a 'corkscrew-picket-iron half submerged' evokes Arthur's sword Excalibur (I, 25 and XXI, 5). The sight of the sleeping men recalls the tradition of the dead monarch sleeping in the hills until such time as his country needs him again. This widespread tradition, here associated with the *fer sídhe* and Mac Og, also embraced Arthur and several other medieval monarchs. It is perhaps most memorably expressed in the epitaph attributed to Arthur at the end of the *Morte*: HIC IACET ARTHURUS REX QUONDAM REXQUE FUTURUS. David Jones has an interesting note on the subject, and the topic has been dealt with as regards Arthur by R. S. Loomis in *Arthurian Literature in the Middle Ages* (pp. 64–72). The motif is, of course, the focal point of *The Sleeping Lord*, where it is explored in a multitude of connexions and ramifications. The allusion in 'Starlight Order' arises from the visual situation, but the sense of touch, the cold and the numbness take over as the allusion leads on to Arthur's expedition to the Otherworld to capture the magic cauldron which would not boil the food of a coward. This story is contained in the Welsh poem known as *The Spoils of Annwfn* in the *Book of Taliesin* and is one of the very earliest poems to deal with Arthur in any language. It is particularly instructive to note how the eeriness and uncertainty of this night sequence is intensified by the allusions to episodes of supernatural power and magic in the Arthurian tales.

Day follows night, and the allusions change accordingly. Part 4 bears the heading 'King Pellam's Launde'. We are here perhaps more in the realm of Jessie Weston than of King Arthur, for her book strongly colours David Jones's approach to the Grail theme. King Pellam is king of the Waste Land in Malory (XVII, 3):

> 'And hit was in the realme of Logris, and so befelle there grete pestilence, and grete harme to both reallmys; for there encresed nother corne, ne grasse, nother well-nye no fruyte, ne in the watir was founde ne fyssh. Therefore men call hit—the londys of the two marchys—the Waste Londe, for that dolerous stroke.'

The 'dolerous stroke', referred to on many occasions by David Jones, is the thrust inflicted by Balin on King Pellam by 'a mervaylous spere strangely wrought' (II, 15), the wound from which he could not be healed until Galahad came in the quest of the Holy Grail. As a result of the stroke Pellam's castle fell down, killing most of its inhabitants, and the people of the three countries round about were destroyed. The Dolorous Stroke in this account occurs in an ordinarily motivated encounter, for Pellam is wounded by Balin in an attempt to avenge the death of his brother, Garlon, at Balin's hands, whereas many of the versions of the Grail story make the wound in some sense a punishment. In fact, Malory confuses the issue by giving two accounts, in the second of which the Maimed King is called Pelleaus and receives the wound 'thorow both thyghes' for his audacity in entering the ship of Faith and trying to take the sword which only the perfect knight might have (XVII, 5). This second version is not referred to by David Jones, who thinks of the Grail hero, the knight who heals the Maimed King, in terms of the Peredur of the *Mabinogion*. According to Jessie Weston the conclusion of the Waste Land theme is brought about by the successful quest of the Grail, and the healing of the king causes the 'freeing of the waters' whereby the land is fructified. Curiously enough, there is no mention of this idea either in Malory or in *Peredur*. The English author concentrates all his attention on the ideal of knighthood achieved by Galahad, the Maimed King retiring without further ado to 'a place of religion of whyght monkes' (XVII, 21) and nothing more said, while the Welsh romance contains no healing motif at all. David Jones, however, is clearly more interested in Jessie Weston's ritual archetype, and his composite references use the dual sources to evoke a conjectural form of the Grail story. The title of Part 4 sets the tone for the sequence, in which particular details are mentioned later in Dai's boastful catalogue: 'I was the spear in Balin's hand / that made waste King Pellam's land' (p. 79). The last few lines of the boast allude to the motif of the question which the Grail hero should have asked in order to release the Maimed King from his misery. This whole complex of ideas recurs in the disastrous encounter of Part 7 in the grim rhetorical question 'who gives a bugger for / the Dolorous Stroke'. But then comes a catalogue of heroes who in death 'fructify the land', among them the name of 'Peredur of steel arms'. The allusion here is not very exact, as the fructification of the land has to be understood in two different senses—with Peredur in the ritual sense of the Waste Land theme, with the other heroes by transference in the nobility of their deeds.

'King Pellam's Launde' begins with an anonymous reference to

Lancelot, providing a connexion with the allusions to him in the preceding section and making the transition from night to day: 'So thus he sorrowed till it was day and heard the foules sing, then somewhat he was comforted' (XIII, 19). This quotation is peculiarly apt, as it shows us the Lancelot who by virtue of his sin and wickedness is unable to achieve the quest of the Holy Grail. A further moment of crisis in Lancelot's career is spotlighted in the wood sequence (p. 66), where his madness is alluded to. This episode occurs in Malory (XI, 8) where Lancelot has been deceived into sleeping with Elaine, being under the impression that she was Guinevere. In his sleep he talks so loudly of his love for Guinevere that the queen in her nearby chamber hears him, coughs loud and wakes him up. Lancelot immediately recognizes Guinevere's cough, realizes that he has been with Elaine and reacts to the queen's accusations by fainting and then leaping out of a bay-window into the garden and then 'he knew nat whothir, and was as wylde woode as ever was man'. The lively details of this episode make it one of the most memorable in Malory. Elaine, for example, tells Sir Bors, 'And whan he awoke he toke hys swerd in hys honde, naked save hys shurte, and lepe oute at a wyndow wyth the greselyest grone that ever I harde man make.' The reference in *In Parenthesis* requires perhaps a subtle mind to remember that Galahad, Malory's successful Grail quester, is the fruit of Lancelot's bewitched union with Elaine, so that this is yet another ramification of the Waste Land theme.

In the list of John Ball's companions appears that of Dai de la Cote male taile. The allusion to Malory's Knight of the Evyll-Shapyn Cote (IX, 1) is, I think, a purely visual one, since the Arthurian knight's motive for wearing his badly fitting garment— 'to have my fadyrs deth in remembraunce, I were this coote tyll I be revenged'—does not chime in with the sentiments of David Jones's dedication including 'the enemy front-fighters who shared our pains against whom we found ourselves by misadventure'. But Dai's glory in the book is the long boast asserting the identity of human action throughout the ages of man's history, behind which stands Christ's assertion 'Verily, verily, I say unto you, Before Abraham was, I am' (John, viii, 58). The catalogue is modelled on

183

the boast of Taliesin at the court of Maelgwn in the *Hanes Taliesin*[1] and recalls also the Anglo-Saxon poem *Widsith*. Dai's boast is full of Arthurian matter, of which the Waste Land motifs have already been mentioned. Even the allusion to 'Abel when his brother found him/under the green tree' is Malorian (XVII, 5) and not exclusively Biblical, as one might expect. The reference to Longinus, the legendary soldier who pierced Christ's side with a lance, also has a place in Malory, as his lance is identified with the spear associated with the Grail (II, 16). 'The adder in the little bush' is the unsuspected catalyst of the final battle in the *Morte* (XXI, 4), since the drawing of a sword is the sign for the opposing sides to slay each other, and a knight first drew his sword to kill the adder that stung his foot. 'And never syns was there never seyne a more dolefuller batayle in no Crysten londe.' There then follows the list of Arthur's twelve victorious battles against the Saxons, as given by Nennius in his *Historia Brittonum*. Arthur is referred to by many native titles as the Bear of the Island, the Island Dragon, the Bull of Battle, the War Duke, the Director of Toil. But despite Arthur's glorification as defender of Britain in the Welsh and early historical sources, he himself brought about his downfall through his hubristic assumption of the defensive role of supernatural forces in the shape of the head of Brân the Blessed, buried under the Tower of London. Arthur's action here was 'the third woeful uncovering' alluded to in the Welsh Triads.[2] Again the final tragedy of the *Morte* is referred to in the person of Agravaine, who first openly counselled that action should be taken against Lancelot for the disgrace that his liaison with Guinevere brought on Arthur and the Round Table. All these Arthurian allusions emphasize types of encounter either in or leading to battle.

The only other Arthurian allusion of Part 4 is a Welsh one of considerable force in David Jones's imagination—it is the boar Twrch Trwyth, which was the object of Arthur's great expedition undertaken to help Culhwch in winning the hand of Olwen, daughter of the giant Ysbaddaden. This episode from *Culhwch and*

---

[1] Included in *The Mabinogion*, tr. Lady Charlotte Guest (London, 1877), pp. 482ff.
[2] See Rachel Bromwich in *Arthurian Literature in the Middle Ages*, ed. R. S. Loomis, pp. 45ff.

Olwen echoes through the rest of *In Parenthesis* and is of such compelling power as to form the main subject of one of David Jones's most recently published pieces, *The Hunt*. In this extraordinary chase the role of Menw was to transform himself into a bird to snatch one of Twrch Trwyth's treasures, the comb and shears hidden between his ears, but he failed in his task and was poisoned into the bargain. Llaesgeven appears in *Culhwch* as Llaesgymyn, a name which means 'slack hewer'. Between them, he and Menw represent something of the extremes of disparity between effort and reward, characteristic enough of life as of battle.

Part 5, 'Squat Garlands for White Knights', with its more leisurely account of day-to-day activities outside the immediate range of battle, has only one Arthurian sidelight. The cook is compared with 'the worshipful Beaumains/the turner of broches [i.e. spits]/the broth-wallah' (p. 119), i.e. to Sir Gareth of Orkney, Gawain's brother, who worked himself up from the humblest beginnings in Arthur's court to being a knight of the Round Table (the particular reference is to VII, 2 and 5).

Everywhere in Malory the pavilions of the title to Part 6 abound as tournaments and preparations for battle take place. The initial lines of this sequence of preparations are typical Malorian phrases culled from disparate sources. The arrival of Elias the Captain (X, 29) marks the call to battle that he, 'a passynge good knyght' (X, 30) made to Mark and Tristram. His is a brief role in the lengthy *Book of Sir Tristram*, but one of great dignity. It is interesting to know that Elias is not simply Malorian, but belongs to David Jones's real-life experience: 'It so chanced that Elias was the name of our Captain & Adjutant at the date of the Somme battle, and he did "come on the morn" of the battle—or rather on to the field of bivouac. I can see him now, a jolly nice chap, with very thick spectacles—very dapper, a Welshman, a lawyer, I think, in civil life. I don't know what happend to him. He *may* have been killed later on, for we had a new Adjutant sometime in 1917. So anyway 'Elias the Captain' survived the attack on Mametz Wood.'[1] In the rest of this section of *In Parenthesis*, which has once again the more

[1] In a letter to me dated 6 November 1966.

naturalistically descriptive prose of Parts 1 and 2, the attitude of the soldiers is cast in the linguistic framework of that of Arthur's party in the *Morte* (XX, 1). There is no allusion to any particular knight in this section apart from Elias, who represents the enemy. It is an evocation of mood, not of event or character.

The precise prose of 'Pavilions and Captains of Hundreds' yields to a greater allusiveness in 'The Five Unmistakable Marks'. This final section provides a summation of most of the Arthurian references already made. Thus, the death of Aneirin Lewis, 'who sleeps in Arthur's lap', brings references to Olwen, Ysbaddaden and Twrch Trwyth. The battle, naturally enough, is aligned with that between Arthur and Mordred (XXI, 3) at Salisbury, where Malory situated the fatal battle of Camlann of the *Annales Cambriae*. The whole atmosphere reeks of death. We are told, as was Galahad, how the green tree under which Abel was killed 'bore scarlet memorial'. The Dolorous Stroke is invoked only to be immediately dismissed as irrelevant in the extremity of the circumstances. Lancelot's dread experience of the Chapel Perilous is recalled. The names of the great heroes are read before us—Tristram, Lamorak de Galis, Alisand le Orphelin, Beaumains, Balin and Balan the unwitting fratricides, and Peredur—and that knight is mentioned who, at the moment of death, ate grass as a token of the sacrament (David Jones couldn't track down this Malorian reference, nor have I been able to). The action of the enemy is compared with the truncheon of Garlon, the invisible knight (II, 12ff.), and the mention of the 'ferocious pursuer / terribly questing' reminds one of the Boar Trwyth as well as the Questing Beast that crops up in several places in Malory as the special pursuit of Sir Palomides. The conduct of battle resembles that of Mark and Tristram against the Saxons (X, 29), while the picture of death in the trenches is reminiscent of Mordred's siege of Guinevere in the White Tower (XXX, 1). The words 'and but we avoid wisely there is but death', which David Jones attributes to Mark, I have not been able to trace, but their context is not especially important —it is rather the plain words that matter.

Such, then, are the Arthurian *momenta* of *In Parenthesis*. The sources and types of allusion are as varied as their effects. But perhaps they can be summed up in two ways—as particularizing the events, characters and moods of the war experience, and as providing a recognized and valued tradition of experience in battle against which to see the *disjecta membra* of the soldier's life. The dislocation of warfare in the trenches especially gains some kind of relevance and meaning through the reference, in this case, to the Matter of Britain. It is a standard which gives a certain objective, as opposed to emotional or sentimental, value to the soldier's otherwise meaninglessly amputated existence.

The *Anathemata* is a more difficult work to define than *In Parenthesis*. Its theme is more abstract, being concerned almost more with a mode of seeing than with what is actually seen, and although its descriptions of particulars are as precise and finely wrought as those of *In Parenthesis*, they are given not simply for themselves, but as aspects of the archetypes of history (whether factual or imagined) and human experience. In this more ambitious framework the Arthurian allusions have a somewhat different significance from those of the earlier work. Many of them take up materials already used in *In Parenthesis*, though in a context which is more deeply concerned with the essence of things, the coherence of observed phenomena, and perhaps especially of religious phenomena, where the data of anthropological investigation into ancient and primitive rituals, for example, are seen as part of the same fabric as the revealed wisdom of Christianity.

The anthropological substructure is immediately apparent in the first section, 'Rite and Fore-time', with the 'cult-man [who] stands alone in Pellam's land'. The reference here, more than in *In Parenthesis*, is to the fertility ritual associated with the Grail story, and Pellam's name merely serves to invoke this idea. But in the later references to this theme the anthropological motif is linked to the idea of Christ as both Redeemer and the Maimed King. This is lightly sketched in in the query 'at any hour the maimed king/pays a call?' in the section 'Keel, Ram, Stauros' (p. 179), to be amplified in 'Mabinog's Liturgy' and 'Sherthursdaye and Venus-Day', for among the titles applied to Christ are those of 'Freer of the Waters' and 'Chief Physician' associated with Peredur (pp. 207, 225). The Grail theme is further alluded to in the use of the unusual term

'Sherthursdaye', for this is the word used by Caxton (and regarded by Vinaver as corrupt, as it is not found in the Winchester MS. of Malory's works) when Christ appears out of the Holy Grail and tells Galahad that it is 'the holy dysshe wherein I ete the lamb on sherthursdaye' (XVII, 20). This name for Maundy Thursday is now generally obsolete in English, but it is still used in Scandinavia (cf. Norw. *skjaertorsdag*), the first element being cognate with English 'sheer', i.e. pure or bright.

The context of ritual includes references to the hill-places on which ancient ceremonies and sacrifices so frequently took place. Here we are reminded of the *colles Arthuri* (p. 55) and the tradition of the sleeping king; and the later reference to 'dragons and old Pendragons' (p. 68) with their abodes in such areas as the Snowdon range also evokes Arthur's father, Uther Pendragon, from whom Malory's tales take their beginning. The delving into prehistory and the search for origins in this section of the poem relate the archaeological evidence of potsherds and dog-bones to 'the dish / that holds no coward's food' of *The Spoils of Annwfn* and the dogs 'that quested the hog' in *Culhwch and Olwen* (p. 79). Both these exploits of Arthur are, as we have seen, adventures into the unknown world of the supernatural.

'Middle-Sea and Lear-Sea' is concerned with the definition of time and a change of place from the Mediterranean to Britain, expressed in imagery of the sea. The period of the Crucifixion is determined by a number of events, including the making of the sixth century B.C. 'Beautiful Korê', and in the list of paragons of female beauty hereby evoked there figures Gwenhwyfar, the name of Arthur's wife in Welsh tradition, the Guinevere of Malory. Later, in the sequence devoted to the Blessed Virgin in 'Mabinog's Liturgy', Gwenhwyfar is again recalled, though this time to suffer, even at her best, by a comparison with Mary (p. 195). In the progress from the Mediterranean to Britain Cornwall is the first part of the land to be reached, and it is singularly fortunate that Cornwall should play such a distinctive role in the Arthurian myth. Mark is an ignominious figure in Malory, but when the Scillies are hailed as 'the horse-king's *insulae*' (p. 97)—Welsh *march* means 'horse'—and reference is made to the kingdom of Lyonesse as 'Mark's lost hundred' (p. 101), it is the incorporation of these regions into the mythological setting that matters and not especially the associations of Mark. The mention of Igraine, the wife of the Duke of Cornwall who by magic became Arthur's mother, is more significant, in the same way as that of Uther Pendragon. This Cornish sequence has another peculiarly felicitous coalescence of ideas in 'Morgana's fay-light', since the original *fata morgana*, referring to a mirage in the Straits of Messina, is accommodated ' 'twixt Uxantis and the Horn' and assimilated into the character of Morgan le Fay, Arthur's sister, whose supernatural powers shimmer through much of Malory's story. Morgan le Fay was 'put to schole in a nonnery, and ther she lerned so moche that she was a grete clerke of nygromancye' (I, 2), as David Jones tells us also of the Lady of the Pool (p. 135).

The title of the section 'The Lady of the Pool' sets up a number of intricate associations, for Arthurian legend knows of both a Lady of the Lake and a Lady of the Fountain. The Lady of the Lake, otherwise known as Nyneve, is the mysterious figure who gives Arthur the sword he sees raised above the water of the lake by an arm clothed in white samite. She even gains power over Merlin (p. 159), whose infatuation with her is such that she can imprison him under a great stone (Malory, IV, 1). In the supernatural world she, together with Morgan le Fay, who is also connected with the Lady of the Pool, is Merlin's female counterpart and 'allwayes fryndely to kynge Arthure' (IX, 16). The Lady of the Fountain, in the tale from the *Mabinogion*, is not specifically referred to in this section, but appears in the final one expressly as 'the lady of the *ffynnon*' (p. 237) in the Passion sequence. In the medieval romance she marries Owain in order to secure a proper protection for the fountain, and here, as in the Passion sequence, the theme of salvation is paramount.

On the whole, however, 'The Lady of the Pool' is an evocation of the long history of London, antedating Arthur by recalling Belin (pp. 124, 163), whose imperial dignity Arthur discovered in searching through the chronicles of the land (Malory, V, 1). Belinus occupies an important position in Geoffrey of Monmouth's *History of the Kings of Britain* (III, 1–10), the most important source of the alliterative *Morte Arthure*, which in its turn was the chief source of Malory's version. From such glimpses into the mist of early times the Lady of the Pool provides us with a plethora of data and associations, swearing to them by a hotch-potch of authorities abounding with Arthurian significance. But the Lady of the Pool has only a limited place for Arthurian reminiscences, and when she has managed to include the '*rexque futurus*' (p. 164), she goes on to other things. There is plenty more Celtic material, to be sure, but what is specifically Arthurian is here almost submerged beneath the rushing waters of memory.

In 'Mabinog's Liturgy', which is basically concerned with the celebration of the birth of Christ, Guinevere appears in a position analogous to that of the Blessed Virgin, as we have already noted. Arthur is mentioned by his titles of Bear of the Island and Director of Toil (pp. 196f.), but more by virtue of being her husband than for his own sake. Guinevere's death in the *Morte* (XXI, 11), one of Malory's most poignant episodes and one in which the liturgy plays an impressive part, is referred to for the fine cloth of her shroud. The *Morte* is further alluded to in Mordred's incestuous compulsion to take Guinevere as his wife, which she resists by retiring into Tower of London (XXI, 1), the allusion again seeking to underline the purity of the archetypal Mother. Even the Welsh tradition that Arthur had three successive wives all named Gwenhwyfar (or Guinevere or Gaynor), an idea invoked by the Lady of the Pool, takes its place among the associations chosen to enhance her position.

Such other Arthurian motifs as there are in the section tend to deepen the numinous atmosphere appropriate to the celebration of a liturgy. In this sense Merlin is mentioned (p. 201); and the 'nine crones of Glevum', the witches of Caer Loyw (Gloucester) that are killed by Arthur and his men at the end of *Peredur*, are thought of as active on the night of the Nativity. It is hard here, as indeed elsewhere, to draw the line between clearly Arthurian allusions and the more generally Celtic mood, since the two are in any case mingled in the deposits of literature and tradition, as they are in David Jones's imagination.

The culmination of liturgy and ritual, connecting the beginning and the end of *The Anathemata*, is expressed in the final section, 'Sherthursdaye and Venus-Day', to which the coherence of a number of images has already led us. Only one new allusion remains to be mentioned, and this links up with the Grail theme that runs through the whole work. In the concluding lines the definition of place in the Last Supper sequence fixes on 'Sarras city', where 'in the spirituall palleys' Galahad learns the mysteries of the Holy Grail (XVII, 20). In Malory's conception of the Arthurian legends the quest of the Sankgreal is the achievement solely of the perfect knight. Need more be said?

The types of Arthurian reference in *The Anathemata* certainly differ from those of *In Parenthesis*. Though some of the motifs recur in both works, they are used in such a way as to reinforce the differing themes of the two books. The scope of *The Anathemata* is wider than that of *In Parenthesis*, not being controlled by a clear-cut linear narrative. Accordingly, its Arthurian allusions deal more with those aspects of the matter of Britain that border on the realms of the supernatural and the numinous. Neither Merlin nor Morgan le Fay is mentioned in *In Parenthesis*. The Anathemata deals more in moods and figures of a universal character than in events, and its mysterious relationships backwards and forwards through time and place are perhaps best captured in the Fool's words from *King Lear* (III, 2), which serve as an epigraph to the whole book: 'This prophecie Merlin shall make for I liue before his time.'

Among the shorter pieces that comprise the work in progress only two—*The Hunt* and *The Sleeping Lord*—contain an important Arthurian element. *The Wall* and *The Fatigue*, which are basically concerned with the situation of the Roman Empire around the time of Christ, do, however, contain certain motifs incidentally. It is significant that in his preoccupation with the composition and decomposition of civilizations David Jones continually returns to the ritual basis of the Waste Land theme, which is the only image associated with the Arthurian legend that is found in these two pieces. Christ is seen both as 'the maimed king in his tinctured vesture, the dying *tegernos* of the wasted *landa*' (*The Wall*) and as the man who 'Frees the Waters' (*The Fatigue*). In so far as a good deal of the material in the work in progress consists of dialogue or interior monologue spoken in an imagined historical situation, it is appropriate that the allusions should refer to what underlies (or may be held to underlie) the Grail legend and not to figures or events of the Matter of Britain.

The most clearly Arthurian of all David Jones's poems is *The Hunt*, modelled on the story of Arthur's pursuit of the boar Twrch Trwyth from *Culhwch and Olwen*, and this theme is also referred to a number of times in *The Sleeping Lord*, though this latter piece is generally more Celtic than specifically Arthurian in the range of moods that it seeks to evoke. *The Hunt*, unlike David Jones's other poetry, is Arthurian in its primary theme, though there are further complementary allusions which broaden the field of reference. One of 'the riders who would mount though the green wound unstitched' is Tristram, called upon to fight for Mark against the Saxons in Malory (X, 30), while Mark himself would certainly be included among 'those who would leave their mounts in stall if the bite of a gadfly could excuse them'. Arthur, 'the diademed leader/who directs the toil' is here alluded to by one of his many traditional titles (most of which are used in various sections of *The Sleeping Lord*). It seems, however, to be the case that such additional Arthurian details in *The Hunt* serve a more decorative function than those in *In Parenthesis* and *The Anathemata*. It is the re-creation of the myth in terms of modern poetry that is the main thing in *The Hunt*; and here, with the precise touches of close observation, the wide-ranging imagery, the technique of parallelism and anaphora, the balance of phraseology, David Jones has been singularly successful.

The Arthurian myth is only one of his circles of images, perhaps not even the most important. But David Jones uses it carefully and extensively to explore the depths of his chosen themes. It is not there to provide a mere literary background or a pseudo-medieval flavour, but because it is a way of stating his conviction of the essential unity of the Island of Britain.

9
Conclusion

What is the nature of David Jones's achievement as a poet? Where can he be placed in relation to other 20th century poets? and what sort of position does he occupy in the long tradition of literature in the English language? These questions are not susceptible of an easy or straightfoward answer, but some attempt has to be made to provide at least a starting point. Part of the problem lies in the fact that the lyric or short poem is the dominant poetic form and that by and large it currently contents itself with circumscribed pirouettes around the surfaces of personal triviality. The situation has been set out clearly enough in Kathleen Raine's recent book *Defending Ancient Springs*, where it forms the background to her discussion of a number of poets who she feels are faithful to the spiritual depth of 'true poetry' and find new ways of exploring and expressing it. David Jones is not explicitly dealt with in this study, though he is mentioned on several occasions, but like Vernon Watkins, Edwin Muir, David Gascoyne, Yeats and St. John Perse he is one of the defenders of the 'ancient springs'. Add to these names those of Pound and Eliot, Hopkins, Joyce, Blake, Hugh MacDiarmid and (despite all the decrying that she is at present subjected to) Edith Sitwell, and one probably has a fair context, and a diverse enough one, for David Jones's work. Vernon Watkins is the Welsh poet with whom he has the closest affinity; St. John Perse he explicitly recognizes as a kindred spirit; and Pound, together with the Eliot of *The Waste Land*, is the person whose technique of poetic collage most nearly resembles his own. Hugh MacDiarmid seems to me to possess a similar toughness and exactitude of language, a delight in particularity, and an even greater range of literary and cultural continuities, while Edith Sitwell expresses in much of her later poetry a kind of mystical numinosity, a sense of involvement with the obscure sufferings of the world, and an incantational element that derives ultimately, in the West, from the rites and insights of Catholicism. It is possible, however, that the most important of all these literary affiliations or correspondences is to be found in Joyce. Not so much the Joyce of *Ulysses* as the Joyce of *Finnegans Wake*. David Jones doesn't go in for the Joycean pun (or at least not on the same, bewildering scale), nor does he share the negative side of Joyce's obsession with Catholicism, but his use of language is motivated by a similar kind of philological delight and he employs its cross-fertilizing powers. Moreover, what he has to say is based on a comparable perception of the permanence of mythological structures. This similarity has been remarked on before by such critics as Kathleen Raine and Edwin Muir, and it is probable that David Jones would confess to Joyce as a 'master', while rejecting any other specific influences. *The Anathemata* could be regarded as a counterpart in the field of poetry to *Finnegans Wake*, though whether the common distinctions of poetry and prose have much relevance here is a matter open to dispute. *The Anathemata* is certainly more readable.

David Jones's work, whether one takes his poetry, his essays, or his complex drawings such as the *Aphrodite in Aulis*, bears all the marks of what the Germans would call a *Spätzeit* or 'late time'. The First World War was the effective close of an era in Europe, and the experience of it that David Jones distilled in *In Parenthesis* has remained with him. The old order had, of course, been long crumbling, and the War shattered most of what was left. *The Anathemata* can, in some ways, be construed as a threnody on the situation which the First World War brought about and the Second exacerbated—the decay of a unified civilization and the loss of the ability to think intuitively in terms of symbols or even to apprehend that they might mean anything at all. This well-nigh fatal impoverishment of the human spirit has been extensively commented upon and discussed by C. G. Jung in many of his

CONCLUSION

psycho-analytical writings, which have a considerable bearing on what David Jones has tried to create. David Jones has followed up the themes of *The Anathemata* by relating the problems of the present day to the axial time of the Incarnation in the Roman Empire in the various fragments of the work in progress. Perhaps Rome was not quite in its *Spätzeit* then, but the Golden Age was already turning into the Silver. The old gods were dying, and the new cult-hero was born that was to determine the development of the West for nearly 2000 years. The Romans' unawareness of what was happening at that time, of what seeds were being sown to spread a new kind of life in the future, is an apt parallel for the Spenglerian analysis of our own situation.

The poetry of a *Spätzeit*, certainly that of our own, fluctuates between being an act of salvage and transitoriness. The task of the poet is to preserve what he conceives to be of value and to possess beauty and significance. I think we can see David Jones's poetry—more especially *The Anathemata*—as the creation of a museum. Not the sort of museum, I might add, that is housed in a fusty, old building with bad lighting, indiscriminately lumped together, and poorly explained, but one that provokes unexpected enthusiasms in both the casual visitor and the informed expert, a museum in effect that is true to its etymology and is a real *mouseion*, a 'sanctuary of the Muses'. This is the kind of thing that David Jones has tried to make in the form of a poem. Not all the Muses are equally invoked, but Calliope, Clio, Melpomene, Polyhymnia, and Thalia certainly receive their due measure of devotion from *In Parenthesis* onwards. The 'devoted objects' are collected and arranged with care that is more than careful of their mere beauty: they are set to some purpose, to illustrate the 'inward continuities' of man's life as a 'maker' and as a spiritual being.

Perhaps because David Jones's poetry invites analysis in terms of non-literary categories, discussion of it has frequently touched upon the problem of how it should be categorized in literary terms also. This discussion has continually circled around the notion of epic, which is probably, after all, the genre to which his work is most nearly akin. The reason for this desire to class both *In Parenthesis* and *The Anathemata* as epics is the fact that both works are felt to be in some strange way representative and suprapersonal. This is, however, only one aspect of the nature of epic, which ignores such other characteristics as its narrative basis and the concept of the hero. In *Parenthesis* has a narrative structure, but it can hardly be said to have a hero in a way that makes for sense in an epic. Neither *The Anathemata* nor the work in progress has a narrative element in the commonly understood sense, and there is no hero figure in them at all. In fact, the notion of epic seems to be raised simply in order to have some criterion by which to judge David Jones's work a failure. His poems are characterized as (the modern equivalent of) epics; the true nature of epic, as derived from, say, Homer, Vergil, the *Chanson de Roland*, *Beowulf*, and the *Poema de mio Cid*, is set forth; in comparison David Jones's work does not conform to the pattern, and it is thereby neatly adjudged a failure. It seems to me fairer to his work not to try to fit it into such moulds. That it has certain qualities usually associated with epic is undeniable, but we need not therefore classify it as epic *manqué*.

I think we have to agree that *The Anathemata* is the central work in David Jones's poetry, though many people will regard *In Parenthesis* as the 'more successful' book, or at least the one they like better. *The Anathemata* in John Holloway's view is 'less successful', but 'much the more ambitious'.[1] In this view and in his assumption that David Jones is writing epic John Holloway is expressing a fairly general attitude, but the norms by which he is judging are not, to my mind, relevant to what David Jones has tried to do. He talks of 'that constant leaning on Celtic legend, Welsh language, and Roman ritual, which in the end seems to introduce into the poem a radical distortion and asymmetry, a lapse from objective to subjective, public to idiosyncratic and private' and goes on to state:

> And this is wholly at odds with the status and intention of epic which the poem indisputably claims. Nor is this in any way a matter of the critic's subjectivity against the author's, of the former telling the latter what to write about. It is to challenge the general validity, as a resurrection of the *mythos* of the people of Britain (or let us say England and Wales) of a work which tracks down every London city

[1] John Holloway, *The Colours of Clarity. Essays on Contemporary Literature and Education* (Routledge and Kegan Paul, 1964), p. 116. The following quotation is from pp. 119–20.

CONCLUSION

parish, but is silent over Durham, Canterbury, Winchester and the great wool churches; which is full of Geoffrey of Monmouth and the *Mabinogion*, but barely hints at Shakespeare; or which draws on the Mass of St Gabriel and the Feast of the Exaltation of the Cross, but makes nothing of St Aidan, Ockham, Wycliff, the English Prayer Book, or the Authorized Version.

Holloway's catalogue of omissions appears to have as its aim the creation of a balanced picture, but it is more than questionable whether David Jones intended this kind of balance. His work is not meant as a guide-book to Britain or to the great tradition of English literature. There are in any case plenty of Shakespearian allusions in his writing, and the Authorized Version and the *Book of Common Prayer* are far from neglected. That, however, is a minor point. The major point about David Jones's work is that his selection of material *is* a personal one and that through this personal element, which may certainly be idiosyncratic, but which is *not* private, a more brightly focussed vision is reached. But, unfortunately, we do not possess the poem in which the great cathedrals, William of Ockham and Shakespeare are allotted their measured place, so that comparison is rendered impossible.

The only really comparable endeavour is Pound's *Cantos*, against which John Holloway would level very similar criticisms to what he has to say about *The Anathemata*. David Jones only began to read Pound after having completed *The Anathemata*, so the question of literary dependence does not arise. Both poets, however, are concerned to shape, by means of a partial literary collage, some kind of picture of the whole world as they see it. Pound ranges far more widely for his material, seeing the whole of the globe as his garden and thus including Chinese ideograms side by side with 'the Bros Watson store in Clinton N.Y.' But the *Cantos* as a whole are far less comprehensible than anything David Jones has written. Even Pound's most consistent admirers tend to take their refuge mainly in the claim that the collection contains some very fine passages of poetry. This no one would deny, but it is hardly an adequate justification for the sheer impenetrability of most of the work. David Jones may be judged difficult and idiosyncratic, but he is not careless of his readers in the way that Pound is. Pound seems to assume that the reader has direct access to all the poet's personal experience and reading, for he explains nothing and postulates a familiarity with Old Provençal, Italian, Latin, Greek, German, French and other less easily identifiable languages into the bargain. All of which points to the fact that Pound has written chiefly for himself and of a private world. With David Jones it is easier to sense a purpose in his writing; one can see the unifying, ordering factors at work, one can appreciate his themes of birth, death, creation and sacrifice. The strictly personal element in his work is minimal: he is not guilty of the strictly in-group aside or the use of private jokes.

Pound has, most people will agree, a very good ear, and his musicality is what redeems a great deal of his later work (though his colloquial passages lapse often enough into a barbaric yawp, and his use of archaic grammatical forms is irritating). I mention this because John Holloway levels something like the reverse of this criticism against David Jones. '*The Anathemata*,' he declares, 'save for a handful of rather striking and very uncharacteristic passages, is poetically a work of almost astonishing boredom.... Boredom, mind you, strictly from the standpoint of poetry...' He then goes on to isolate 'first an idiosyncrasy, and ultimately a kind of erudite triteness, which do not create poetry but preclude it.'[1] I must admit that I find it difficult to understand what sort of distinction Holloway is trying to make, for earlier in his essay he writes very positively about the modernism of David Jones's technical resources, and he clearly finds *The Anathemata* a work of very considerable interest. That it has its patches of awkwardness and obscurity, I would be prepared to admit, but the over-all conception of the book is so forceful as to carry the reader along in the magnificent sweeps of its vision. At the present moment all definitions of art and poetry are in the melting pot. People may ask themselves whether computerized haiku or concrete poems are really poetry and whether the kind of things that the Institute of Contemporary Arts displayed at its recent Cybernetic Serendipity exhibition properly fall within the ambit of art, but what is important is really whether they add some new perception or

[1] *Op. cit.*, pp. 122f.

CONCLUSION

dimension to man's appreciation of his ambience and his creative potentiality within it. David Jones's work is supremely concerned with the ambience of twentieth century man, both physically and spiritually, and in the kind of juxtapositions that he makes, surprising as many of them are, he can evoke a sense of wonder and newness that is characteristic of man's deepest experience.

David Jones is not concerned solely with appearances or the contactual realities of life, keenly though he is interested in them. He is at pains to point beyond this to spiritual intangibles and underlying harmonies, to the Queen of the Woods on the battlefield of the dying, and to the *lux perpetua*. His books and his paintings and engravings are full of this mystery of the beyond. Many of his pictures give one the impression that something is just about to happen, something faintly strange and disturbing, and his poetry leaves one feeling that one has understood something, but there is still a great deal more to be understood. This understanding is not based on an intellectual comprehension of the literal meaning of his words, but is communicated through something else and is related to the experience of power through incantation and the stirring of folk-memory. It is the kind of quality that pervades Edith Sitwell's visionary poems such as 'The Coat of Fire' and 'The Shadow of Cain', though there is a romantic opulence about her poetry that is foreign to David Jones, and what she says is phrased more personally. It is also found in such very different poems as Vernon Watkins' 'Ballad of the Mari Lwyd' and 'Taliesin and the Spring of Vision', which are far more classical and restrained in their language and metre. Both in their particular modes are seeking to express a universal reality through primordial images and symbols, reinforced by the rhythmical patterns of liturgy and primitive poetry. It is this pattern and range of images that makes David Jones's poetry (I return deliberately to the word) so impressive. It is the same kind of thing that causes one to recognize the *Te Deum* as great and magnificent poetry aside from any theology.

The element of incantation is the original impetus of poetry. The goal of such poetry is the achievement of insight or a psychic transformation focussed on some object of the external world. This transformation can only be obtained through the invocation of spiritual powers. It is hardly accidental that charms and riddles, in which ritual is combined with poetic form, no matter how simple or rudimentary, are among the earliest pieces of literature that we know in English, German and Norse, together with fragments of myths that connect man with his beginnings. Such poetry is an attempt to manipulate the external environment (or at least one's manner of apprehending it) and to produce ultimately a state of harmony between it and the life of man. In this early stage, where prehistory is becoming history, poetry and religion are indivisible because both are concerned with the depths of man's experience as a whole. For this reason all great poetry is at bottom religious, from *Gilgamesh* and the Homeric epics to Hölderlin and the *Four Quartets*. It is a quest for knowledge, a search for identity, through the power of names to bring down the gods to the earth and initiate order. This is the kind of thing that David Jones is attempting in all his poetry from *In Parenthesis* onwards. Everywhere he is concerned with transformations at the deepest possible level. Here the rational mind comes to a halt and the world of myth takes over, because it is the only way in which further progress can be made. As far as Britain is concerned, the myths are Celtic and this determines the dominance of the Welsh in David Jones's *materia poetica*. There is nothing in the strictly English tradition that can mediate the reality of myth. What is numinous in English literature derives from sources that are other than English, i.e. the Matter of Britain, the Bible, Greece and Rome.

Possibly the best illustration of the incantatory mood in David Jones's work is Dai's boast in *In Parenthesis* (pp. 79–84). It is certainly typical enough, and it takes up the most famous transformation myth of medieval Welsh literature in the shape of the legend of Taliesin, who was born of the goddess Ceridwen after a series of metamorphoses from being the stirrer of her cauldron of Inspiration and Knowledge under the name of Gwion, through various animal and vegetable forms, back to human shape as the court poet of Elphin, son of Gwyddno Garanhir, ruler of the lost cantref of Gwaelod. Taliesin, who made his first appearance in English literature in Gray's Pindaric Ode 'The Bard', is celebrated in Welsh tradition as the great early master of poetry, and legend

CONCLUSION

has made of the historical man a figure of mythological importance. In the legend one of his functions is to release his master Elphin from capture by Maelgwn, king of Gwynedd, and it is in the course of this effort that he utters the boast, known as the *Hanes Taliesin*, that is the model for Dai's boast:[1]

> I was with my Lord in the highest sphere,
> On the fall of Lucifer into the depths of hell:
> I have borne a banner before Alexander;
> I know the names of the stars from north to south;
> I have been on the galaxy at the throne of the Distributor;
> I was in Canaan when Absalom was slain;
> I conveyed the Divine Spirit to the level of the vale of Hebron;
> I was in the court of Don before the birth of Gwdion.
> . . .

The boast of Taliesin and his powers of transformation as shown in the legend seem to link up very closely with the multifarious forms of the 'child archetype' in the collective unconscious. Jung does not mention the legend of Taliesin in his essay on 'The Psychology of the Child Archetype', but he notes several points which would be relevant in a full consideration of the figure of Taliesin, namely:[2]

> . . . the mythological idea of the child is emphatically not a copy of the empirical child but a *symbol* clearly recognizable as such: it is a wonder-child, a divine child, begotten, born, and brought up in quite extraordinary circumstances, and not—this is the point—a human child. Its deeds are as miraculous or monstrous as its nature and physical constitution.... Moreover, the mythological 'child' has various forms: now a god, giant, Tom Thumb, animal, etc., and this points to a causality that is anything but rational or concretely human.

Later on in the same essay (p. 164) he says:

> . . . the 'child' paves the way for a future change of personality. In the individuation process, it anticipates the figure that comes from the synthesis of conscious and unconscious elements in the personality. It is therefore a symbol which unites the opposites; a mediator, bringer of healing, that is, one who makes whole.

This tallies very closely with the role that Taliesin plays in the

[1] Quoted from *The Mabinogion*, tr. Lady Charlotte Guest (London, 1877), p. 482.
[2] C. G. Jung, *The Archetypes and the Collective Unconscious* (New York, 1959), p. 161.

Welsh legend, and the psycho-analytical explanation helps to show why this particular motif has such a peculiar force. This concept of the 'child' archetype, which is often simultaneously a hero or saviour figure, also illuminates the sections entitled 'Mabinog's Liturgy' and 'Sherthursdaye and Venus Day' in *The Anathemata*. But returning to Taliesin, we can see something of his numinous significance in the twentieth century in the variety of poems that have used him as a key figure. In 'Taliesin's Voyage' and 'Taliesin and the Mockers'[1] Vernon Watkins gives a characteristically limpid, supple version of part of the legend together with a completely new vision of the Boast; while his 'Taliesin and the Spring of Vision'[2] uses a number of motifs from the legend to make an utterance about the nature of poetic understanding:

> In a time of darkness the pattern of life is restored
> By men who make all transience seem an illusion
> Through inward acts, acts corresponding to music.
> Their works of love leave words that do not end in the heart.

Not only in this poem, but in many others also, Vernon Watkins concentrates in lyric form his sense of a guiding spirit in the universe, his awareness of the elemental powers of nature, and his involvement with the central traditions of European literature. It is an experience that he shares with David Jones, though he expresses it in a quite different way. Taliesin's Boast is taken up once more by R. S. Thomas in a short poem called 'Taliesin 1952',[3] where it relates more than elsewhere to the things of Wales, but concludes nonetheless on a universal note:

> Taliesin still, I show you a new world, risen,
> Stubborn with beauty, out of the heart's need.

It is again the idea of Taliesin as the seer who has been everywhere and seen everything that Charles Williams seizes upon in order to make the legendary poet the central figure of his Arthurian vision in *Taliessin through Logres* and *The Region of the Summer Stars*. But here the old Welsh tale and the Boast at Maelgwn's court, though fully used as always, form only the point of departure for Williams's

[1] Vernon Watkins, *Affinities* (Faber, 1962), pp. 73ff.
[2] Vernon Watkins, *Cypress and Acacia* (Faber, 1959), pp. 20f.
[3] R. S. Thomas, *Song at the Year's Turning* (Hart-Davies, 1955), p. 105.

CONCLUSION

more comprehensive, and not always convincing, narrative.

If it is not so much the figure of Taliesin as his famous Boast and intricate poetry that stand behind David Jones's work as a formative influence, there are other poets who can testify to similar poetic goals. Among these Hugh MacDiarmid stands out as particularly coherent and articulate, and his poem 'The Kind of Poetry I want' expresses with a peculiar cogency the qualities that poetry needs to give it backbone, vigour and seriousness. Most of what he sets out as his programme, which is demanding and sublime, is very close to David Jones's aims:

> A poetry the quality of which
> Is a stand made against intellectual apathy,
> Its material founded, like Gray's, on difficult knowledge,
> And its metres those of a poet
> Who has studied Pindar and Welsh poetry,
> But, more than that, its words coming from a mind
> Which has experienced the sifted layers on layers
> Of human lives—aware of the innumerable dead
> And the innumerable to-be-born,
> The voice of the centuries, of Shakespeare's history plays
> Concentrated and deepened,
> 'The breath and finer spirit of all knowledge,
> The impassioned expression
> Which is in the countenance of all science.'

This is merely the beginning of his demands, but it immediately strikes a chord for the reader of David Jones's poetry. Later on in this same poem MacDiarmid picks on Taliesin as the prototype of this kind of poetry and even quotes from Charles Williams's *Taliessin through Logres* to make one of his points:

> And above all a learned poetry, knowing how
> Taliesin received the hazel rod
> From the dying hand of Virgil
> Who in turn had it from Homer
> —A poetry full of milk
> 'Milk rising in breasts of Gaul,
> Trigonometrical milk of doctrine,'
> In which it is more than fancy
> That brings together the heroes of Arthur,

DAVID JONES: ARTIST AND WRITER

> The founders of Rome and of New Rome,
> Moslem and Manichean,
> Joseph of Nazareth and Joseph of Arimathea,
> Lupercalian and Lateran rites,
> The pagan and the Christian,
> And groups them kaleidoscopically
> Around Taliesin, our 'fullest throat of song'
> —A poetry covering 'the years and the miles'
> And talking 'one style's dialects
> To London and Omsk.'

It is surprising how almost exactly David Jones fits these aims of poetry. There are further affiliations between him and MacDiarmid, arising from the fact that both turn to Celtic life, history and poetry as well as to English, but deepened in the devotion of both to philology and omnivorous reading. They are not among the ranks of those poets who appear to have read nothing else apart from their own poems and perhaps the *Daily Mirror*.

The name of Vergil among MacDiarmid's celebrations of poets reminds one of his fundamental importance in the European tradition. There is probably no other single poet with whom David Jones has so much in common or whose influence is so pervasive. In addition to being the greatest of the Roman poets, Vergil was venerated throughout the Middle Ages as both a prophet and a necromancer or magician, becoming a potent legendary figure. This was principally on account of the Fourth Eclogue, which was universally regarded as a prophecy of Christ, and by reason of the knowledge of the underworld that he evinces in the sixth book of the *Aeneid*. Both the poet and the seer of legend loom large in David Jones's imagination, and it is remarkable how often the words of Vergil echo through his work. Quotations and paraphrases from the Fourth Eclogue are easily recognizable in his inscriptions and also in 'Mabinog's Liturgy', and reference is made to the degrading death of Hector in 'Middle-sea and Lear-sea' as well as in *The Fatigue*, to mention the most prominent examples. But the influence is really more pervasive than simple quotation suggests. The significance of Troy in *The Anathemata* owes more to Vergil than to Homer, though it owes a great deal too to Geoffrey

CONCLUSION

of Monmouth, 'now deemed the most incontinent liar on record' (*A*, p. 152). This is the Vergil whose technique of synthesis and adaptation and whose use of ancient, half-forgotten symbols and ideas have been so productively explored by W. F. Jackson Knight in *Vergil's Troy* and *Cumaean Gates*, two books that David Jones eagerly assimilated. Indeed, the main movement of the first half of *The Anathemata* runs parallel to the narrative structure of the *Aeneid* in its concern with origins and the voyage to a new land. Both the *Aeneid* and *The Anathemata* are concerned with the preservation of the past in the continuous sweep of history, and both poets look forward to later events than those they are directly chronicling: Vergil frequently tells of what came after the arrival of Aeneas on the soil of Latium and often hints allegorically at the events of his own time, while David Jones uses Roman culture and history as a type of our twentieth century megalopolis and speaks, for example, of what '*will* be called / The Tumulus' (in *The Fatigue*). Equally striking are the similarities in attitude that make Vergil interpret the story of Aeneas as part of the supernatural struggle between the gods and especially between Venus and Juno and that cause David Jones to link all he has to say with the religious impulse. How often both poets refer to ritual and sacrifice as the sustaining element in human life! The poetry of Vergil has endured for 2000 years, focussed as it is in the *Aeneid* on the destiny of one man, though attempting the history of a people. That is perhaps the key to its success. The difference in David Jones lies in his choosing the method of universality and abstraction in order to delineate a similar view of man. For him one feels that the concrete and the particular exist not so much for themselves, but rather as necessary embodiments of a numinous power. He would agree with what Blake said in *The Marriage of Heaven and Hell*:

> If the doors of perception were cleansed everything would appear to man as it is, infinite.
> For man has closed himself up, till he sees all things thro' narrow chinks of this cavern.

David Jones is attempting, with a method of composition and vision that he shares with Vergil as well as Joyce, to open up again the narrow chinks of this cavern.

Select bibliography

The following list attempts only to give a more or less complete account of David Jones's own writings. For a list of the books he has illustrated the reader is referred to the catalogue of the Arts Council of Great Britain's 1954 exhibition. Letters and articles included in *Epoch and Artist* are not listed separately. In the secondary literature brief reviews and slight notes have generally been omitted. For a more complete list the reader should consult the bibliography appended to Charles J. Stoneburner, *The Regimen of the Ship-Star. A Handbook for 'The Anathemata' of David Jones* (Ph.D. dissertation, University of Michigan, 1966), of which a microfilm copy is available in the University Library, Manchester.

A = article.
L = letter.
Agenda, SI = *Agenda*, vol. V., nos. 1–3, Spring–Summer 1967, David Jones Special Issue; reprinted October 1967 with two additional illustrations.

Writings of David Jones

In Parenthesis (Faber, 1937; paperback edition 1963 without the illustrations, but with a Note of Introduction by T. S. Eliot)
'King Charles' Statue' (L, written with Arthur Pollen) (*Times*, 30 May 1941)
The Anathemata (Faber, 1952)
The Wall (*Poetry*, vol. LXXXVII, no. 2, November 1955, pp. 68–74; reprinted *Agenda*, SI, pp. 6–10)

'Welsh Affairs' (L) (*Times*, 13 March 1956, p. 11)
'The Holy Week Liturgy' (L) (*Tablet*, 7 April 1956, p. 330)
'Langland's "Piers Plowman"' (L) (*Listener*, 4 April 1957, pp. 563–4)
'Third Programme' (L) (*Times*, 16 May 1957, p. 13)
The Tribune's Visitation (*Listener*, vol. LIX, 22 May 1958, pp. 843–5; republished with an introduction and notes Fulcrum Press, 1969, no pagination)
'Lost Languages' (L) (*Times*, 20 August 1958, p. 9)
Epoch and Artist. Selected Writings, edited by Harman Grisewood (Faber, 1959)
'The Dying Gaul' (A) (*Listener*, 7 May 1959, pp. 791–3)
The Tutelar of the Place (*Poetry*, vol. XCVIII, no. 4, January 1961, pp. 203–9; reprinted *Agenda*, SI, pp. 18–22)
Foreword to *Arthur of Albion*, by R. W. Barber (Barrie & Rockliff, with Pall Mall Press, 1961), pp. vii–ix
'Amends to a Prophet' (L) (*Times*, 12 August 1961, p. 7)
'Use and Sign' (A) (*Listener*, 24 May 1962, pp. 900–1)
'Welsh Magic' (L) (*Times*, 18 August 1962, p. 7)
'Fr Desmond Chute' (L) (*Tablet*, 20 October 1962, p. 994)
The Dream of Private Clitus (*Art and Literature*, vol. I, no. 1, March 1964, pp. 9–17; reprinted *Agenda*, SI, pp. 11–7)
Foreword to Samuel Taylor Coleridge, *The Rime of the Ancient Mariner* (New York: Chilmark Press, 1964), not paginated
'Looking Back at the Thirties' (A) (*London Magazine*, New Series, vol. V, no. 1, April 1965, pp. 47–54)
The Hunt (*Agenda*, vol. IV, no. 1, April–May 1965; reprinted *Agenda*, SI, pp. 23–7)
'Christianity and Poetry' (L) (*Times Literary Supplement*, 22 July 1965, p. 616)
The Fatigue (Cambridge: Rampant Lions Press, 1965; privately printed for David Jones's 70th birthday, 1 November 1965, limited edition of 298 copies)
The Sleeping Lord (*Agenda*, SI, pp. 28–54)
Le Coeur du temps, by Jean Mambrino, S.J., translated by David Jones (*Month*, New Series, vol. XL, nos. 1–2, July–August 1968, p. 45)

SELECT BIBLIOGRAPHY

Secondary literature

(1) *General*

Michael Alexander, 'David Jones, Hierophant' (*Agenda*, SI, pp. 116–23)
David Blamires, 'Kynge Arthur ys nat dede' (*Agenda*, SI, pp. 159–71)
Louis Bonnerot, 'David Jones: "Down the Traversed History-Paths"' (*Agenda*, SI, pp. 124–7)
Neville Braybrooke, 'David Jones: Painter and Poet' (*Apollo*, vol. LXXXVII, no. 12, February 1963; also in *Queen's Quarterly*, vol. LXX, Winter 1963, pp. 508–14)
Aneirin Talfan Davies, 'A Note on David Jones' (*Poetry Wales*, Spring 1966; *Agenda*, SI, pp. 172–5)
T. S. Eliot, 'A Note on "In Parenthesis" and "The Anathemata"' (*Dockleaves*, vol. VI, no. 16, Spring 1955, pp. 21–3; from a broadcast on the Welsh Home Service of the BBC on 29 October 1954)
Michael J. Fleming, 'David Michael Jones: The Artist and His Tradition' (*Sequoya* [St John's University, Jamaica, New York] Winter 1965, pp. 7–12)
Kenelm Foster, O.P., 'David Jones on Art and Religion' (*Blackfriars*, vol. XL, no. 474, September 1959, pp. 421–5)
Harman Grisewood, 'David Jones' (*Blackfriars*, vol. XXXII, no. 373, April 1951, pp. 151–5)
——, 'David Jones' (*Month*, New Series, vol. XXXIV, no. 5, November 1965, pp. 310–2)
——, *David Jones. Writer and Artist*, Annual Lecture for 1965 of the BBC in Wales (BBC Publications, 1966)
René Hague, 'A Personal Memoir' (*Blackfriars*, vol. XXII, no. 251, February 1941, pp. 90–4)
——, 'David Jones: A Reconnaissance' (*Twentieth Century*, vol. CLXVIII, no. 1001, July 1960, pp. 27–45; *Agenda*, SI, pp. 57–75)
Donald Hall, 'Correspondence' (*London Magazine*, New Series, vol. VII, no. 1, January 1960, pp. 61–3)
Peter Levi, S.J., 'The Poetry of David Jones' (*Agenda*, SI, pp. 80–9)

Donald Nicholl, 'A Historian's Calling' (*Downside Review*, vol. LXXVI, 1958, pp. 275–92)

Peter Orr (editor), *The Poet Speaks* (Routledge & Kegan Paul, 1966; transcript of an interview with David Jones, pp. 97–104)

John Petts, 'David Jones: An Introduction' (*Dockleaves*, vol. VI, no. 16, Spring 1955, pp. 10–7)

Stuart Piggott, 'David Jones and the Past of Man' (*Agenda*, SI, pp. 76–9)

Kathleen Raine, 'David Jones' (*New Blackfriars*, vol. XLIX, no. 569, October 1967, pp. 44–9; same article entitled 'Solitary Perfectionist' *Sewanee Review*, vol. LXXV, no. 4, October–December 1967, pp. 740–6)

Nesta Roberts, 'Sign of the bear' (*Guardian*, 17 February 1964)

N. K. Sandars, '"The Inward Continuities"' (*Agenda*, SI, pp. 92–6)

Peter Steele, 'David Jones: Precision as Presence' (*Twentieth Century* [Australia], vol. XVIII, Winter 1964, pp. 335–45)

(2) *Visual arts*

Catalogue to *David Jones: An Exhibition of Paintings, Drawings and Engravings*, organized by the Welsh Committee of the Arts Council of Great Britain, 1954, with a Note by way of preface by Saunders Lewis (reprinted *Agenda*, SI, pp. 90–1) and an Introduction by John Petts

Catalogue to *Paintings and Drawings from the Private Collection of Miss Helen Sutherland*, Scottish National Gallery of Modern Art, 1962

Catalogue to *Decade 1920–30*, organized by the Arts Council of Great Britain, 1969, with an Introduction by Alan Bowness

Catalogue to *Helen Sutherland Collection*, organized by the Arts Council, 1970–1, with an Introduction by Nicolete Gray

Kenneth Clark, 'Some Recent Paintings of David Jones' (*Agenda*, SI, pp. 97–100)

H. S. Ede, 'David Jones' (*Horizon*, vol. VIII, no. 44, August 1943, pp. 125–36)

——, 'The Visual Art of David Jones' (*Agenda*, SI, pp. 153–8; adapted and amplified from the previous article)

Eric Gill, 'David Jones' (*Artwork*, no. 23, Autumn 1930; reprinted

SELECT BIBLIOGRAPHY

without the illustrations in *Essays by Eric Gill* (Cape, 1947), pp. 147–53)

Basil Gray, *The English Print* (Adam & Charles Black, 1937; reprinted University Microfilms Ltd, 1969)

Nicolete Gray, 'David Jones' (*Signature*, New Series, no. 8, 1949, pp. 46–56)

——, 'David Jones and the Art of Lettering' (*Motif*, no. 7, Summer 1961, pp. 69–80; reprinted without most of the illustrations *Agenda*, SI, pp. 146–52)

René Hague, 'David Jones at the Tate Gallery' (*Studio*, vol. CXLIX, no. 745, April 1955, pp. 106–9)

Robin Ironside, *David Jones* (Penguin Books, 1949)

Clare Leighton, *Wood-Engravings and Woodcuts* (London: The Studio Ltd, 1932; new edition 1944)

H. D. C. Pepler, *The Hand Press* (Ditchling: St Dominic's Press, 1934)

Bryan Robertson, John Russell & Lord Snowdon, *Private View* (Nelson, 1965), pp. 190–2.

John Rothenstein, *Modern English Painters. Lewis to Moore* (Eyre & Spottiswoode, 1956), pp. 289–309 (reprinted Grey Arrow Books, 1962)

A. C. Sewter, *Modern British Woodcuts & Wood-Engravings in the Collection of the Whitworth Art Gallery*. A catalogue with an introduction (Manchester: Whitworth Art Gallery, 1962)

Review of the Chilmark Press edition of the *Ancient Mariner*, *Times Literary Supplement*, 25 February 1965

(3) *'In Parenthesis'*

Bernard Bergonzi, *Heroes' Twilight. A Study of the Literature of the Great War* (Constable, 1965), pp. 198–212

J. A. V. Chapple, *Documentary and Imaginative Literature 1880–1920* (Blandford, 1970), pp. 313–9

John H. Johnston, *English Poetry of the First World War. A Study in the Evolution of Lyric and Narrative Form* (Princeton University Press, 1964), pp. 284–340

Earle R. Swank, 'David Michael Jones: "In Parenthesis"', *Lectures on Modern Novelists*, by Arthur T. Broes and others

(Pittsburgh: Carnegie Institute of Technology, 1963), pp. 67–78

(4) *The Anathemata*

W. H. Auden, 'A Contemporary Epic' (*Encounter*, vol. XII, no. 2, February 1954, pp. 67–71)

David Blamires, 'The Ordered World: "The Anathemata" of David Jones' (*Review of English Literature*. vol. VII, no. 2, April 1966, pp. 75–86; reprinted with slight modifications *Agenda*, SI, pp. 101–11)

William Blissett, 'David Jones: Himself at the Cave-Mouth' (*University of Toronto Quarterly*, vol. XXXVI, 1966–7, pp. 259–73)

Desmond Chute, 'Anathemata' (*Blackfriars*, vol. XXIV, no. 403, October 1953, pp. 455–60)

Christopher Devlin, 'Teste David cum Sibylla' (*Month*, New Series, vol. IX, no. 2, February 1953, pp. 110–4)

John Holloway, *The Colours of Clarity. Essays on Contemporary Literature and Education* (Routledge & Kegan Paul, 1964), pp. 113–23

J. C. F. Littlewood, 'Joyce—Eliot—Tradition' (*Scrutiny*, vol. XIX, no. 4, October 1953, pp. 336–40)

Howard Nemerov, 'Seven Poets and the Language' (*Sewanee Review*, vol. LXII, 1954, pp. 305–19)

Robert Speaight, 'The Anathemata' (*Times Literary Supplement*, 6 August 1954, pp. xxxii–xxxiii)

Charles J. Stoneburner, *The Regimen of the Ship-Star. A Handbook for 'The Anathemata' of David Jones* (Ph.D. dissertation, University of Michigan, 1966)

Review in *Times Literary Supplement*, 14 November 1952, p. 744

(5) *The work in progress*

Le Rêve du simple soldat Clitus, translated by Louis Bonnerot (*Agenda*, SI, pp. 128–34)

Peter Orr, 'Hear the Voice of the Bard' (*Review of English Literature*, vol. VIII, no. 1, January 1967, pp. 74–83)

Tony Stoneburner, 'The Work in Progress' (*Agenda*, SI, pp. 135–45)

(6) *Epoch and artist*

Frank Kermode, *Puzzles and Epiphanies. Essays and Reviews* 1958–1961 (Routledge & Kegan Paul, 1962), pp. 29–34

Saunders Lewis, 'Epoch and Artist' (*Agenda*, SI, pp. 112–5)

Harold Rosenberg, 'Aesthetics of Crisis' (*New Yorker*, 22 August 1964)

'Relic of the Celtic Twilight' (*Times Literary Supplement*, 22 May 1959, p. 299)

Index

A, a, a, *Domine Deus* 151
abstract art 30f.
'Abstract Art' 30
Aeneid 205
Agag 61
Agate, James 74
Aisopou tou muthopoiou logoi hepta 47, 64
Alison 118
The Anathemata 1, 2, 4, 7, 10, 11, 12, 13, 34, 46, 47, 54, 66, 69, 70, 71, 72, 73, 113–50, 151, 152, 153, 165, 171, 176, 178, 179, 187–91, 192, 194, 195, 196, 197, 198, 204, 205
  'Rite and Foretime' 120, 141–3, 147, 148, 165, 187f.
  'Middle-sea and Lear-sea' 137–9, 145, 148, 149, 188, 204
  'Angle-land' 122, 145, 179
  'Redriff' 2, 122, 132, 145
  'The Lady of the Pool' 117f., 122, 135, 143f., 145, 146, 147, 148, 189f.
  'Keel, Ram, Stauros' 122, 187
  'Mabinog's Liturgy' 122f., 139f., 145, 149, 187, 190, 202, 204
  'Sherthursdaye and Venus Day' 123, 145–50, 187f., 191, 202
  Preface to *The Anathemata* 16, 23, 29, 31, 32, 34, 60, 116f., 127, 134, 135, 137, 144, 174, 177
The Ancient Mariner, Rime of 5, 47–50, 64, 86, 87
Aneirin 82, 119, 171
  see also *Y Gododdin*
The Annunciation (to Shepherds) 9, 63, 70, 72
Anwyl, Edward 83
Aphrodite in Aulis 4, 9, 67–9, 70, 73, 76, 194
Aquinas 19
archaeology 130, 131f., 188
'Art and Democracy' 9, 22
'Art and Sacrament' 9, 17, 23, 26–8, 29, 115, 120
Arthur 9, 13, 65, 84, 139, 140, 146, 163f., 165, 174, 176, 177, 180, 181, 184, 186, 188, 189, 190, 192
Arthurian material 46, 58, 64, 65–7, 106, 116, 123, 174, 176–92
Auden, W. H. 31, 135
Augustine, St (of Hippo) 119, 170

Balin (and Balan) 87, 178, 179f., 181, 182, 186
Ball, John 77, 85, 86, 88, 92, 93–6, 100, 107, 108, 110, 183
Balston, Thomas, 45
Barber, R. W. 177
The Battle of Brunanburh 12, 84
The Battle of Maldon 84
Baudelaire 19, 20, 116
Bawden, Edward 7, 51
Bayes, Walter 4
BBC and broadcasting 46, 76, 112, 114, 170, 174
Beardsley, Aubrey 3
La Belle endormie 70
Belloc, Hilaire 9, 174, 177
Benn, Gottfried 89f.
Beowulf 76, 84, 196
Bergonzi, Bernard 64, 65, 75, 79, 81, 100

215

INDEX

Bible 13, 85, 88, 101, 102, 103, 106, 147, 158, 184, 197, 200
Blake 1, 4, 193, 205
Bliss, Douglas Percy 45
Blunden, Edmund 79
Bodkin, Maud 48
Boniface, St 103
Borrow, George 170, 172
Botticelli 63
Bradshaw, Ebenezer 2, 54, 132
Brân the Blessed 27, 56, 169, 184
Braque 51
Braybrooke, Neville 35, 71
Breughel 91
The Bride 46
Bridges, Robert 9, 87
Britain 33, 65, 70, 81, 82, 100, 115, 121, 143, 152, 164, 168, 169, 170, 176, 177, 178, 180, 184, 187, 188, 191, 192, 196, 197, 200
Brockley 2, 6
Bromwich, Rachel 184
Brooke, Rupert 78, 95
Burroughs, William 77

Caesar 82
Caldy Island 6
calligraphy 11, 71–3, 204
The Cantos 2, 13, 100, 114, 115, 134, 197
  see also Pound, Ezra
Capel-y-ffin 6, 42, 57, 169
Carroll, Lewis 88
  see also *Through the Looking Glass*
Cath Gartref 61
Catholicism 4, 8, 17, 20, 25, 26, 87, 100–6, 114, 115, 116, 128, 129, 137, 174, 194
Caxton 177, 188
Celts and Celtic material 81, 116, 119, 122, 132, 154, 161, 164, 171, 173, 175, 190, 192, 196, 200
Cézanne 21, 51
Chagall 65
Chapel in the Park 8, 57, 90
The Chapel Perilous 7, 58, 146
Chaucer 13, 37, 82, 84
A Child's Rosary Book 39
Chrétien de Troyes 146, 176
Christ 3, 11, 19, 29, 43, 48, 68, 69, 102, 104, 105, 106, 116, 117, 118, 122, 123, 138, 142, 144, 146, 148, 149, 150, 154, 157, 161, 163, 183, 184, 187, 188, 190, 191, 204

Christianity and Art 42, 43f.
Chute, Desmond 5, 38, 39, 47
Clark, Kenneth 54, 58, 63, 70
Claudel, Paul 20, 64
Cleverdon, Douglas 47, 112
Cohn, Norman 164
Cole, Herbert 3
Coleridge 13, 47, 48, 86
  see also *the Ancient Mariner*, *Rime of*
Common Prayer, Book of 148, 197
Compton-Burnett, Ivy 76
Coomaraswamy, Ananda 21, 22
Coventry, Francis 40
Cows 61
Curtained Outlook 59
Culhwch and Olwen 84, 163, 184f., 186, 188, 192

Dai 100, 131, 183
Dai's boast 95, 111f., 171, 182, 183f., 200, 201
Dancing Bear 2, 4, 35
Daniel, Book of 105
Dawson, Christopher 13
the Deluge, *Chester Play of* 5, 7, 42, 44f., 47, 48, 49, 50, 54, 73
Disney, Walt 177
Ditchling 5, 6, 7, 17, 19, 35, 36, 39
Dixon, R. W., 87
Dolorous Stroke 87, 181f., 186
Donne, John 172
The Dream of Macsen Wledig 170
The Dream of Private Clitus 151, 152, 153, 154, 159f., 161, 162
The Dream of the Rood 161
Drinkwater, John 39
Dunbar 13, 94
Dürer 70
Durrell, Lawrence 76
'The Dying Gaul' 173

Ede, H. S. 2, 44, 47, 50, 59, 61
El Greco 1
Elias the Captain 185f.
Eliot, T. S. 2, 7, 11, 13, 14, 31, 33, 70, 71, 76, 89, 114, 134, 136, 193
  see also *Four Quartets*; *The Waste Land*
Elizabeth II 170
English Window 59
engravings 36–50
epic 76, 79, 80f., 101, 114, 195–7
Epoch and Artist 2, 11, 17, 29, 30, 31, 71, 168–75, 176, 177

216

INDEX

Epstein, Jacob 39
Eric Gill 62
eucharist 29, 66, 68, 104, 144, 145, 157
 see also liturgy; mass; ritual
Everyman 45f.

Factory Coast 54
Farjeon, Eleanor 40
Farleigh, John 36
The Fatigue 11, 76, 151, 152, 153, 155, 157, 160f., 191, 204, 205
The Fens 57
Finnegans Wake 13, 114, 115, 121, 194
First World War 3, 4, 8, 12, 64, 74–112, 132, 147, 153, 171, 180, 194
Flora 28, 60, 63, 135, 154
Flora in Calix-Light 60
Four Quartets 200
The Four Queens 9, 65, 66f., 70, 72, 176
Fragonard 91, 92
Frazer, James 13

Galahad 123, 149, 179, 182, 186, 188, 191
The Game 38
Gascoyne, David 193
Geoffrey of Monmouth 98, 176, 189, 197, 204f.
'George Borrow and Wales' 172
Gibbings, Robert 36, 37, 40, 41
Gill, Eric 5, 6, 7, 8, 11, 15, 16, 17, 18, 20, 21, 22, 37, 38, 39, 40, 42, 43, 49, 57, 62, 63
Giraldus Cambrensis 172
Glyn Dŵr, Owain 169, 173
Y Gododdin 12, 80, 81, 82f., 84, 85, 86
 see also Aneirin
Golden Cockerel Press 7, 37, 40, 41, 42, 44
Grail 123, 146, 149, 179, 181f., 183, 184, 187f., 191, 192
gratuitousness 20, 23, 117
Graves, Robert 79, 84
Gray, Basil 46
Gray, Nicolete 7, 44, 46, 47, 48, 49, 72
Gray, Thomas 200, 203
Greece and things Greek 69, 116, 118, 119, 123, 129, 132, 200
Greene, Graham 174
Gregynog Press 37, 42
Grisewood, Harman 46, 61, 144, 145, 168

Gruffudd ab yr Ynad Coch 172
Guenever 1, 9, 64, 65f., 67, 70, 76, 176
Guest, Charlotte 184
Guinevere 65f., 67, 140, 183, 184, 186, 188, 190
Gulliver's Travels 40f., 50
Gwenhwyfar 139, 140, 188, 190
Gwyl Ddewi 60
Gwyn, Captain 97, 101

Hague, René 6, 44
Hague's Press 61
Harris, Derrick 41
Hartrick, A. S. 3
Hassall, Joan 36
Hector 138, 161, 204
He Frees the Waters 46
Helen of Troy 140, 147
Helena 170
Henry V 12, 82, 84, 86
Hepworth, Barbara 7
Hermes, Gertrude 36, 37
Hermia 46
Hierarchy—Still Life 61
Hill Pastures—Capel-y-ffin 52, 53, 64
History of Pompey the Little 40
Hitchens, Ivon 7, 51
Hobbema 91
Hodgkins, Frances 51
Hogarth 30
The Hoggot, Cumbria 54
Holloway, John 196f., 198
'The Holy Week Liturgy' 175
Homer 33, 196, 200, 203, 204
 see also *Iliad*; *Odyssey*
Hopkins, Gerard Manley 9, 13, 68, 84, 87, 88, 170, 193
Hügel, Friedrich von 13
Hughes-Stanton, Blair 37
Human Being 62
The Hunt 3, 151, 152, 153, 161, 163f., 176, 179, 185, 191, 192

Iliad 126
Incarnation 27, 152
In Parenthesis 1, 2, 3, 4, 6, 8, 9, 10, 11, 12, 50, 63, 64, 74–112, 114, 118, 124–7, 146, 152, 153, 157, 171, 176, 178, 180–7, 191, 192, 194, 195, 196, 200
 Part 1 86, 87, 101–3, 107f., 180, 186
 Part 2 86, 180, 186

217

INDEX

Part 3 87, 103, 108–10, 180
Part 4 87, 157, 181, 182–5
Part 5 87, 185
Part 6 88, 185f.
Part 7 86, 88f., 92, 104–6, 180, 186
In Petra 38, 40
Irenaeus, St 116
Ironside, Robin 2, 35, 44, 52, 53, 57, 58, 60, 61, 62, 63, 66
Isaiah, Book of 138, 164

Jackson, Kenneth 83
Jaguar 61
Jenkins, Lieutenant 91, 96–8, 108, 109
Jerusalem 99, 147f., 154, 156, 157, 159, 160
John, Augustus 39
John, Gospel of 102, 105
Johnston, John H. 75, 80, 81, 89, 92, 95
Jonah, Book of 7, 41f., 48, 49
Jones, Gwyn and Thomas 56
Jones, James 2
Joshua, Book of 105
Joyce, James 21, 89, 171, 173, 193, 194, 205
see also *Finnegans Wake*; *Ulysses*
Jung, C. G. 194, 201

Ker, W. P. 22
Klee, Paul 65
Knight, W. F. Jackson 205
Knox, Ronald 39

Lamb 70
Lancelot 58, 65f., 67, 178, 180, 183, 184, 186
landscape painting 51, 52–9
language 106–12 (*In Parenthesis*), 140–4 (*The Anathemata*)
Lascaux 24, 131
Latin 11, 71, 72, 73, 111, 121, 129, 141
Leafless Tree 69
Leighton, Clare 44, 45
Leonardo da Vinci 21
Leopard and Tiger 35
Levi, Peter 71
Lewis, Aneirin Merddyn 98f., 100, 102, 107, 186
Lewis, Percy Wyndham 1
Lewis, Saunders 72, 174
Libellus Lapidum 39, 40
Lillywhite, Major 93, 98
Lion 35

Littlewood, J. C. F. 113f.
liturgy 101–4, 111, 124, 137, 139, 162, 174, 175, 190
see also eucharist; mass; ritual
Llyfr y Pregeth-wr 42f., 44, 46
Llywelyn 99, 169, 170, 172
Longinus 155, 184
'Looking Back at the Thirties' 31
Loomis, R. S. 174, 177, 181, 184
Lycidas 32
Lynx 61

Mabinogion 27, 46, 56, 80, 82, 84, 116, 163, 170, 172, 177, 179, 182, 184, 186, 188, 189, 197
MacDiarmid, Hugh 2, 114, 193f., 203f.
Maimed King 112, 146, 156, 182, 187, 191
Malory 7, 9, 12, 13, 57, 58, 65, 66, 67, 80, 82, 84, 87, 88, 116, 140, 146, 177, 178f., 180, 181, 182, 183, 184, 185, 186, 188, 189, 190, 191, 192
Manawydan's Glass Door 55, 56, 57, 58, 146
Mann, Thomas 76
Manning, Frederic 75, 79, 81
Mare terraque 57
Maritain, Jacques 17, 18, 19, 20, 23, 26, 29, 37
Mark 185, 186, 188f., 192
Martha's Cup 61
Mary, Virgin 39, 63, 68, 100, 106, 118, 140, 144, 188, 190
mass 29, 143, 197
see also eucharist; liturgy; ritual
Maxwell, George 5
Meninsky, Bernard 4
Merlin 65, 189, 190, 191
Merlin Appears in the Form of a Young Child to Arthur Sleeping (*Merlin-Land*) 7, 65
Middle Ages 18, 58, 63, 86, 124, 132, 164, 165, 176, 177, 204
Milton 13
Montes et Omnes Colles 53, 57, 90
Moore, Henry 7
Moore, Marianne 134
Mordred 140, 186, 190
Morgan le Fay 66f., 189, 191
Morley, Frank 71
Morris, William 1
Muir, Edwin 113, 193, 194
'The Myth of Arthur' 9, 174, 177–9

218

INDEX

Nash, John 36, 51
Nash, Paul 36
Nativity 144, 145, 149, 190
Nennius 116, 184
Nicholson, Ben 7, 51, 52
Nicholson, Winifred 51
Nonesuch Press 37

O'Connor, John 17, 64
Odin 103, 146, 161
Odyssey 126
The Old Animal from Tibet 61
Orr, Peter 29
Out Tide 54, 55
Owen, Wilfred 78, 101
Oxyrhynchus Papyri 150

Palestine 11, 121, 132, 152, 153, 154, 155, 160
Panthers 61
Parker, Agnes Miller 36
Passion 27, 104f., 123, 138, 144, 148, 149, 154, 155, 160, 161, 164, 171, 188, 189
'Past and Present' 34
Paul, St 158
Pepler, Hilary 5, 37, 38, 39
Peredur 46, 146f., 182, 186, 187, 190
Perse, St. John 193
Pertinent and Impertinent 39
Petra 6, 62, 63
Petra im Rosenhag 63
Picasso 21, 51
Piggott, Stuart 131
Pigotts 57
Pigotts under Storm 57, 90
Pinwell 3
Piper, John 7
Pontius Pilate 149, 157
Portrait of a Boy 62
Portrait of a Maker 62
Poston, Elizabeth 112
Pound, Ezra 2, 31, 89, 100, 114, 134, 193, 197f.
    see also *The Cantos*
Powell, T. G. E. 173
Preface to *The Anathemata* 16, 23, 29, 31, 32, 34, 60, 116f., 127, 134, 135, 137, 144, 174, 177
Pre-Raphaelites 3, 21
prosody (of *The Anathemata*) 136–40
Psalms 53, 106, 137, 138, 148, 162f.
Purney, Harold 39

The Queen's Dish 61
question form 145, 156, 165f.
Quilter, Corporal 98, 99, 101, 108, 153

Raine, Kathleen 13, 113, 193, 194
Raverat, Gwendolen 36
Ravilious, Eric 36, 41
Read, Herbert 31, 74, 79
The Reefed Place 57
'Religion and the Muses' 17, 21
ritual 100–6, 120, 124, 145, 157f., 162, 165, 166, 175, 187, 188, 190, 191, 194, 196, 205
    see also eucharist; liturgy; mass
Roland's Tree 57
Roman Land 53
Rome, Romans and things Roman 3, 11, 68, 69, 116, 118, 121, 123, 129, 132, 135, 147, 149, 152, 154, 155, 156, 157, 158, 159, 160, 161, 164, 165, 166, 170, 171, 191, 195, 200, 204, 205
Rossetti, D. G. 1
Rothenstein, John 1, 2, 47, 54, 63, 67, 68
Rousseau, Douanier 52

sacrament 23, 24, 25, 26, 27, 28, 29, 32, 120, 157f.
    see also sign
St Dominic's Press 7, 17, 37–40, 46
Salies de Béarn 6, 53
Samuel, First Book of 61
Sandars, N. K. 131
Sandys 3
Sassoon, Siegfried 78, 79, 84
Saunders, Pte Bobby 99
Savage, Reginald 3
Scanlan, J. F. 17
sea 41, 42, 43, 45, 49, 54, 55, 56, 57, 122, 149
Seven and Five Society 7, 51, 52
Shakespeare 13, 20, 56, 82, 84, 86, 191, 197, 203
    see also *Henry V*
Shaw, Bernard 39
Shewring, W. H. 46, 74
ships and boats 41, 43, 49, 50, 54, 57, 122
sign 23, 24, 25, 27, 28, 29, 30, 32, 34, 72, 116, 120, 124, 127, 128
    see also sacrament

219

INDEX

Signorelli 91, 92
Sitwell, Edith 134, 193, 194, 199
The Sleeping Lord 151, 152, 161, 164–6, 167, 169, 181, 191, 192
Snell, Sergeant 96, 99
Song of Roland 6, 12, 80, 81, 82, 84, 196
Sorley, Charles 78
Speaight, Robert 5, 7, 15, 16, 17, 21, 38, 62, 63
Spengler, Oswald 180, 195
The Spoils of Annwfn 188
Steuart, R. H. J. 64
Stock, Noel 134
Stoneburner, Tony 152, 163
The Storm Tree 69
Surf 57
Sutherland, Helen 7, 52, 54, 57, 58, 59, 60, 61, 62, 63, 70
Swank, Earle R. 106, 107, 110
Swift 40, 41
see also *Gulliver's Travels*

Tacitus 103
de la Taille, Maurice 29
Taliesin 131, 176, 181, 184, 199, 200–4
Taylor, A. J. P. 77f.
Taylor, Eva 13
Tenby from Caldy Island 53
Ten Commandments 38
Tennyson 13
The Terrace 55
Thomas, R. S. 202
Thorn Cup 1, 60
Through the Looking Glass 87
see also Carroll, Lewis
Tir y Blaenau 52
The Town Child's Alphabet 40
Trade Ship passes Ynys Byr 57
transubstantiation 29, 101
The Tribune's Visitation 71, 76, 151, 152, 153, 154, 157–9, 160, 161, 162
Tristram 178, 185, 186
Troy 68, 98, 99, 138, 147, 161, 204
Trystan ac Essyllt 9, 54, 65, 70, 176
Tucker, P. E. 178
The Tutelar of the Place 151, 152, 153, 161–4
Twrch Trwyth 131, 163, 166, 184f., 186, 192

Uccello, Paolo 91
Ulysses 76, 115, 194
Underwood, Leon 37

'Use and Sign' 29
'The Utile' 21, 115

Van Gogh 60
Venantius Fortunatus 69, 118
Venus of Willendorf 131f., 143
The Verandah 55
Vergil 20, 161, 196, 203, 204f.
Vexilla Regis 9, 54, 67, 69, 70
'The Viae' 172
Vinaver, Eugène 58, 177, 188
Violin 61

Wales 6, 7, 10, 51, 60, 72, 86, 163, 165, 168, 169–73, 202
see also Welshness and things Welsh
'Wales and the Crown' 170f.
The Wall 11, 151, 152, 153, 154, 155f., 157, 158, 161, 166, 191
Wallis, Alfred 52
Walterson, Francis 42
Waste Land theme 46, 87, 146, 182, 184, 191
The Waste Land 9, 11, 13, 89, 114, 118, 134, 193
water 32f.
watercolours 35, 36, 50–70, 145
Watkins, Vernon 193, 199, 202
Webb, Beatrice and Sidney 39
Welshness and things Welsh 2, 3, 8, 9, 10, 13, 82f., 84, 98f., 106, 116, 121, 141, 146, 162, 167, 169–73, 177, 178, 184, 188, 190, 193, 196, 200, 202
see also Wales; Celts and Celtic material
Welsh poetry 119, 171f., 203
'Welsh poetry' 171
Weston, Jessie L. 87, 179, 181, 182
White, T. H. 177
Whitman 118
Widsith 184
Wilenski, R. H. 65
Williams, Charles 176, 202, 203
Williams, Gwyn 13, 119, 171
Williams, William Carlos 2, 114
Window at Rock 58
Wittgenstein 115
Wolf in the Snow 35
Wood, Christopher 51, 52
Wright, David 2

Yeats 31, 193